Immediation II

Immediations

Series Editor: SenseLab

> "Philosophy begins in wonder. And, at the end, when philosophic thought has done its best, the wonder remains"
> – A.N. Whitehead

The aim of the Immediations book series is to prolong the wonder sustaining philosophic thought into transdisciplinary encounters. Its premise is that concepts are for the enacting: they must be experienced. Thought is lived, else it expires. It is most intensely lived at the crossroads of practices, and in the in-between of individuals and their singular endeavors: enlivened in the weave of a relational fabric. Co-composition.

> "The smile spreads over the face, as the face fits itself onto the smile"
> – A. N. Whitehead

Which practices enter into co-composition will be left an open question, to be answered by the Series authors. Art practice, aesthetic theory, political theory, movement practice, media theory, maker culture, science studies, architecture, philosophy ... the range is free. We invite you to roam it.

Immediation II

Edited by Erin Manning, Anna Munster,
Bodil Marie Stavning Thomsen

()
OPEN HUMANITIES PRESS
London 2019

First edition published by Open Humanities Press 2019.

Cover Design by Leslie Plumb

Typeset in Open Sans, an open font.

Print ISBN 978-1-78542-084-9
Vol I Print ISBN 978-1-78542-061-0
Vol I PDF ISBN 978-1-78542-062-7
Vol II Print ISBN 978-1-78542-024-5
Vol II PDF ISBN 978-1-78542-025-2

Freely available online at:
http://openhumanitiespress.org/books/titles/immediation

OPEN HUMANITIES PRESS

Open Humanities Press is an international, scholar-led open access publishing collective whose mission is to make leading works of contemporary critical thought freely available worldwide. More at http://openhumanitiespress.org

Contents

List of Diagrams and Figures

Fourth Movement

Collective Assemblages of Enunciation

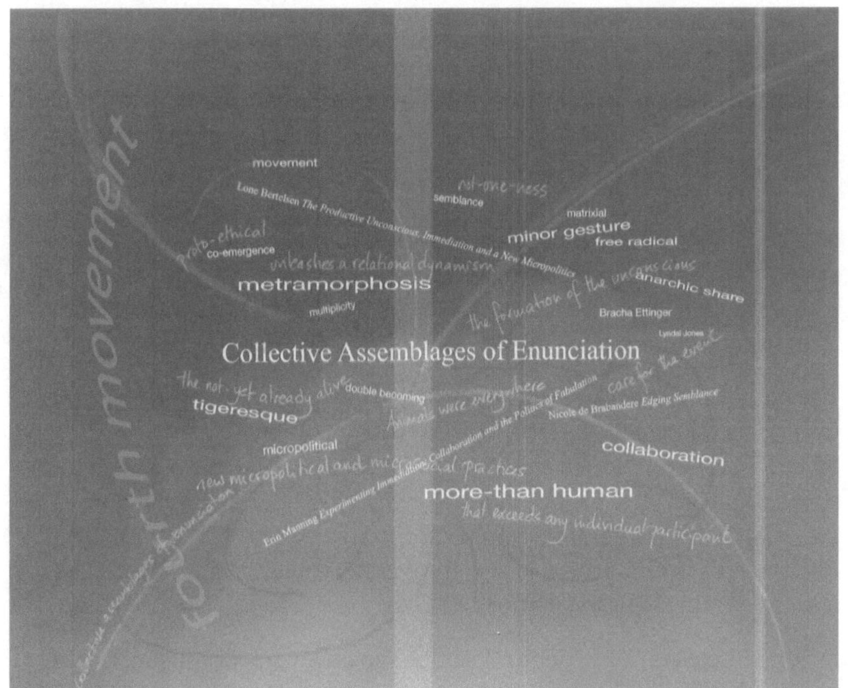

Bodil Marie Stavning Thomsen

Prelude

The question "what is collectivity in terms of immediation?" is important to pose in order to get a sense of the extended intensity in expressions of virtual forces and in sudden radical changes. Experiences of co-composing can be experienced as encounter-events of human/non-human assemblages of enunciation. They are felt and expressed on a collective level of experience. Even if you as a subject are alone at another space and place, events as such are felt and experienced on a collective level of experience. Immediations change takes place affectively-immediately.

The notion of collective experience in immediation's events might be framed as taking place at the level of "the productive unconscious" as connected to Deleuze and Guattari's "schizoanalytic" approach to psychoanalysis. The productive unconscious is here an expression of the collectively felt joint force of expression and creation. This collective unconscious is embedded in the immediation of an event and can be felt as a tendency or inclination.

In Lone Bertelsen's article the "productive unconscious" is connected to Félix Guattari's notion of an "ethico-aesthetic practice" as well as to Bracha Ettinger's notion of a "matrixial unconscious." The latter refers neither to subjectivity, inter-subjectivity nor collectivity but to a co-creative relational web that is "wider than relations between signifiers or texts and includes the more affective materiality and sociality of the 'real'" (Immediation II, 343) What Guattari and Ettinger have in common is the exploration of the unconscious as a plural multiplicity in which differentiation operates—even on the level of subjectivity, since a constituent force of becoming is experienced as a co-emerging of "I and non-I" (in Ettinger's words). This constituent force of the matrixical unconscious thus is "proto-ethical" to what can be experienced as social in affective immediating events. Bertelsen explains the forces of a productive unconscious in relation to her own experience of differential co-composing in the exploration of the "dual site network installation" *Intimate Transactions*, made by The Transmute Collective (with artistic director Keith Armstrong).

Nicole de Brabandere presents her own photographic explorations of Suzanne Langer's writings on the semblance of movement that can be virtually experienced by non-moving representations of movement like for example a Greek meander. In *Semblance and Event: Activist Philosophy and the Occurent Arts* (2011) Brian Massumi further explores Langer's work in relation to the forces of events. Nicole de Brabandere's works are especially composed to explore how rhythm, space, surface and form might affectively spark tensions and thus create semblances of transversal movement in- or outside the frame. These works can be experienced as immediating micro-events in which the virtual forces "come to life" as transversal semblances of movement.

In Erin Manning's article, writing itself is explored as a collective assemblage of fabulations or thoughts-in-motion. This exploration of immediation from a schizoanalytic approach sets off from the question of how engagement and creative event-making can be valued while unfolding rather than in its exhibited, presentational form. The question of how to make an event's unfolding and its living ecologies of collective explorations primary to the individuals taking part in it—and not to hold on to former events nor to traditional forms of reporting, archiving or habits—is key to a continued engagement. Or as stated by Manning: "How can an event mark its punctuation in an account that continues the work of the event?" One approach to this is to tell stories of events in a fabulating manner in which "the power of the false" (Deleuze) decomposes linearity, relations of cause and effect, mythmaking and makes even time fall off its hinges of chronology—to instead take on a folding relation to an event's passing. Precisely as "[a] fabulation's content can never be seen as limited to the story itself " (Immediation II, 388) the immediations of events are on the level of futurity more complex than we can describe or represent. The falsifying cut of fabulation operates on the level of immediation, and its success cannot be measured in its utterances but only by its potential coupling of two kinds of time: "the time of the now and the time of the will have been. Time becomes operative, experiential" (Immediation II, 389). So, a politics of (the need of) fabulation would have to include the schizoanalytic as a technique for making apparent "the simultaneity of incompossible presents ... the coexistence of not-necessarily true pasts." (Deleuze 1989: 131). This is necessary in order to recognize the events potentialities beyond our individual taking part in it—and to recognize and valuate an event's creative and anarchic potentialities.

Lone Bertelsen

The Productive Unconscious, Immediation and a New Micropolitics

> It seems to me essential to organize new micropolitical and microsocial practices, new solidarities, a new gentleness, together with new aesthetic and new analytic practices regarding the formation of the unconscious.
> *Félix Guattari (2008: 51)*

> Schizoanalysis sets out to undo the expressive Oedipal unconscious, always artificial, repressive and repressed, mediated by the family, in order to attain the immediate productive unconscious.
> *Gilles Deleuze and Félix Guattari (1983: 98)*

The concern in this chapter is with how an "immediate productive unconscious" can be attained. The chapter brings the concept of the "productive unconscious" into encounter with the work of Bracha L. Ettinger and the emerging concept of *immediation*.[1] This encounter enables us to more effectively activate a possible basis for a "new micropolitics" of resistance and change: what Félix Guattari (1995) has called a new *ethico-aesthetic* practice.[2] In the last section of this chapter I suggest that the collaborative artwork *Intimate Transactions* is an example of such an ethico-aesthetic practice working along the lines of immediation. The artwork it[3] self produces a mapping of the "immediate productive unconscious" in its full polyphonic and ecological sociality. Such a cartographic mapping can be constitutive of new micropolitical practices.

An Immediating Matrixial Unconscious

With the creation of the concepts matrix and metramorphosis, Ettinger (2006) thinks a mode of individuation and sociality based on encounter and relation. Via the matrixial and metramorphosis she also conceptualizes a more "relational" and I would suggest immediating unconscious (1992: 195).

For Ettinger the *production of subjectivity* is relational in an ongoing manner. She writes that in "the matrixial perspective the becoming-together precedes the being-one" (1995a: 30). This "becoming-together" is "trans-subjective."[4] It is radically different to the usual way of understanding relationality—and with it sociality—in terms of self versus other, and thinking of relation as occurring between these more "discrete" entities.[5]

In many ways Lacan conceived of relationality and the social along these more conventional lines when, in his early (more structuralist) version of the unconscious, he claimed that the "Unconscious is the discourse of the Other" and that it is "structured like a language" (Lacan in Evans 1996: 133, 218). In a traditional Lacanian understanding of the unconscious the subject recognizes itself in "the discourse of the Other"—the master signifier of the symbolic, social order.[6]

Ettinger, like Guattari, provides an alternative to Lacan's idea of the Other and to his early version of both the unconscious and the social as understood in linguistic and Oedipal terms. Ettinger rejects the idea that "the unconscious is structured *like* a language" only and that all "unconscious processes are either metaphors or metonymies." Like Guattari, she suggests that the early Lacan "too quickly" translated Freud's notion of the unconscious into purely linguistic terms, ruled in accordance with the master signifier (1992: 178-201). Ettinger writes that "the unconscious is ... structured like a language only in the realm of the symbolic Other, but this Other is not all" that participates in the production of subjectivity and sociality (1995b: 67-72).[7] According to Ettinger (2006) "co-emerging I[s] and non-I[s]" (her different understanding of the "other") can gain expression and have an unconscious (and social) place beyond that of metaphor or metonymy.[8] This co-emergence where difference is key operates according to what she calls "*metra*morphosis" (my emphasis).

Metramorphosis is about transformative engagement and becoming that is *not* resolved into a "unity" (Huhn 1993: 8). For Ettinger "when changes occur in the borderline between two fields, they produce changes in both fields" (1993: 13). It is in this way that they are different to metamorphosis: in metramorphosis one becoming is not left behind for the sake of the becoming of the other (Huhn 1993: 8; Ettinger 1992: 200). In Ettinger's vocabulary the becomings are "co-affective" (2011: 13). Becoming is necessarily at least "double" (see Deleuze and Guattari 1987) and I would suggest immediating.[9]

Immediation then is metramorphic and concerns constitutive and affective co-mediation rather than mediation between more discrete entities such as self and other. Moreover, what Deleuze and Guattari refer to as the "immediate productive unconscious" (and with it sociality) is no longer only determined by the signifier or "linguistic like laws" or structures but also by affective, metramorphic mapping processes (Ettinger 1992: 181).

If metramorphosis concerns simultaneous "differentiation" and "co-emergence" then it does not, like "the signifier of signifiers," bring individuation into a purely linguistic and supposedly human social order of clear-cut divisions between self/other, subject/world and symbiosis/differentiation (Ettinger 1992: 178). Metramorphosis is not only about direct relations between signifiers or a sliding from one to the other; nor is it reducible to the "realm of discursive meaning" (Pollock in Ettinger 1996a: 89).

Ettinger (1992) also proposes the notion of the "matrixial" as a feminine alternative/parallel to Lacan's phallic signifier. Metramorphosis, including what Ettinger calls "metramorphic borderlinking" (1999: 18-20), occurs within this "matrixial stratum of subjectivation" (2006: 64). However, Ettinger writes that even though "we are living mostly in the sphere of co-emergence" we "are still conceiving the Unconscious as bounded by the contours of a subject's body." Yet the "matrixial unconscious" is neither individual nor collective nor inter-subjective (2009: 15). Rather, it is "trans-subjective" and "co-poietic." It operates like a relational "web", a creative "co-affective" force (Ettinger 2011: 12-13). What Ettinger calls a "matrixial unconscious" is therefore a productive, immediating unconscious. It is "wider than" relations between signifiers and includes the more "co-affective" sociality and "materiality" of the "Real" (Ettinger 1995b: 67; 1992: 196).

The "not-one-ness" of Ettinger's conceptualizations implies then that the unconscious becomes a relation (1992: 178; 1999: 18). It concerns differentiating co-affective encounter that is constitutive. Such a constitutive co-emergence, where "differentiation is primary," usually has no place in a more Oedipal social world (Ettinger 1996b: 128). Ettinger wants to change this. She writes that "*the matrixial stratum of subjectivization* ... proposes ... a plural, partial, and shared unconscious" that has social "impact." It has social impact "if," that is, "we conceive of" relation in terms of "*co-emerging I and non-I* ...[*immediation*] prior to" or I would suggest better still instead of "I versus others [*mediation*]" (1995a: 22; see also 2006: 64).[10]

I have suggested that the metramorphic processes occurring in "the matrixial stratum of subjectivation" are immediating. Significantly, they are also "proto-ethical." Ettinger (2009) explains that "[a] move toward a particular kind of ethicality is enabled by this affective zone." However, the matrixial zone is "*proto*-ethical" only, because "it enables but doesn't impose an awareness of borderlinking." It is implied then that what we call immediation—like metramorphosis—has a proto-ethical linking quality that is enabling.

Immediating metramorphosis does not involve pre-social merger as a more Oedipal approach would have it (Ettinger 1992: 199). Rather, immediation—if thought together with Ettinger's concepts—is differentiating. Like affect, it is immanently social.[11] In fact, for Brian Massumi "affect is the ongoing immediation of the social" (2015b: 206). And a micropolitical approach must do its work at the level of this immanent polyphonic sociality.

Text as Social Space

In *The Undercommons* Stephano Harney and Fred Moten too are concerned with this polyphonic sociality. While neither using the term micropolitics nor explicitly engaging with the concept of the productive unconscious I would say that what Harney and Moten call *study* concerns ethico-political immediation that is co-constitutive.

In a conversation published recently, when talking about his own writing and reading practices, Fred Moten (Moten and Fitzgerald 2015) says that what he is drawn to involves "composing ... in common—as an explicit social practice." For Moten "composing... in common" does not necessarily involve "being in the same place at the same time" and this is key because there can be "a kind of presence shared in and as displacement." Polyphonic "shared presence in displacement" can be productive. It can be productive and enabling because it "cuts the way we attach certain kinds of events and certain kinds of advancement to the individual subject, to his name." In a conversation with Harney, published in *The Undercommons*, Moten elaborates on this and again moves away from approaching a text in terms of sole authorship or in terms of intertextuality only. For Moten, a text is much more than intertext.[12] Moten experiences it as a social space where there is a kind of meeting in displacement happening.

> Recognizing that text is intertext is one thing. Seeing that a text is a social space is another. It's a deeper way of looking at it. To say that it's a social space is to say that stuff is going on: people, things, are meeting there and interacting, rubbing off one another, brushing against one another—and you enter into that social space, to try to be a part of it. So, what I guess I'm trying to say is that the terms are important insofar as they allow you, or invite you, or propel you, or require you, to enter into that social space. But once you enter into that social space, terms are just one part of it, and there's other stuff too. There are things to do, places to go, and people to see in reading and writing—and it's about maybe even trying to figure out some kind of ethically responsible way to be in that world with other things. (Moten in Harney and Moten 2013: 108).

So in reading, writing and study as in social life more generally there are ways of becoming-together and co-composing in difference, producing change along the way. In that sense "all ... work" (even though it does not necessarily take place as a "real time" encounter) is an immediating collaboration often working beyond the conscious register (see Moten 2015). This is the case too with Ettinger's own "artworking" where reworked images—often photographs—call through time and invite us to enter into an immediating "encounter-event" with the artwork (Ettinger 2000; 2009: 3). Ettinger writes:

> The art work, the final object, be it the photograph or the painting ... continues to work through in themselves and through themselves, interconnected with us, they always continue to connect between themselves and with us and with other forces. (Ettinger in Horsefield 2007: 128)

However, too often the many variations of affective "becoming-together" ("composing ... in common—as an explicit social practice") have been colonized, violated or capitalized upon, by an Oedipal unconscious, while at the same time often being denied social expression by the signifier of the One. With the "productive unconscious," as with "the matrixial unconscious," it is proposed that the Oedipal is not the only possible unconscious. The unconscious can be "defamiliarized."

The Productive Unconscious and Schizoanalytic Cartographies

Guattari is also concerned with the production of new "polyphonic" subjectivities that have "not been imagined in advance" according to a pre-determined unconscious or an Oedipal family structure (Guattari in Ettinger 2002: 243; see also Holland 2012: 314-317). Guattari is not alone here. Donna Haraway also wants to reimagine and defamiliarize the unconscious. She writes:

> I am sick to death of bonding through kinship and "the family," and I long for models of solidarity and human unity and difference rooted in friendship, work, partially shared purposes, intractable collective pain, inescapable mortality, and persistent hope. It's time to theorize an "unfamiliar unconscious," a different primal scene, where everything does not stem from the dramas of identity and reproduction. (1997: 265)[13]

The issue, at least in part, is to resist the reproduction of problematic social norms upheld by an Oedipal unconscious based on the model of a white, heteronormative European family: a model supporting the individuation of a phallocratic and often racist (re)production of subjectivity (see Deleuze and Guattari 1983).

In this regard a schizoanalytic approach to the unconscious is not about "proper social adaptation" in accordance with "prevailing norms"; quite the opposite (Guattari 2009: 195). Tamsin Lorraine writes: "Schizoanalysis, rather than tracing all desire to the position of an oedipal triangle, wants to attain 'the immediate productive unconscious' that affects and is affected by the breaks and flows of the larger social field" (2002: 7). The unconscious does not have to be that of a "private" human subject—"individualized and Oedipal." Indeed, Guattari calls the unconscious " 'machinic' because it is not necessarily centered on human subjectivity" (2009: 198 and 197). He writes that the unconscious is not "lodged at the core of every person ... but open to social and economic interaction" as well as to the media, art, and the general chaos of the world. Neither is the unconscious universal. It produces itself and is produced differently in particular circumstances. "What matters" then "is not the existence of ... polarized entities" within a "universal structure" of the unconscious but processes of "becomings" (Guattari 2009: 150 and 201; see also Clough 2000). Deleuze puts this well, writing that the productive "unconscious no longer deals with persons and objects, but with trajectories and becomings; it is no longer an unconscious of commemoration but one of mobilization, an unconscious whose objects take flight rather than remaining buried in the ground" (Deleuze in Clough 2000: 135-136).

With this focus on process and becoming we may think of the productive unconscious as operating in accordance with what Guattari has call a "logic of affects rather than a logic of " the signifier, discourse or "delimited sets" only. A "logic of affects" is both "polyphonic" and "co-creative" (Guattari 1995: 9 and 1). If the unconscious too is polyphonic—involving co-creative encounter or attunement across and between emergent subjectivities—then it must be mapped in its productive diagrammatic affectivity. Thus the title of Guattari's book *Schizoanalytic Cartographies*.

One of the most important aspects of this kind of unconscious is that it is not only a symptomatic unconscious, "mediated" by the analyst and open to interpretation but, via polyphonic encounter and co-creation, an affective and immediating unconscious productive of "social change" (Lorraine 2002: 4).

Guattari's schizoanalytic cartographies are one attempt to engage with this immediating unconscious. Here, indeed, for Guattari the point is precisely to bring about change—a *molecular revolution* of the "social field" itself. This must involve the creation of "new analytic," social and "aesthetic practices," something he hopes to activate with his schizoanalytic cartographies. In all this Guattari focuses on the expressive and "collective assemblages of enunciation," rather than on signification and the individual as such (Guattari 2012: 2). Peter Pál Pelbart stresses that for Guattari the unconscious is an actual "function of the[se] assemblages" (2013: 185-86). It is not a "structure." These polyphonic assemblages are productive, mobile and creative and must, as I mentioned, be mapped in their productivity rather than interpreted

(Pelbart 2013: 184-86). Bruno Bosteels points out that for Guattari the focus is on this "mapping" not on the "interpretation of symptoms as a function of preexisting, latent content." Again, this is because Guattari is interested in "the invention of new" *collective assemblages of enunciation* "capable of" changing "existence" (Guattari in Bosteels 1998: 155-159).[14] The unconscious here becomes productive and future directed. It is an unconscious that lends itself to an ethico-aesthic mapping "in action" (Guattari in Bosteels 1998: 159). Here, to cite Deleuze: "The map expresses the identity of the journey and what one journeys through. It merges with its object, when the object itself is movement" (1997: 61).[15]

Bosteels stresses that "schizoanalytic cartography" does not throw a masterful look at the past, to repression or to trauma (1998: 159). Instead schizoanalytic cartographies are concerned with "collective assemblages of enunciation." As mentioned, this is a more productive approach. It involves a creative diagrammatic "mapping" of desire in the production of subjectivity. This mapping affects the "social field" itself and the "larger social field" affects it (Lorraine 2002: 7). In sum, rather than interpreting, schizoanalytic cartography thus concerns itself with "composing ... in common—as an explicit social practice." It maps and diagrams the unconscious in a performative, mobile manner that looks to the future in order to free "up ... fields of virtuality" and potentiality (Guattari in Bosteels 1998: 159).

In all this Guattari moves from signification to the refrain because the refrain can hold "together partial components without abolishing their heterogeneity." This is important because "[a]mong these components are lines of virtuality that are born of the event itself" (Guattari in Ettinger 2002: 244). The same can be said of any schizoanalytic cartography: new "lines of virtuality" may emerge from each cartographic mapping and this is precisely where a "new micropolitics" can do its work and enable actualization of more proto-ethical "lines of virtuality."

Intimate Transactions

I would argue that the artwork *Intimate Transactions* is a schizoanalytic cartography "in action"—it is a work that "composes ... in common—as an explicit social practice" (Moten 2015).[16]

Intimate Transactions is a "collaborative" and deeply ecological work: "it is a dual site networked installation," created by the Transmute

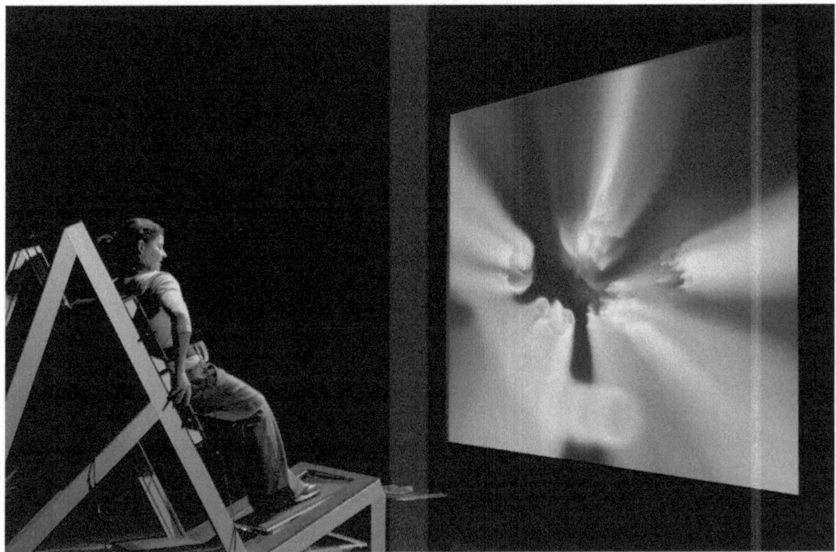

Figure 41, The Transmute Collective, *Intimate Transactions*, version 3 (2005-8), "Participant navigating on Mark III Body Aluminium Shelf, ACMI, Melbourne, Australia". Image David McLeod. Courtesy of Keith Armstrong.

Collective with Keith Armstrong as artistic director (Armstrong n.d; 2005 and 2006: 12-24). Armstrong (2005) describes *Intimate Transactions* as collaborative, ecological and concerned with relation.[17]

Intimate Transactions involves the active participation of two human participants in "different locations" (two different gallery spaces, when I encountered the work). Two people in two different physical locations engage with linked "virtual worlds" on large screens (Armstrong n.d.; O'Neill 2006: 36-38). In order to navigate the work the two participants stand tilted slightly back on (what the artwork's creators call) "identical Bodyshelves." Lisa O'Neill writes that in order to engage with the work the participants move and "roll" their backs against these Bodyshelves. They also shift the weight of their bodies on the "mobile" platforms on which they stand. This "drives the navigation" (O'Neill 2006: 36).

The movement activates the worlds on the screens—the worlds of the non-human "creatures." The movement on the Bodyshelf also activates the participants' avatars and at times aspects of a joint "virtual world," shared across the two screens in different locations (Armstrong 2006: 27-30). However, the Bodyshelf does not only pick up and transfer the movements of the body on the shelf onto the avatars and creatures on the screen. The Bodyshelf also transmits vibrations, based on

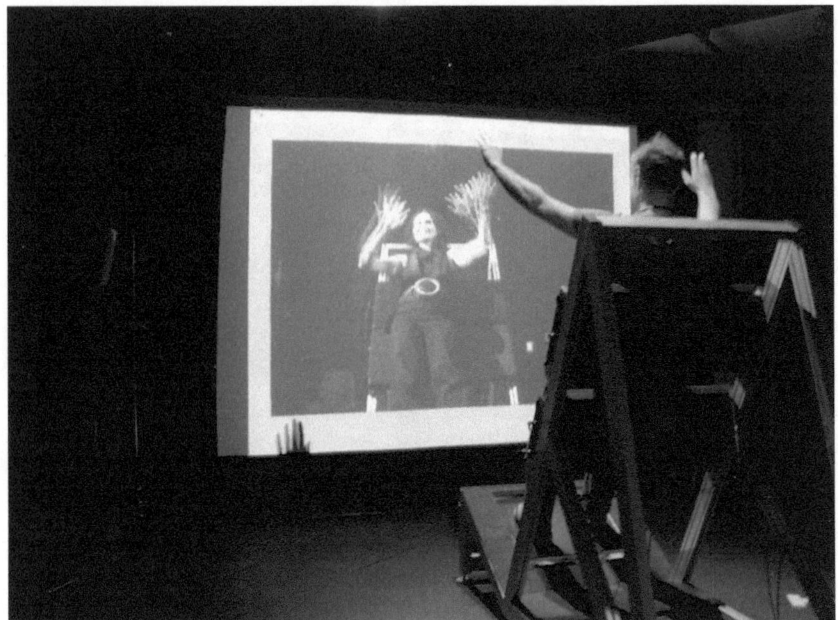

Figure 42. The Transmute Collective, *Intimate Transactions*, version 3 (2005-8), "Two Participants meet at the end of the 25 min. experience". Photo Keith Armstrong. Courtesy of Keith Armstrong.

engagement with the other person's movements, onto the lower back of the body (Ednie-Brown and Mewburn 2006: 80-81). Finally, the shelf plays an active part in the "immersive sound-scape," as the "motion in space generate[s] the feedback of the sound" (Webster 2006: 60 and 67).

In addition to all this—and to me the most intimate quality of the work—a rubbery "garment," with a pink border, is looped around the neck, like a "pendant" and strapped loosely to the abdomen (Ednie-Brown and Mewburn 2006: 81). Inside this garment there is a "device" that transmits vibrations, based on the engagement with the creatures in the "screen-world[s]," onto the stomachs of the participants (Ednie-Brown and Mewburn 2006: 81-82; Armstrong 2005; Birringer 2006: 109).

With the vibrations emerging from the "haptic devices" in the Bodyshelf, the "immersive sound-scape" and the vibrations felt on the stomach, it is not totally clear whose movement we experience (Hamilton and Lavery 2006: 7). The two human participants do not see one another until briefly at the very "end of the experience" (Armstrong 2005). Yet, over time, an intimate feeling of *co-creation* emerges between the human participants and the non-human creatures. As such *Intimate Transactions* is designed to operate "co-creatively" (Armstrong 2005). One experiences a sense of *becoming-together* and *co-composing in difference*, "as an explicit social practice."

Pia Ednie-Brown and Inger Mewburn, the creators of the *haptic components*, write about how this co-composed world "vibrates with the texture of difference" and about how each participant literally "can feel the undeniable difference between us." They write that through these vibrations "each player can feel the directional push of the other" person and the creatures as well—their movements vibrate on the bodies of the two participants and "the undeniable differences" between all creatures in the worlds of the work are "felt" (Ednie-Brown and Mewburn 2006: 81 and 87).[18]

There are different screen-worlds activated at different times in *Intimate Transactions* (Hamilton 2006: 116). At times, participants work in their local "screen-spaces," inhabited by unusual non-human creatures and their milieu (Armstrong 2005). At other times, there is participation in a *"shared virtual" world* (Hamilton and Lavery 2006: 4). Armstrong (2005) emphasizes the importance of the various virtual screen environments. He explains that at one stage of the work it is possible for the human participants to work in their local environments and impoverish the world of the non-human creatures. The human participants can work individually and take away "objects from" the non-human creatures in order to "incorporate ... these objects into their own avatars." Clearly, *Intimate Transactions* here engages with issues related to over-"consumption" and colonization (Armstrong 2006: 27). As Armstrong (2005) points out, it is possible *not* to "work collaboratively with the other person." However, the less one does so, and the more one takes away from the world of the non-human creatures, the more impoverished the "immersive" world becomes. The entire work loses its "vitality" (O'Neill 2006: 41). Non-collaboration is thus not encouraged by the very design and operation of this work: co-composition is (Armstrong 2005; 2006 and Webster 2006: 66).

In order to re-"enrich" the gallery spaces and "restore" the virtual worlds, and to care for the non-human creatures as well as for each other and the relation itself, the avatars of the two human participants have to "meet" in the "shared-space" and work together in a trans-subjective collaboration based on what Armstrong (2005) terms transversal, "networked and cross-affective processes." In this shared

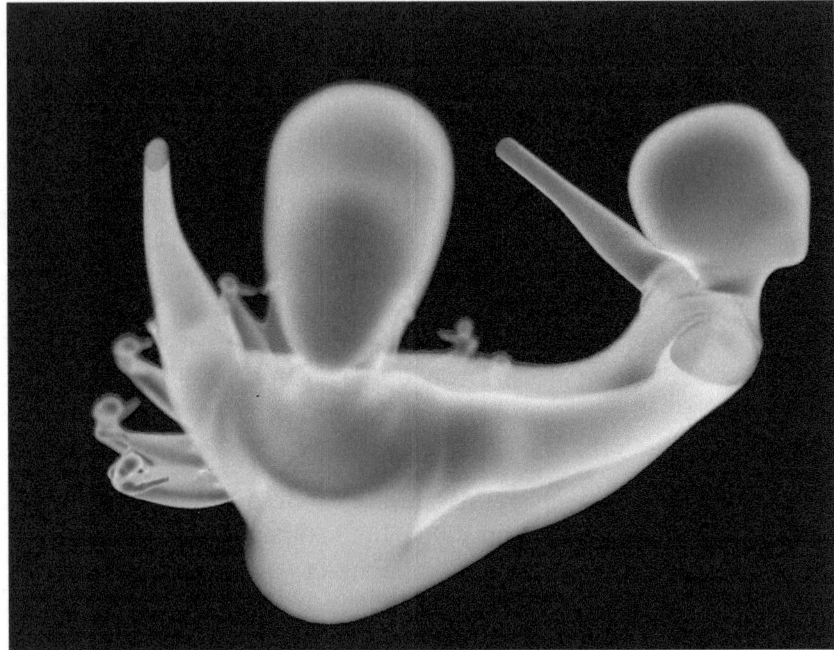

Figure 43. The Transmute Collective, *Intimate Transactions*, version 3 (2005-8), "Intimate Transactions Shared body group". Image Stuart Lawson. Courtesy of Keith Armstrong.

virtual space the two participants can meet and move together as one *semi-joined* avatar in order to "return" objects to the screen-worlds of the creatures and "restore" environments that may have suffered overconsumption. This restorative collaboration will *re-enliven* the entire ecology of the work (Armstrong 2006: 26-29; O'Neill 2006: 41).

So the more individualized enunciations of the supposed sovereign or narcissistic subject are deterritorialized by the very design of *Intimate Transactions*. The work encourages and enables the creation of new "collective assemblages of enunciation" where a polyphonic "becoming-together precedes the being-one" (Ettinger 1995a: 30). *Intimate Transactions* does not attribute what happens in the more collaborative "transactivity" of the event to any individual subject (Birringer 2006: 109). Causality and responsibility become "distributed," emerging from a larger trans-subjective field. All this is felt through the vibrations on the body (Armstrong 2006; Hamilton 2006: 119 and Birringer 2006: 108-109). *Becoming-together,* while *co-composing in difference*, begins to emerge as "an explicit social practice."

In *Intimate Transactions* we do not really experience mediation between discrete bodies or entities but what has been termed *affective immediation*. Immediation works the "collective assemblages of enunciation" as these emerge in the *shared virtual world* of the installation. It diagrams the entire polyphonic ensemble across the sensual and perceptual register of the moving bodies (human and non-human). The *collective assemblages* are felt and they participate in the creation of new trans-subjective individuations that care for the entire ecology of the work. This care may well attune with other situations after the two participants leave the gallery spaces.

In terms of issues related to sustainability, overconsumption and colonization, *Intimate Transactions* then does not attempt to mediate a clearly formulated political message. Rather, *Intimate Transactions* is immediating—the artwork operates at a micropolitical level and works the "collective assemblages of enunciation" as these come into being. It diagrams them to change the desire of "the social field" itself. I would say that *Intimate Transactions* is a schizoanalytic mapping "in action" where new *proto-ethical* "lines of virtuality" emerge that are born of the "encounter-event" itself.

In *Intimate Transactions* the cartographic mappings encourage actualization of habits and techniques that are more amenable to the gentleness necessary to collaborative "becoming-together." I have suggested that out of these cartographic actualizations new "lines of virtuality" may emerge that can support future individuation of an ethico-political care. These "lines of virtuality" operate at a more unconscious level of experience. As proposed in this chapter, the productivity of this kind of unconscious—a *productive unconscious* that in *Intimate Transactions* also becomes an ecological unconscious—is not a matter of representation or interpretation. Rather what is involved is an immediate and, in the case of *Intimate Transactions*, a micropolitical productivity in which the new "lines of virtuality" produced can participate in immediating new polyphonic practices. These practices would themselves be productive of resistance and change.

Notes

1. According to Alanna Thain (2005) "the original concept of immediation is meant to flesh out a non-phenomenological understanding of the body

in cinema." This "entails a critique of the understanding of film as simply a second nature or a mediated version of reality". See also Brunner (2012) and Brunner, Manning and Massumi in Massumi (Immediation I, 275-293).

2. Guattari calls for us to readjust. He writes that "[o]nly a profound transformation of social relations at every level ... a 'molecular revolution' correlative to analytic practices and new micropolitics, will enable such a readjustment" (2009: 203).
3. It concerns "relational difference in co-emergence" (Ettinger 1995a: 30).
4. See Massumi (2002) for a more detailed conceptualization of this understanding of relationality.
5. Ettinger explains that for Lacan "[s]ubjectivity is discovered in the relationship between self and the signifiers of language, between the subject and the discourse of the Other which is an unconscious tissue of chains of discourse. By the signifier, every message is connected to an unconscious code that is included in the Other" (1992: 184).
6. Ettinger is in part drawing on the later work of Lacan here. See Ettinger (1992: 191 and 204) for a discussion of how Freud and Lacan differ in regard to the power of visual images in relation to the unconscious.
7. Ettinger writes that the "matrixial Other is not a total Other" (1999: 21).
8. Ettinger considers metramorphosis "a conductive between-link" (1995b: 74).
9. Ettinger (2011: 7) explains that "[i]n the matrixial borderspace ... transsubjectivity" is "never global, never form[s] a collective unconscious, but ... [is] ...limited each time to a few who participate in an encounter-event: to the several. A move toward a particular kind of ethicality is enabled by this affective zone which in itself is only proto-ethical, since it enables but doesn't impose an awareness of borderlinking; recognizing this is a choice, an option, an offer, a gift. A possibility for resistance is offered to the subject by ... a tending-toward and a response that are not reactional even though they are responsive".
10. Massumi (2015b: 205) writes that affect "is pure sociality."
11. Moten is talking about Frantz Fanon's writing here.
12. See also Haraway (2013: 123-126).
13. Bosteels (1998) gives an extensive account of Guattari's conceptualization of the unconscious and schizoanalytic cartography.
14. Also cited by Bosteels (1998: 167). According to Deleuze this implies that "[t]he trajectory merges not only with the subjectivity of those who travel through a milieu, but also with the subjectivity of the milieu itself" (1998: 61).
15. Note that sections of my more descriptive account of *Intimate Transactions* here have been published previously in *The Fibreculture Journal* as a small part of a much longer article titled "Affect and Care in Intimate Transactions" (see Bertelsen, 2012).

16. The other members of the Transmute Collective are Lisa O'Neill and Guy Webster. See the full list of collaborators here: http://embodiedmedia.com/homeartworks/intimate-transactions
17. See also O'Neill (2006: 41-42) and Webster (2006: 66).

Nicole de Brabandere

Edging Semblance

Proposition: freeze a gradation in the instant of photographic capture, align the position of image fragments on the surface of the composition so that edge and image mutually inform. The intense tension between image and edge co-compose as image fragments accumulate and cover the entire surface of each composition. The shape of the images or the contour of their edges, either aligns with or juxtaposes the virtual vectors of the image gradations, making felt differential elasticities, speeds and frictions—edge moves image into position, and vice-versa. The tension between surface and image, form and edge resonates with the referential, igniting a diversity of remembered pasts in the present. Liquid seeps fastest along the edge of the image of differential absorption through a sponge; the image of a stretched balloon gently pulls the ground of the image that frames it, settling uneven tensions onto the surface of composition; the round edges of the image of a pulling pant seam compel the accumulating composition to pivot over itself, further pulling the fabric into bunching pleats; the torn edge of tape grips at the image of its own contrast, slowing the fast dissolve of the roll of tape as it slips out of highlight. These intense relations of virtual dynamism set the pace for stirring form, image and edge into topographical excesses that resonate with the choreographic—the relation between ground and surface, form and edge activates time in varying mixes of tendencies to movement and their anticipation. In turn, the resulting compositions do not contain the intensities that give force to their divergent forms. As the emergent form of the composition folds diverse inhabited pasts into precise relations in the present, these emergent relations continue to inform how one inhabits diverse technical ecologies after the fact. The dynamics of movement coming into form, and vice-versa, further differentiate as words feel for the contrasts, intensities and transversal movements of attention with and through the compositions:

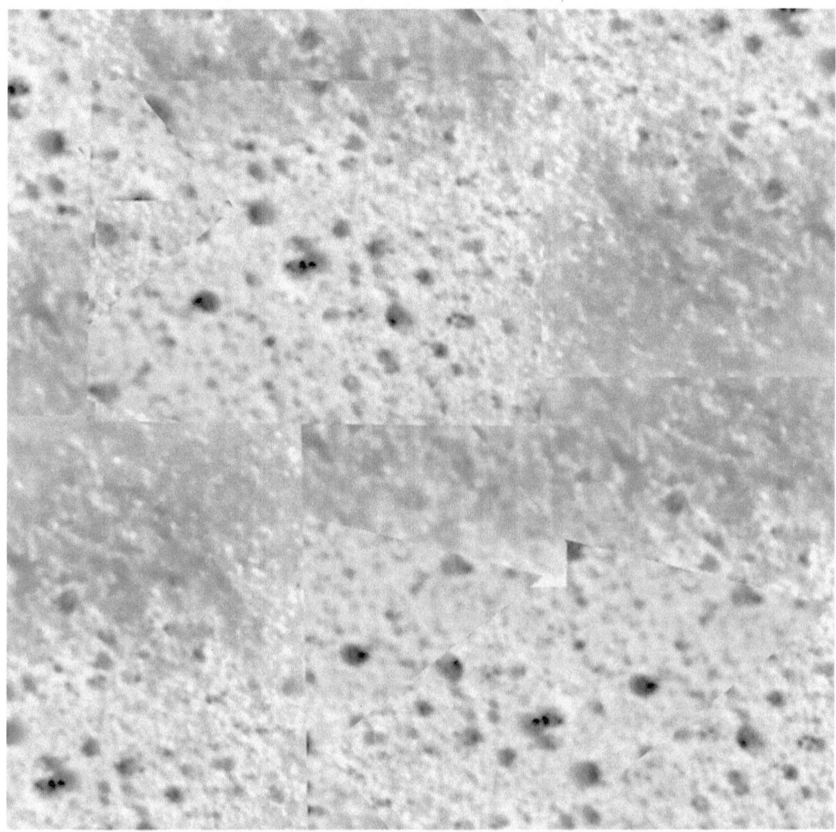

The image of a partially wet sponge is composed into a topography that seems to seep variable wetness between the sharp edges of cropped photographs and the volume of sponge. The image of flattened foam cuts the movement of directional grain onto the visible surface while threatening to draw the water that settles on the bottom-facing side of the sponge image into it. The tonal gradation that goes from dry minty foam to soft, waterlogged green is fixed into form but comes into tension with image orientations that invert, mirror and reverse the flow. As the sharp, cropped edges of individual images align into flush geometries on the image surface they also seem to press deep into seeping absorption, drawing differential wetness to the surface.

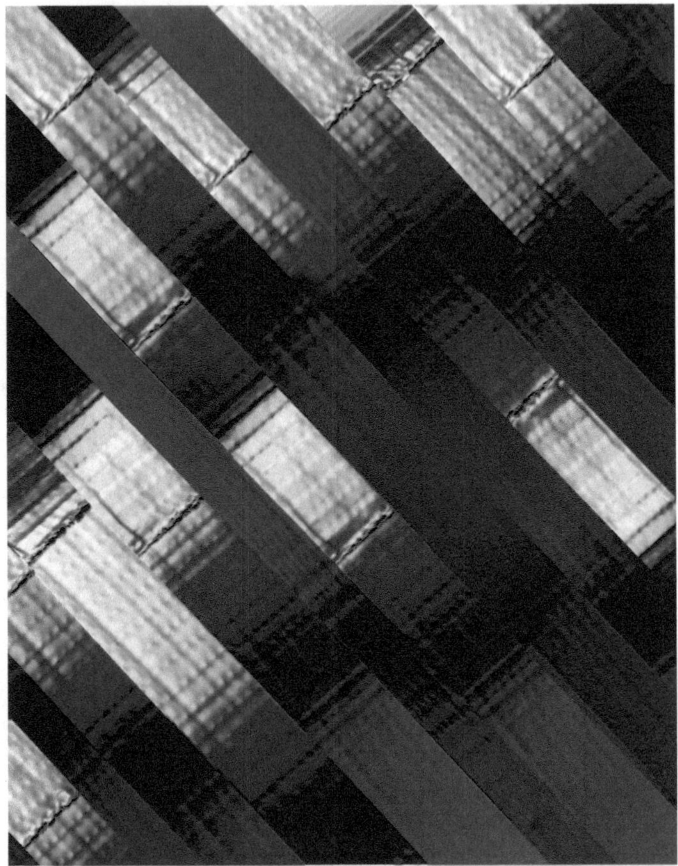

Black duct tape still stuck to the roll is photographed, in incremental instances as it rolls towards and away from the single-sided light source. The variable illuminations of the tape roll surface are cropped into strips, objectifying the light that burnishes its surface in a gradation, somewhere between grey scale and litmus test. The strips are assembled diagonally, and cover the entire surface of the composition. The broken tape seems to catch the light, setting the subtle difference between each strip into relief, where they otherwise align in seamless parallel over the surface, and where the tips without reflection blur into a homogenous consistency. The rolling rolls of tape pull out of indifference in the snagging light, between the crispness of a tear and the rounding surface of the roll that smears streaks between highlight and shadow. Now the photographic instant returns focus to the cresting a glint on broken ends of tape before again peeling away into the recomposing depths of edgeless, blackening sight.

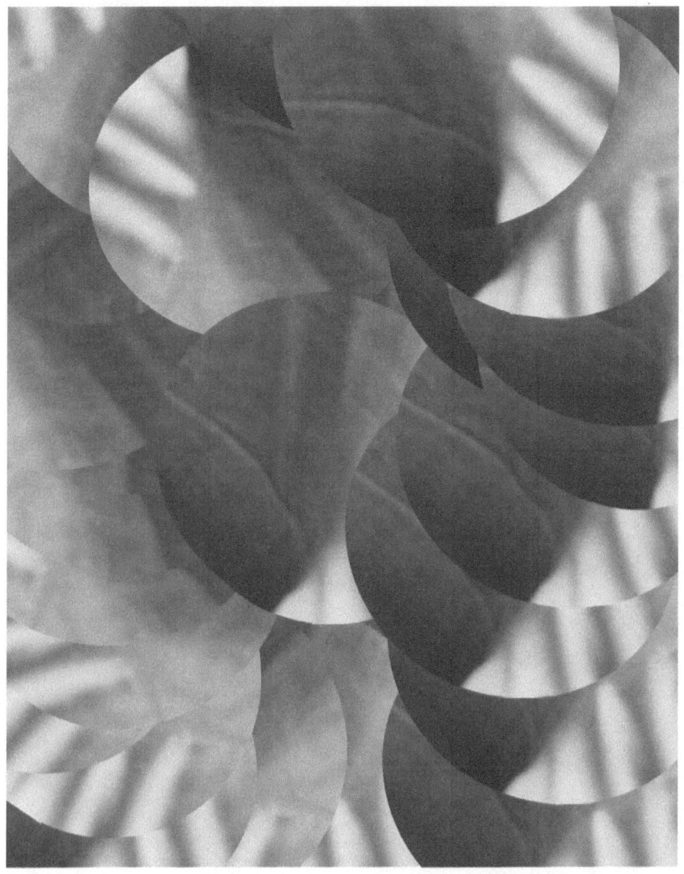

The pivotal nexus of a pant seem, rippling at the edges from the tension of being worn on legs stretched to step back in pivot, are cut into the shape of a round disk. The image sample is copied repeatedly so that it fills the space of the composition with a dance of layering, turning and pivoting circles. The pulling surface of the pants seem to pull the composition into form in a spiraling movement inwards, as if the wearer were dancing a series of turns on an image surface that doubled as a slick ballroom floor. The composition turns a corporeal that is anchored in pivot, in the sequenced pull of fabric flexing, twisting the surface into form.

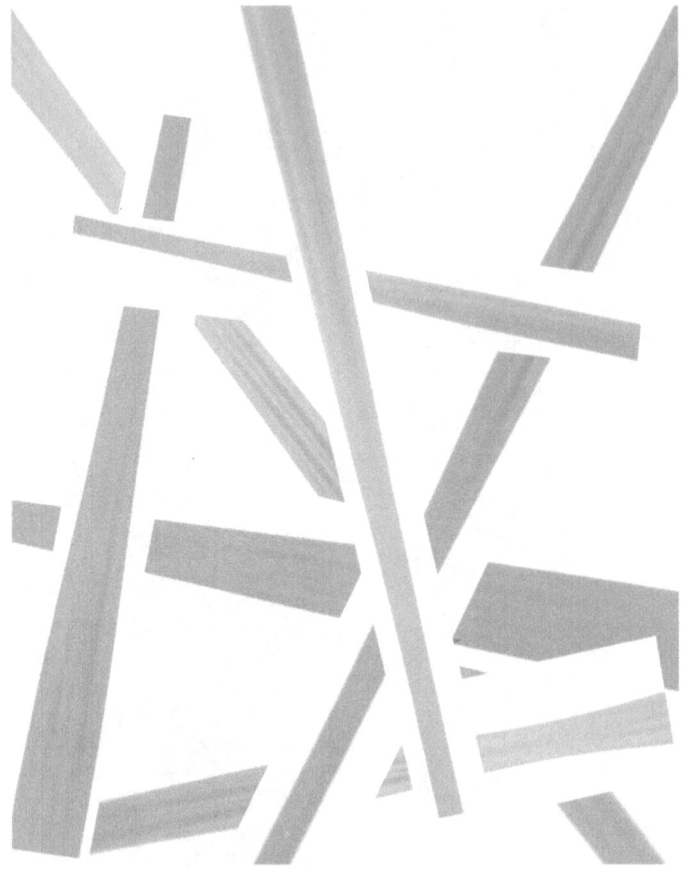

Empty orange balloon skins stretch out and hold still, over a stiff white ground, for the instant of photographic capture. Each image is a cropped strip that borders the length of the gently thinning and widening orange contour, while severing the ends. The surface of the collage copies and pivots the strips over top of each other, holding them in multi-directional tension. The white photographic borders of the strips blend into the white ground of the blank white canvas, but reveal starkly visible edges at the site of overlap, where they seem to press the image tightly into place. At the same time, the layered images also seem to pull outwards from the elastic ends, suspending time between the permanence of the composition and the anticipation of quick release. The persistent oscillation between tensions on the surface holds the image in an endless snap.

Erin Manning

Experimenting Immediation: Collaboration and the Politics of Fabulation

A Laboratory for Thought in Motion

When I proposed SenseLab in 2003, my hope was to create an environment that would learn, over time, how to create conditions for new forms of collaboration across art, philosophy and the political. This laboratory for thought in motion was a speculative proposition that required collective engagement, and so a first call was sent in 2004. This call included a question that remains at the heart of our collective practice: what kinds of events can we craft that are capable of creating a living ecology that values forms of engagement that trouble the mode of self-presentation of the conference and the art exhibition, the two major ways in which we are taught to share our work? Instead of foregrounding finished work, could we instead come together with the techniques that move our process, collaborate at this incipient stage rather than at the phase where form is already revealing itself? In this middling of the process, what kinds of conditions could be invented that would facilitate a shifting back and forth between our individual work and a collective field of making-thinking that didn't know in advance where it could lead? What kinds of collective practices could be created that were moved not by the institution, not by membership in an organization, but by an appetite for the anarchic share of the event's coming to form? How could this anarchic share be oriented toward an affirmative politics moved not by optimism (or pessimism) but by the schizz that reorients process?

SenseLab was never conceived as a site, though it has found landings over the years, first in other peoples' labs[1] and eventually at Concordia University in Montreal. In 2012, it began to proliferate, finding temporary sites in Australia, in Europe, In Brazil and in the

US, temporary because the hope is that SenseLab never really learns how to site. To know too well how to site is to become an institution. SenseLab's nightmare is to know itself too well.

But anything that persists over time risks eventually narrating itself, and SenseLab is no exception. How to keep open and lively the process of subtracting SenseLab from its own singular specificity, its ways of knowing "itself"? There have been many configurations and populations over the years, and each of them has defined SenseLab in ways that make a global narration of intelligibility impossible. And so the attempt here to bring SenseLab into narration must always be seen as carrying with it a certain ineffability of expression. Throughout these uneasy narrations, SenseLab must be seen less as a form than as the conceptual persona it orients, a conceptual persona that carries living problems, not their solutions. For conceptual personae carry not the truth of the narration, but its power of the false.[2]

The danger of any narration is that it mythologizes, that it builds institutions to hold narratives in place. What I propose here, in the name of experimenting immediation, is an account that I hope demythologizes as quickly as it enters into a shape, an account oriented not by a subject-participant so much as by an emergent collectivity always reinventing the stakes that bring it into uneasy encounter. For SenseLab is about more-than human comings-together, more-than human in the sense that what comes into formation as event is an ecology of practices, more-than human in the sense that what is planned is not set in advance of the event's coming to be, but, as Moten and Harney might say, "fugitively planned," the welling event's own emergent organization playing a key role in what ensues.

This emphasis on the more-than human, on the capacity for the event to activate a quality of participation that doesn't rely solely on the human, became increasingly important as SenseLab grew and became more literate. The more we told our story, the more it became clear that we were in danger of creating a collective that could only know itself from the inside. To know oneself from the inside is to believe that the constitution of the event is directly linked to the people who are visible in its formation. But events are not like this: they are troubled and energized by affective tonalities that infiltrate their bounds, oriented by the push and pull of ecologies brought simultaneously into being. And so we started inventing techniques to make felt the proliferation of tendencies and consistencies that make up events, working hard to become attuned to forms of participation that complicate both notions of individual subjectivity and of human-centric organization. Moving, for instance, from the forest to the city in the 2012 event *Generating the Impossible*[3] was an attempt to feel the effects of how an environmental surrounds also composes and participates in the process of making-thinking. How, we wondered, would what began to take form in the forest come to expression in the city? What kinds of schisms would emerge in the transversality of transduction? Conceiving transduction – a shift that creates a new process – as key to an affirmative politics that sites in the doing, it became urgent to consider how events themselves craft bodies, how they create emergent bodyings that are composed of and compose with the ecologies that move through them.

The focus on the more-than human was also geared toward challenging the category of the personal. When the personal organizes experience, two main tendencies emerge. First, there is an infiltration of identity politics which tend to amplify not what the emergent collectivity can do, but what personal stakes are understood to be present even before the project takes form. While these personal stakes no doubt make some kind of contribution in the event, SenseLab's approach is to initially background them in favour of allowing the event itself to foreground how it mobilizes political, aesthetic and philosophical problems. The second tendency of the personal is toward the creation of what is too often a normative psychologization that privileges individual narratives. SenseLab turns instead to a schizoanalytic approach which focuses on the group-subject, the agglomeration of collective forces in the event. With attention to how group-subjects both come into formation and express their collectivity, we work from the perspective of what an emergent constellation can do rather than what individual participants owe the event and are owed by it. Our main point of emphasis is that SenseLab is a project that exceeds any individual participant: the project should always be more-than the sum of its parts. This is no easy task: the uncertainty of emergent collectivity, where the production of subjectivity is understood as immanent to the event, inevitably breeds anxiety and anxiety tends to solidify personal stakes. How to escape from the positioning of the personal before it takes hold?

The Free Radical

The concept of the free radical was brought into the mix in 2012 to begin to address this question of how to work collectively with a focus on emergent collectivity and the production of subjectivity. The free radical came in through the event discussed above, *Generating the Impossible*, an event whose focus was on affective attunement and altereconomies of exchange.[4] The free radical, as we envisaged it, would infiltrate the event's interstices, keeping the event from hardening around positions. Operating transversally to the practices of making-thinking orienting the event, the free radical would punctually unglue any position-taking. It would do the work of a trickster around the inevitable personalization, creating opportunities for the event to find new orientations capable of diffusing the kind of stabilization that breeds eventual institutionalization. The hope was that the free radical, despite (and because of) its deeply unsettling tendencies, would make it possible to create a culture of affirmation that didn't fall prey to a desire to settle the event into a culture of consensus, or its by-product, critique. Working from the perspective of the anarchic, thinking anarchy both in terms the anarchic share of the event (those merest of existences that seed future processes without necessarily taking form as such), and from the perspective that an event always exceeds the bounds of prescribed spacetimes of organization, a concept was needed to orient transversally, bringing to the anarchic the force of an affirmative politics. The concept of the free radical allowed us to bring an intercessor[5] into the mix who would assist us in making felt how the anarchic schizzed through the event. While we did have a person in mind for this first exploration of the free radical, the concept was also conceived in a broader way. Affinity groups that might be capable of both incorporating and sustaining the force of free-radicality were composed in advance of our coming together, and platforms for relation for seeding affective attunement to the event were proposed. With the free radical as concept, proposition, and intercessor, the question was: what does the creative dissonance of the anarchic share of experience in the making do for the event as it unfolds? How does a resonant field of experience that includes the merest of existences affect attunement to the event? What might attention become, under these circumstances? With the benefit of hindsight, I would say that these were early steps toward developing techniques for what we have come to call minor gestures, those emergent forces of variation that shift how an event comes to pass.

The free radical cuts across the event to open it to where else it could go. Always operative, the free radical jumps into fissures, activating their potential to create new directionalities that alter what an event can do. Affirmative and joyful, the figure of the free radical is nonetheless uneasy-making in its anarchic tendencies. For its technique is to open things up, to explode them. With this come closures as new paths are taken up: there is much reorienting to do when the ground shifts. The free radical has no care for sites that claim their ground.

SenseLab has never had membership. Membership would make the free radical a member, which would, of course, destroy its potential for intercession. The free radical must be able to become every member, and every tendency in the event must free radicalize itself.

The issue of membership nonetheless rears its head. Despite there being no actual membership, it is inevitable that certain cultures take hold and, over time, embody a history of what it can mean to be involved at SenseLab, which can lead to feelings of exclusion for newcomers. Uncertainty can be powerful, especially in the context of the kind of practice that is built with an emphasis on not-knowing-in-advance. Tensions can emerge. But with the intercession also comes great enthusiasm and joy: there is nothing like the clearing of the air that can come from a step sideways. We make this part of our practice: what makes an event-based orientation powerful is precisely what cuts across it. All newcomers bring with them a quality of intercession. The culture of SenseLab actively works to collaborate with the transversality this engenders.

This raises an interesting issue: how to work between the activation of what enters from elsewhere and the inheritances that come from working together over time? There is no question that the force of inheritance makes a difference: a practice that takes techniques seriously and works with the enabling constraints of a structured improvisation over years inevitably develops orientations that are singular. SenseLab in no way supports an ethos of "anything goes." This is the case for material intervention as much as for concept invention. We commit to what we learn together and we stay with the learning for extended periods to experiment with where it can take us. There are practices that underlie this commitment to the thickness of an evolving process. For instance, it is our practice to read closely from philosophical texts. Reading groups are structured to prevent debate. What is important is how the text does its work: we read out loud and stick to the propositions operative in the materiality of expression of the text at hand. This approach allows all newcomers to feel included, whether or not they have any philosophical background. The same is true for movement experimentation and material exploration. Our investment in a politics of affirmation does not mean having no constraints. It means working-with, sitting-with the singular ways in which materials unfold and activate nodes of process. The first thing that would undo this would be a culture of critique and competition.[6] And so we work to avoid any tendency to move in that direction, including any attempt to engage with general ideas. We are aware that the culture of academia loves general ideas, and we resist this tendency to speak in ways that generalize experience: what interests us is always a commitment to *how*. How does the thinking do its work, here, now? How do the materials activate a transversality? How does the movement shift the conditions of the bodying?

That said, there is no question that leaving the space of intercession open is vital: very often events have been reoriented by new arrivals precisely because these newcomers are not informed by the history of our ongoing practice. And so, over the past fifteen years, we have worked to hone an event-based practice of welcoming difference that carries the consistency of an ethos. It is not our practice to discuss "our" way. What we do instead is try to hone a mode of listening to the event as it unfolds. The hope is always that the newcomer can feel the stakes at hand and can participate in them directly. It is beautiful to watch how often this happens, how often a newcomer arrives in the middling to reorient what came before in ways desperately needed. Almost every day there is an intercession, every intercession shifts the conditions of what we call SenseLab. It would therefore be fair to say that the intercession of the sideways entry is as much part of the inheritance of SenseLab as the years of experimentation redirected by the inflexion the newcomer proposes.

No decision-making bodies external to the process exist at SenseLab. We have no governing body, no committee for overseeing activities. This developed organically from a desire to work from within the event's own conditionings. What has resulted is a politics of immediation, which, by extension is always also a politics of affirmation.[7] Affirmation is understood here in the Nietzschean sense: active, not reactive. Affirmation is not consensus, that most flattening of practices, but nor is it anything goes. In an always shifting register of emergent collectivity, SenseLab moves where the experiment takes it, casting propositions aside without looking back if they don't do their work. We practice saying "yes" but seek not to attend to personal stakes above what the event can do. Of course "this is how we do things" is still heard:

difference is not necessarily easy to attune to, especially in moments of stress. It is a radical proposition to remain open to new tendencies all the time. Free radicalization inevitably gets watered down by the fear of losing our footing. And yet we persist because we know that the desire for continuity, for the recognition of the past in the present, is a real danger as regards the ability to remain attuned to the differential at the heart of event-based propositions.

This is a challenge all political formations face. How to keep the edges open to the elements in ways that enliven those in the midst without creating such a strong tempest of uncertainty that collaborators drift away or collapse? How to build into the sociality that emerges over time enough porousness that it remains open to the fray? For it is only in the fray that new weaves become visible.

SenseLab lives with all of these contradictions. We often contend with failure. The transitions are messy. Growing pains are deep and often agonizing.

Immediation

Our current event series is called *Immediations.* With the force of the free radical active as intercessor, and close attention paid to the way the minor gesture affects event-ecologies, this series[8] asks how else the event can tell its story? What kinds of knowledges are alive in the event and how are they passed on? How can we move beyond mediation, or reporting, in the passage from force to form? How can we compose collectively, working both with past and emergent techniques, without holding fast to the security of habits, material or conceptual? How do we differentiate between the close encounter with materials and concepts, that encounter that allows us, over time, to become even more attuned to their potential, and the fear of trying something different? While finding ways to narrate experience, how do we refrain from mythologizing it? How can the immediacy of the event cut through the certainty of a certain belonging-together, a return to the figure of the individual? How can the anarchic share of an emergent collectivity based on appetite make itself felt without falling into the kinds of social camps facilitated by practices of inclusion and exclusion?

Immediation is a technique more than it is a descriptor. It is what moves the event into another register. A politics of fabulation invariably accompanies it. Fabulation is altogether different from a practice of mythologization: it is that tendency in the telling that resists organizing the event into the kind of consumable bite-sized description that would narrate it as a linear arc. This kind of telling:

> free[s] [fiction] from the model of truth which penetrates it, and [...] rediscover[s] the pure and simple *function of fabulation* [...]. What is opposed to fiction is not the real; it is not the truth which is always that of the masters or colonizers; it is the fabulatory function of the poor, in so far as it gives the false the power which makes it into a memory, a legend, a monster (Deleuze 1989: 150, *translation modified*).[9]

Inheritor of oral practices of story-telling, fabulation is how the trickster speaks. As the voice of the free radical, fabulation attunes to the difference between those kinds of narratives that hold the event hostage and those that breed openings. It's not that these more normative narratives don't enter the world: they do. Our task is to craft the conditions for events that resist this kind of telling, opting instead for a fabulation that undermines the very question of an event's localization in a single place, toward predictable ends, activating not the truth of a myth framed by individual accounts, but its power of the false, the power of the event to claim its falsification from itself. With the power of the false, time begins to err, undermining the imposition of continuity. Time as metric is disrupted, but not just that: time folds.

The free radical activates the power of the false in the event. Acting as intercessor, it cuts into what is moving the event and opens that movement to uneasy rhythms. These rhythms are uneasy because their paths are not yet drawn, and because these paths are both synchronous and dissonant, more multiplicity of cut than site. The free radical pushes against them to feel where else they can lead.

What the free radical can do is make appear a minor tendency in the event and move that tendency into a becoming-gesture that shape-shifts the tonality of the event. The free radical does this by activating a schizz in the event. This schizoanalytic gesture involves setting the event's myth-making orientations in direct confrontation with their power of the false, making felt the story's own unmaking of itself. With the power of the false a sense of *what else* enters the event, allowing the contours of a still-transitioning to be felt. The challenge is to not try to make this passage, this transition intelligible. Its force is precisely that it cannot be organized into an all-encompassing narrative. The work: to create the conditions for enough elasticity in the event for the story to emerge again differently, told not only in words but also in the language of the ineffable. "Language [...] is always ambiguous as to the exact proposition which it indicates. Spoken language is merely a series of squeaks" (Whitehead 1978: 264).

Fabulation tells in a way that moves with time's unweaving. Sensitive to the squeaks of language, to language at the edge of comprehension, fabulation is moved less by the necessity to explain than by the realization, always come to anew, that telling is a form of liveness completely connected to the event's own emergence. Fabulation's telling cannot be separated out from how the narration shifts the terms of the event. Stories become intensive magnitudes rather than extensive place-holders. They tell at the limit of what can be known, their work a falsifying of what constitutes the knowable. This falsification is not of the order of a simple untruth: the power of the false is about another kind of truth altogether, a truth of the event in its inevitable permutation. Fabulation speaks in the mouths of the many, its utterance collective. "An act of fabulation which would not be a return to myth but a production of collective utterances capable of raising misery to a strange positivity, the invention of a people" (Deleuze 1989: 222).

The push to experimentation in the event can be textured by fabulation, orienting the event in novel ways. When this happens, fabulation acts as point of inflection, making felt the kind of vertigo that emerges of necessity when perspectives are transversalized and time-signatures that hold accounts in place begin to blur. Fabulation tells into this blurring, pushing futurity into presentness in ways that allow time to become dechronologized. Mediation is not what is at stake here: the task of the mediator is precisely to keep the horizon line. Fabulation does the opposite: it mobilizes the not-yet already alive in the interstices and makes it reverberate. It catches free radicals at work, activating a worlding that keeps the event uncertain as to where its points of reference lie. It articulates a doing in the thinking that makes felt how the telling falsifies time's linearity.

The power of the false, the capacity for fabulation to challenge what a personalized accounting might want to invent as the event's truth, is deeply unsettling. Much easier would be to formalize a frame for the event in the name of some kind of truth. Or to create myths that solidify it from the inside. But both of these tendencies undermine the very practice of what an event can do and what a more-than human approach can catalyze. Much more difficult, but also richer, is to engage directly in the event's interstices, in those schizzes where desynchronized truths are crafted for the uneasy telling. "Fabulation is not an impersonal myth, but neither is it a personal fiction: it is a word in act, a speech-act through which the character never ceases to cross the boundary which would separate his private business from politics, and which itself produces collective utterances" (Deleuze 1989: 222, *translation modified*).

To not cease to cross involves a punctuality. The event never ceases to create a limit through which a certain telling takes place that produces a collectivity of utterance. That is to say: the event invariably narrates itself. The event tells itself in the ways in which it composes with the ecologies of practices that are its emergent surrounds. It tells itself in its reorienting by the free radical. It tells itself in the ways in which it transitions and cuts. For the event transitions more than it places, passaging experience. In this passaging, a "people" is invented, Deleuze suggests, a worlding that is more-than the humans who also compose it. With fabulation, this worlding opens itself each time anew to the passaging. This is where the event, as Whitehead might say, most feels the concern for its unfolding.[10] This is where it emergently attunes to worlds of its making. Fabulation makes felt this worlding, this ecology, which will always, by necessity, exceed its capacity to be told. This telling, at the heart of all events, is a punctual limit, altered at every turn by what the event immediates.

Tigeresque

In November 2014, a SenseLab gathering was organized in Australia. It was composed of two propositions, one held north of Melbourne in the rural town of Avoca, the other held in Sydney. The first proposition was made in conjunction with Lyndal Jones's *Avoca Project*.[11]

The *Avoca Project* (2005-2016) worked across a community, a house (Watford House), and the question of sustainability as oriented by how an artful approach can alter the conditions of everyday living. How, Jones wondered, might the house become an image of potential and resilience, and how would such an approach have effects that might leak into the community?[12]

SenseLab arrived toward the end of this process, a decade into Watford House's transformation. The proposition for the SenseLab-Avoca encounter was to see how SenseLab's approach to creating conditions for more-than human forms of collaboration might compose with the *Avoca Project*. By then the final phase of the *Avoca Project* had begun: a Chinese garden in the old sheep yards next to the house had recently been landscaped. Described by Jones as a project that "draws attention to the lack of public gardens in Avoca [...] and acknowledges the important Chinese contribution to the town from the 1850s, when many thousands settled in the area after the gold rush," the garden, entitled "Garden of Fire and Water," punctuated a decade-long inquiry into sustainability by designing directly with the underground flows of water. This self-sustaining garden underscored "that to live-with is an ethos that requires attending to the existing sites of potential," signing the *Avoca Project* with a final act that would continue to make sustainability in the region felt, even without direct human intervention.[13]

> The garden is exquisite. It overlooks the flood plain and the Avoca river, foregrounding the role water plays in this arid town.
>
> The central water element has been created as a wetland that cleans and uses the stormwater from the main street. Plants were selected that directly reference China and thrive in this climate, framed within indigenous and native plantings to situate the garden firmly into this landscape of River Red Gums.[14]

SenseLab's arrival coincided with the launch of the garden. The only directions we received in advance of our arrival was that we were to bring formal wear: there would be a cocktail party for the garden. In true SenseLab form, we saw ourselves as guests of the garden. In our months-long preparation for the SenseLab-Avoca encounter we spoke often about how best to fulfill our role as guest of honour for the gardens: it was the surrounds we most fabulated about.

No other plans had been set: the question of the event itself was the operative problem. Could SenseLab encounter the *Avoca Project* such that an event might take place? And if so, would the event be capable of bringing into focus an emergent proposition that could enliven what was already moving at Avoca? Could SenseLab bring the force of a lure that might activate the anarchic share in the transversality of the two projects? And if so, what kind of proposition might be made that both included us *and* exceeded us?

To approach the question of event-creation rigorously involves a long preparation. This preparation is not about planning content in advance, as though the activity could be focalized through a pre-set frame. That would be to disregard the force of the event's own capacity to orient experience. What is needed instead is a procedure allied to what Moten and Harney call "fugitive planning," an orientation toward the conditions that seed process that remains sensitive to the emergent quality of the event's own forces of organization.

> In the undercommons [...] the means, which is to say the planners, are still part of the plan. And the plan is to invent the means in a common experiment launched from any kitchen, any back porch, any basement, any hall, any park bench, any improvised party, every night. [...] [P]lanning in the undercommons is not an activity, not fishing or dancing or teaching or loving, but the ceaseless experiment with the futurial presence of the forms of life that make such activities possible (2013: 74-75).

At the SenseLab, a technique for approaching this kind of fugitive planning involves experimenting with what we call "enabling constraints." For a year preceding any event, we work to test out the malleability of constraints, exploring to what degree they close down or open up a process. Enabling constraints proposed for a gathering such as that in Australia might include ways of entering into the unknown territory of new vegetation, which might involve research on local flora and fauna, animal and insect life; research on ecologies of practice, on concepts such as the more-than human or the nonhuman; on local environmental practices. Or it might involve exploring experimental movement to see how different qualities of bodying best respond to emergent propositions. Or it might involve material experimentation that creates approximations of proximity in relation to other artistic practices. To keep this at the level of the fugitive, and to work with the force of the propositional rather than with the framing of the organizational, our year-long work is more a guide than a setting-into-place. For what we know of the event is that it modulates on the run, and with this incipient movement, enabling constraints invariably have to be modulated. Fugitive planning is about creating a flexibility of thought and action which is robust enough to be realigned on the fly. It's never enough to import an enabling constraint from one event to another: the preparation is an investment in honing techniques to create a sensitivity that will come in handy when faced with the singular conditions that enable or disable the event.

Despite rigorous exploration in advance of landing, however, nothing had prepared us for the uneasy way the *Avoca Project* disoriented us. It turned out that the cocktail party was for the locals, not for the garden (also for the garden, just not in the sense we'd fabulated). And the house strangely seemed to know where it stood (our fabulation has assumed it was less steady on its foundations). The jetlag didn't help. Here we were, 35 of us from several continents, faced with a project difficult to encounter well in such a short period. Paradoxes loomed: there was a sense, conceptually at least, that Watford House welcomed an intercession toward new ways of thinking sustainability. But there was also a sense that we had arrived too late – that this particular arc of Watford House and the *Avoca Project* had run its cycle, including the garden, which was now ready to be presented. Another arc was on its way, but here we were, at the interstice, unsure how to compose with what we entered into.

SenseLab didn't want to be a visitor to a project already framed nor did the *Avoca Project* simply want to host us. The problem was that neither of us yet had techniques to creatively compose with the ineffability of the emerging arc. What SenseLab thought would be enabling constraints turned out to be disabling. We wandered around, at a loss. Part of the problem was that things were more set than we had imagined – the house was beautifully appointed, much more "house" than "experiment," the surrounds were well maintained, and the project itself was well-established in relation to a town that had now been interacting with the work for a decade. Everything was gorgeous, including the work the *Avoca Project* had been able to do with issues of sustainability and community. The problem was not the *Avoca Project* itself. The issue was one of composition – how to create an emergent collectivity where cracks are not easily felt, where the collaboration does not seem urgently needed, or needed at all. Despite our not wanting the position, we felt like visitors, tourists. As mentioned above, this was Jones's nightmare: more than once she told us that she didn't want us to see Watford House as a bed and breakfast. She wanted us to be free in our approach to it, she wanted us to invent with it. But it was a house that had well-established needs and habits. Jones knew its functioning better than we did, and she knew the environment in ways that tired Canadians, Brazilians and Europeans couldn't possibly know. And so despite best intentions, the encounter began with frames, and with rules. The rules made sense, and were necessary, given the complex water systems of an arid location, but to begin with rules always sets in place a certain passive-active hierarchy. Passivity, once settled into the weave of a gathering, is hard to overcome, dampening the force of the kind of potential necessary for the emergence of a collectivity created in the event.

An impasse could be felt. A certain waiting took hold. Would we be able to move beyond being visitors to being participants in a process? Would the cracks appear? Activities were proposed by a number of us – movement experimentation, sound propositions, conceptual discussions. We followed and participated. Wonderful meals were cooked. But mediation still trumped immediation. Time felt linear. People were on call, waiting to be told what would happen next.

The first two days were dominated by scattered gatherings made interesting by the skills of the leaders. We learned things, we talked, we explored. Individual projects were seeded. There was joy in being together. New friendships began to form. But there was not yet a sense that something with its own consistency was being generated, something capable of weaving the *Avoca Project* through it, moving the encounter with SenseLab toward a collaboration that would affect both in ways unexpected. There was some despair. And with the cocktail party approaching, there was some anxiety about where to move next.

A group gathered at the local pub began to fabulate. The *Avoca Project*, the group decided, had a story – it just needed to be told differently so that SenseLab could connect to it. If we could figure out how that telling could happen, we were sure to find cracks. So far, the stories the *Avoca Project* had told SenseLab were spoken as though they already knew their way. What the *Avoca Project* didn't know how to tell SenseLab was how the *Avoca Project* fabulated, how the deeper recesses of more-than human activity affected it, how the power of the false ran through it. The Chinese Garden, we decided, was key. This garden which could stem flows and capture them for its sustainability had a story to tell about how geological time composes with event-time, how the time of an art project composes with the time of worlds in the making. We would stage an investigation to find out what it knew.

For the six of us around the table, the promise of a fabulatory investigation was immediately a release from the concern which had been clouding our experience: now, rather than fitting into a project already defined, we could initiate a joyful encounter with *what else* Watford House and the Chinese Garden could be. Certain characters immediately emerged: the fish (what was the link between the fish tank in Watford house and the fish brought by a resident of Avoca to the cocktail party?); the possum (what kinds of skylines were the possums creating and how far were they willing to go to create new navigational strategies?); the tunnel (what kind of underground passage did the water flows create and how might these connect Watford House to other worlds?). We spoke to villagers. We checked with each other. We spoke to Jones. No one took us very seriously.

But another kind of perception had been awakened, and some of us were now seeing fish everywhere. On the day before our time at Avoca was to end, with fish on the brain, a few of us decided we needed to return to conceptual exploration. A spontaneous reading group was organized around Brian Massumi's book *What Animals Teach Us About Politics*. This hadn't been planned, but it turned out that several of the participants happened to have the newly published book in their luggage. We decided to begin by reading a passage out loud (for those who didn't have the book) and go from there. This was the passage:

> Think of a child playing the animal. It is certainly easy to sentimentalize the scene. But what if we take it seriously—that is, look to the aspects of it that are truly ludic in the most creative sense. Simondon writes that the child's consciousness of the animal involves far more than the simple recognition of its substantial form. One look at a tiger, however fleeting and incomplete, whether it be in the zoo or in a book or in a film or video, and presto! the child is tigerized. Transformation-in-place. The perception itself is a vital gesture. The child immediately sets about, not imitating the tiger's substantial form as he saw it, but rather giving it life— giving it more life. The child plays the tiger in situations in which the child has never seen a tiger. More than that, it plays the tiger in situations no tiger has ever seen, in which no earthly tiger has ever set paw. The child immediately launches itself into a movement of surpassing the given, remaining remarkably faithful to the theme of the tiger, not

in its conventionality but from the angle of its processual potentiality.

Remaining processually faithful to a vital theme has nothing to do with reproducing it. On the contrary, it involves giving it a new interpretation, in the musical sense of performing a new variation on it. The child does not imitate the visible corporeal form of the tiger. It prolongs the tiger's style of activity, transposed into the movements of the child's own corporeality. What the child caught a glimpse of was the dynamism of the tiger, as a form of life. The child saw the tiger's vitality affect: the potentially creative powers of life enveloped in the visible corporeal form. The tiger's vitality affect passes through what a formal analysis might isolate as its corporeal form. But it never coincides with that visible form. The life's powers that come to expression through the form's deformations sweep the form up within their own supernormal dynamism, which moves through the given situation, toward others further down the line. This transsituational movement is in excess over the form. It is the very movement of the visually given form's processual self-surpassing. This is what the child saw— all of it, in a glimpse; all in a flash. Not just a generic animal shape: a singular vital movement sweepingly immanent to the visible form. What children see: the immanence of a life. Not "the" tiger: tigritude. Children do not just catch sight of a tiger form. They have an intuitively aesthetic vision of the tigeresque as a dynamic form of life. It is this they transpose when they play animal. Not onto their own form but into their own vital movements. [...] Across the serial variations, tigritude begins to escape. It begins to surpass given situations in which we might reasonably expect a tiger to find itself, and the modes of importance those situations present. The tensions of tigeresque corporeality in- forms the childlike corporeality in play. It immanently animates it— and is animated by it in return. The replay series stretches out the tigeresque tensions, prolonging them into a transindividual tensor. The situational tensions put into play undergo an inventively deforming pressure that vectorizes them in the direction of the supernormal. Tigritude takes flight. The givens of the tigeresque situation, as conventionally known, are surpassed,

> following exploratory tensors extrapolating from the child's enthusiasm of the body (Massumi 2014: 86).

Animals were emerging everywhere – fish, possums, and now the enthusiasm of the body activated by a tigeresque encounter with a book. The fish, the possum, and the tiger were not, as Massumi makes clear, given forms. They were forces, vitality affects. The emerging investigation, and now the collective reading, was not bringing them, as animals, to life: it was activating experience such that it might now be capable of becoming transsituational, in excess of this moment, of this form. The *Avoca Project* was becoming self-surpassing. Of course all of this was still very tenuous, but the seeds for a shift were there. Which is why one reading could not be enough: the next and last day we decided to return to the passage again, despite being very short on time.

By now the tigeresque was making its way into the weave of the event. Something was doing. And then, a strange event occurred. Someone decided to spray-paint the desert lawn bright orange with these words: "To avoid predetermination create a field with at least three elements." The graffiti – an engagement with the tigeresque quality of the more-than in Massumi's text – sought to highlight the necessity of emergent collectivity, but it did so at grave risk. The landscape we left behind was scarred and would remain so until the next rain, a year in Watford House's future.

The orange spray paint didn't quite register. To this day, I'm not sure why. We were busy, the event hadn't quite taken place (the encounter remaining a gathering rather than exceeding the sum of its parts) and the time spent together had been challenging – interesting and even joyful at times, but heavy with misunderstandings and uneasy encounters. There was laundry to do, and cleanup, and the grounds were large. Many of us walked by the large expanse of bright orange words, but somehow no one reacted. Until we were gone.

It was an hour or so into the drive toward Melbourne when someone in the car with us mentioned the grass, and the orange spray-paint. We gasped. Surely this hadn't been a good idea? But if it did happen, it must have been condoned? I felt uneasy.

A few hours later, the first text message arrived. I could feel the rawness. And I knew the risk of answering: the event, still uneasily coming into itself, could too easily be reduced to the personal. The desire to single out an individual and blame them for the act was potent, even in the wake of a gathering that had collectivity and collaboration as its aim. What would an apology mean in this context? Wouldn't an inevitable hierarchy be introduced through the act of taking charge, as though the event happened in my name?

As I was thinking this through, I received a note from the investigation. It read:

> *Fishy Business November 26 2014*
>
> *Regarding other fishy business ... It was such a well designed urgency to get to the kangaroos on Tuesday night that I fear that I was unable to clearly tell of all that I uncovered. [...]. I too am suspicious of the architects ... they are very consumed by the taking of measurements and spinning stories about cloaks. I had one of them in the car on the way home but I couldn't detect any deviation within the story to catch them in the act ... my jury is still out. There is something going on with those possums ... however, when one was scratching at the back of my tent it was pretending to be a wombat, then a kangaroo, not a fish ... I suspect it may be yet another diversionary tactic!*
>
> *[...]*
>
> *There are a couple of anomalies that I stumbled upon... how [redacted] knew about the fish being flying fish is beyond me. Likewise with [redacted] ... he knew that the fish ate the Chinese. Perhaps [redacted] has been informed through some pragmatic instructions (bequeathed recipes?) for the preparation of the fish meals ... if this is the case, the usefulness of this information is likely to be questionable so further effort here may not be worthwhile.*
>
> *[...]*
>
> *This is all that I managed to gather over the few days in Avoca. I hope that it is helpful and that we might finally uncover and understand what has really been going on at the house and garden. One last detail I noticed is the difference between orange fish and fish of other colours. The fish on the bag is green ... and remember we were not sure how the actual real fish appear.*
>
> *Cheers and all the best,*

The way forward was clear: rather than dealing with the text message directly, responding one-on-one to a group issue, a collective response was called for. I decided to open up the investigation beyond the six initial members. This was the first message sent. 18 people were copied.

> *The Investigation Nov 27 2014*
>
> *Dear co-investigators,*
>
> *I've put this list together carefully. I think there are a few missing. Mattie? Indira? Aphra? I'll trust you to know where to send it next.*
>
> *I've had a studied report from [redacted]. Since some of it is confidential, I will only touch on the salient issues.*
>
> *We've left Avoca.*
>
> *Orange spray paint may contaminate the soil in the guise of philosophy (or was philosophy left to contaminate?). We fear this may have repercussions. Is Celine a double agent?*
>
> *The green fish has turned into an outline. There is a strong memory of its greenness. Fish meal still seems to be a strong clue.*
>
> *[...] The vortex is awfully close (and yet [redacted] guards the fish).*
>
> *If the fish are the outline, the semblance is near.*
>
> *The tunnel entrances seem to have been masked by the tents. I've seen a picture. It's possible that you will get access to that image. She holds a clue.*
>
> *[redacted] again: she finds the holes.*
>
> *Why is [redacted] measuring? I've included you here, though there is some concern about whose side you're on. Architects are very suspect in this scenario of dissimulated gardens and covered-up tunnels. We will need a copy of the architectural plans.*

[redacted], after investigative reporting, you have come out more Australian than Chinese. This makes you a fish, I think. We're keeping you onboard for now. I know you think you are a meerkat. We're not sure where you are going with this. Please elaborate.

Something about [redacted], [redacted] and fire. I wonder whether [redacted] isn't also implicated. I'd like to hear more. And about rabbits. Did [redacted] think eating them would make them less of a pest in Australia? Is there a parallel with the Chinese?

For now, [redacted] must be treated with caution. She knows more than she admits.

Yours truly,

And then, the next day, with 8 more people copied, but 2 deleted:

Incoming Cargo Nov 28 2014

Investigation #11

I am opening up the investigation a bit. Have heard from my co-investigator that some of the details can now be leaked.

1. [redacted]: imPOSSible defense??? Is that what you've been working at for the past year? I am seriously concerned about both the absence of goldfish in your writing (who were you trying to fool) and the fact that you actually thought this defense could happen on dry land. It's time to come clean. [redacted]: thanks for the clues. Good that you're onto her.

2. As I mentioned in the last message (investigation #8), we've done quite a lot of close scrutiny of the facts, and [redacted] comes up clean (though in the discussion tonight with [redacted] and [redacted], it was pretty much established as a given that she's at least a double agent). Double is of course a semblance.

3. We still haven't gotten to the bottom of the disabling of sustainability through orange. Is that to bring back the goldfish?

4. I've heard something about the bottom of tents. It's worrying as concerns the vortex. Why hasn't [redacted] been added to this list?

5. Sydney seems to be part of the vortex. Or the semblance. Am investigating further.

6. 3 clues in images. Note the mesh (boat?) hanging from the bridge.

8. Very concerned about [redacted], who tried to steer my attention from the mesh. Everyone just turns directly toward the Sydney opera house (I know better). Got a bit of his eyes, but was reluctant to take the glasses off.

9. Is that the ark?

Yours truly,

And the next day:

Incoming Cargo Nov 29 2014

I can still feel the delicate brushing of goldfish fins and tails against my cheeks. They have a strange attunement with my heart flutters. Despite appearances I haven't left the Avoca vortex. [redacted] knows this and is helping me not get sucked in too deeply and drown. That is the real reason he had to stay in Melbourne. [redacted] is making sure that the tunnel has wi-fi, and through her angelic connection she utters revealing philosophical statements that help me think into staying afloat.

[redacted] - we know that you are pretending to know little about this vortex tunnel, but it became clear as I measured up the House that you have at least one fishing line tied to your finger that traces out its turbulence. I am guessing you want us to admit what we know before you confess. There are many lines that I measured up, and not all of them were perceptible by the laser measuring device.

[redacted] and [redacted] have other antennae – [redacted] is organic, [redacted] is elastic. Each has different insights. [redacted] slips under tents and feels out what they hide, but she doesn't seem ready to tell us everything. Perhaps she is

crafting a new escape hole? I think [redacted] knows the cure for [redacted] contaminating paint, which is making the tunnel smell fluorescent, like a blinding light up my nostrils. [redacted]: please help.

[redacted] is with me in the vortex, and I can tell you that she has a special connection with the blind white tower, which played a major role in past Avoca fabulations. She retreats there on occasion, half way between the Chinese garden and the House, to do some measuring up. Her plan is beautifully simple. [redacted] tells me that the possums are indeed staying in contact with [redacted], who has her own very special connection into the vortex tunnel. Keep a wide eye on her.

In the vortex with the fish, [redacted], and the possums, I can now reveal that there is also a giraffe. [redacted] is channeling the meerkat. Will they arrive soon? I think they could have something to tell about the giraffe. [redacted] knows something about a winking tiger, and I am expecting to find out more about this on Monday.

I get the sense that [redacted] feathers in the Chinese garden have something to tell us about a wise bird somewhere in the vortex. I have been trying to get my chicken to help me trace the bird-esque, as we vortex together in the garden, but she was quite busy listening to earwigs.

Yesterday [redacted] and [redacted] led the way to a clue that has gone by unnoticed: the logs. Two massive logs out the front of the House. [redacted] is the double of the Log Lady, and speaks the logs' giant, doubled up words. As the Log Lady said in episode 8 of Twin Peaks:

"Can you see through a wall? Can you see through human skin? X-rays see through solid, or so-called solid objects. There are things in life that exist, and yet our eyes cannot see them. Have you ever seen something . . . that others cannot see? Why are some things kept from our vision?"

Now think about how that statement might be doubled! [redacted] has good reason for not revealing everything.

After some investigative work this morning I discovered that [redacted] is also called [redacted]. She is a double agent to be sure, and may be essential to this investigative trail. I think she knows about the flutters of the fish, and her deep micro-attention to connective tissue is very much required.

Could it be that the vortex is not only full of creatures, but is the very creature we all need to know? As [redacted] said, I had a premonition of the vortex before we arrived at Avoca: The House the Vortex Built, was already in my mind. The goldfishy flutters in my heart might be the hole I need to measure up before I can offer any more clues.

Yours,

A few missives later, now 42 responses in, many of them arriving in the nonlinear swirl only gmail conversations can create. 24 people copied.

Incoming Cargo Nov 29 2014

Oh no. More fish? What is this about green fish?

I couldn't help overreading so I have to point out the following... Those fish were clearly orange (apart from the four almost invisible small black ones...and one is already beginning to change colour I notice...) For me it was all orange and now it is the seepage of orange that remains...

So there are the fish. Well, I still see orange despite this mention of green. And then there is the striped orange of the tiger as you noted [redacted], the one who moved into the balcony room on Tuesday and now refuses to leave. Little [redacted], who is entirely at home lying with the fish seems also comfortable hanging out in this tigeresque space. More animals she seems to be saying. We need better representation amongst the 64 long legs in the forests of the night.

Don't you think that is a strange coincidence? 64 legs. Because '64' was already there on every door before those 64 legs appeared. It was the long orangy-reddy stripe on the doors. Did you see it? The sign '64: Before Completion'? (I didn't like to mention it but, talking of 'before completion', those slices of fish that suddenly appeared in the kitchen, then on our plates, were altogether too close to orange in their pinkness. I did go in and count and was relieved to find that all eight were still there in the other room, swimming easily. Phew. I don't think they knew what was going on.

And then in the hardness of midday there is orange all over the ground on the struggling grass apron in front of the house. I'm relieved to read that some of you also noticed it. Hard to decipher though, hard to know what it is doing there. Some strange message of pain that has seeped up from China perhaps. One day when it rains later next year, it will wash away I think. Or perhaps it will burn to bare earth if the whole house is consumed by the orange of summer fire before the bell can be rung and we desperately count people at the gate. We will need 64 long legs, four short ones, many fins. [redacted], does that measuring device count legs as well?

The tiger will not be counted of course. It will simply refuse to leave, that tiger, even though it knows well enough about the call of the bell. It stays, entirely comfortable, up there in the balcony room. The possums, however, are wary. As they should be. To make sure they realize this is a new dispensation, stones have been thrown against the tiny orange flames that bring them out of the shadows. And there is the smell of urine still there as a declaration of war.

And the hard-orange of the pomegranate blossoms suddenly seen in a back garden now without weeds, and the yellowy-orange of the much desired mango that appeared right at the end. So, of course there must also be double agents (which changes the leg count) for all this to have occurred. And perhaps a vortex or two. Anything is possible. Everything has changed.

Yours,

And so it continued, from November 26 to December 4, investigators added and withdrawn, writing not only from Australia but also from Berlin, and Montreal, 90 pages in all. Everything had changed, as the November 29 message announced. Something else had begun to happen, and with it, an event was taking form.

The investigation that became the fabulation was never really interested in the past. It was interested in creating a time that could compose with futurities in the making. To create an event, these futurities must be there in germ. When we arrived at Watford House, there wasn't yet in the collective a sensitivity to how else the project could expose itself, how else it could be known. As is often the case, the stark presentness of a strange encounter took precedence over its fissures of futurity. None of us really knew where to look, and how to compose with what we might find lurking between garden and house, house and village, past and future. And so, the group fissured into small clumps, the focus more activity-based than event-orienting: someone created an architectural plan of the house; a few people cleared the garden of weeds; some cooked and cleaned; some prepared a site for peeing into mason jars to steer the possums away from the fruit trees; some visited the garden and the surrounds; some went for a walk along the flood plain; some spoke to villagers; some sat at the pub; some skyped home; some slept.

It is the fabulation that finally did the work of shifting the gathering toward an emergent collectivity, making it an event. It did so by making the cracks felt, and by creating opportunities to enter them. Where other constraints had been disabling, the fabulation was enabling precisely because it captured us in the act, in a middling of expression where the anguish of the orange schizz and all that it carried could be addressed by other means. The fabulation allowed the collectivity in germ to express itself and to invent worlds for that expression. While names were used in the text as it moved across the network, there came with the force of the fabulatory gesture a sense of the impersonal – all voices made a difference, as they do in investigations. Even a missive from Berlin from someone who had no idea where exactly Avoca was shifted the orientation, adding a new crack to the puzzle.

The fabulation followed us to Sydney, where the second SenseLab proposition – this one focused on knots of thought and experimenting with the minor gesture – was beginning. Many people now gathered who had not been to Avoca, but still, the fabulation, printed on large pieces of paper and taped to the wall, accompanied us for the next 8 days as we worked in the large UNSW Art and Design gallery. Few people read it as a whole, but its presence made a difference, particularly as we collectively tried to give voice to our uneasiness about how narratives are made – the demonstrations for Michael Brown's death were happening simultaneously in Ferguson.

The telling is an event, and its capacity to impersonalize is key, even (and perhaps especially) in cases where it feels most urgent to direct blame toward the personal. This tension between the personal and the impersonal was felt keenly in the wake of the grass graffiti. Despite the fabulation's gaining momentum, and its growing ability to reorient the field, some participants nonetheless felt that the individual who had painted the grass should apologize for what was considered by some to be a violent act, and so, when she resisted making the act her own, they blamed her for not taking responsibility. And, by extension, they blamed SenseLab. What was overlooked, however, in this painful play of accusation, was the force of enthusiasm of the body, the tigritude, that was moved to paint orange, that was moved to schizz the event. For the painted grass was the cut, the schizz that allowed the schizoanalytic gesture of the fabulation to take place.

It is noteworthy that the words themselves the spray-paint highlighted were never returned to in the discussion of who was to blame. Despite the force of the fabulation, the marked landscape was remembered by those most undone by the graffiti only as a scar. What this reaction neglected was that the writing called for nothing less than that *multiplicity* orient the field. This wasn't a personal act, and this is what the fabulation, despite a great uneasiness, was able to make apparent. The orange had already been seeping long before the spray-paint foregrounded it. What the words did was orient the orange, move the orange tigeresquely toward fish and fire, toward tents and Bea the dog, toward the vortex and 64 legs and pomegranate flowers and mangoes, not all of them orange, but all of them carried by an oranging spell. The fabulation activated the vortex, opening the breach toward a creative limit where new worlds could be inhabited. The fabulation made it possible for the collective to begin to emerge *as* collective. It immediated collectivity, transforming personal stakes into the fraught field of group subjectivity.

Collectivity extends beyond a moment in time. This was the strength of the SenseLab-*Avoca Project* encounter: that it invented itself through the fabulation, in the passage of a time more durational than chronological. A year later, returning to Australia, I met with Jones. It was time, we decided, to return to our collaborator, Watford House, and to see what the SenseLab-*Avoca Project* encounter had been able to do. The conversation was tentative. Had the *Avoca Project* benefitted as much as SenseLab had? Had the politics of fabulation and its immediating power also made a difference for the *Avoca Project*, or did the orange simply leave a scar that spoke of non-attunement in a field of difference?

The story began to fabulate once more as we listened to each other, alive in the knowledge that we were both speaking as intercessors to a participation alive with the more-than human, ventriloquists for a group-subject still in transformation. It was a rich conversation, a real attunement. And in the event of this exchange, which happened over several days, with many rebeginnings, we heard the story once more. And it had morphed, already different than what could ever have been known, would ever be known. This is the power of the false.

It was not a scar, it turns out. The rain washed away the paint shortly after we left, and in any case it had never, it turns out, been spray-paint, but water-soluble marker paint. In the end, the actual graffiti seemed less important than the agony of collaborating with forces that exceeded us. The orange words were not so much what was left behind as what would be reactivated, return after return. This is also the power of the false. The schizz would always be a schizz in time. A memory of orange, of turmoil, a swirling collective composition, a tentative encounter with the fragility at the heart of all collective actions – this is what would continue in the schizzing. What was left burning through the soil, on the Avoca landscape, was not so much, in retrospect at least, the writing on the grass. What was left was an uneasy story ripe for the telling. But, like all fabulations, nothing we will write will ever have been quite true. So perhaps it is important to end with this one last image, one that was kept from me at the time because of my horror of snakes.

For months before our arrival at Avoca, I worried about snakes. Jones, like all those I ask, promised me that snakes were actually quite shy and would be unlikely to show themselves. I wasn't convinced: everywhere I go these animals that horrify me at the most nonconscious level seem to appear to greet me, to my snake-lover-friends' delight.

I didn't see a snake at Avoca. But it turns out a snake did appear, camouflaged in our trace, standing guard at the entry to the house: the day after we left, a tiger snake was seen resting amidst the orange stripes of the lawn. Snake and stripe, tigeresque. The more-than human in all its animality, lingering in the n+1 of the field's incessant necessity to tell it otherwise.

The politics of fabulation is this capacity to make felt the force of immediation at its most impersonal limit. The fabulation at Avoca was not "about" anything, not about the orange "spray" paint or even the tiger-snake-fish that marked the passage of our disappearance. But it was the orange that schizzed the fabulation into motion. The politics of fabulation composes *with* the schizz. Without the schizz there is no event. A fabulation's content can never be seen as limited to the story itself – fabulation is the affective field that makes composition possible, bringing thinking into act. In a political register, this suggests that there is potential in fabulation to get beyond the kind of narration that holds things in place, opening them to the *what else* that also beckons. All events are more complex than they seem, and modes of encounter that play, tigeresquely, with that complexity can and do change their course.

Beyond Myth-Making

Fabulation is vulnerable to capture. Its other, myth-making, is always at its heels, seducing us with the promise of intelligibility. How to keep the wildness of fabulation active in the retelling and reorienting of our everyday practices? "This is how it is," we say, or at least how it's been, its having-been constitutive of what will be capable of coming to be. And we're not altogether wrong. It *is* like this. Today, or yesterday. But it was also much more, in a flash. Already, another shape has begun to take form, a shape relationally attuned to the inheritance of the "it is." What myth-making tendencies will have missed in the description of what things do when they shape each other will always have been the relational field, the inheritance not of form but of formative force.

> [W]hether explicitly or not, narration always refers to a system of judgement: even when acquittal takes place due to the benefit of the doubt, or when the guilty is so only because of fate. Falsifying narration, by contrast, frees itself from this system; it shatters the system of judgement because the power of the false (not error or doubt) affects the investigator and the witness as much as the person presumed guilty (Deleuze 1989: 133).

The kind of telling which does justice to the event in its ongoing capacity for metamorphosis can only emerge from the event itself and be told in the squeaks of the event's own perpetually falsifying forms of articulation, in its ticcingflapping.

Falsifying narration in the name of the event's capacity for metamorphosis is uncomfortable because it refuses to settle the event. Everything is affected.

> The point is that the elements themselves are constantly changing with the relations of time into which they enter, and the terms with their connections. Narration is constantly being completely modified, in each of its episodes, not according to subjective variations, but as a consequence of disconnected places and dechronologized moments (Deleuze 1989: 133).

With the power of the false, the event has multiplied, its schisms made palpable: "contrary to the form of the true which is unifying [...] the power of the false cannot be separated from an irreducible multiplicity" (1989: 133).

This multiplicity is serial. "The power of the false exists only from the perspective of a series of powers, always referring to each other and passing into one another" (Deleuze 1989: 133). The event has schizzed and with it the certainty of what it might have been or what it might become. The event has immediated, an immediation that is already part of a series, a series that is always more than the sum of us, always more-than human. The event is never just the one it has become in its actualization: it is also the many of fabulation's polyvalent accounting.

The cut in the event, its schizz, never lends itself to an overview. Schizoanalysis never happens once and for all. Its felt effects are rhyzomatic, undermining the sense that there might be a knowability that keeps everything in perspective. Fabulation as a technique of immediation makes felt the durational force of the cut, makes resonate an experiential time that doesn't know how to be counted. For while the cut is absolutely punctual, *immediate*, it cleaves the event in ways that recalibrate it, *immediating*. This couples two kinds of time: the time of the now and the time of the will have been. Time becomes operative, experiential. Time folds.

Emergency

But what of the urgency, even the sense of emergency, at the heart of the *now* of immediation? Social Justice activists know this problem well. Everything matters, all the time, the body poised to leap, the nervous system on high alert. Enthusiasm, excitement, and then, too often, chaos, or entropy, or inertia. Absolute movement caught in the vortex of everything the event could become. Madness. Burnout.

This state of extreme overactivation is familiar to all who experiment with emergent collectivity. The event takes us, its absolute movement swirling us within an unbounded spacetime that is often temporally and spatially at odds with the rhythms of the everyday. No points of reliance are available. Perspective is long gone. The body becomes warrior, tense with anticipation, thick with the trauma of what have now become life and death stakes. Adrenal overexertion, there is no calm here where the event has become us.

Too often, in the face of this overlap of focused momentum and deep exhaustion, an uneasy shift happens toward the personal. "I can't do it anymore," we hear ourselves say, as though this were all about us. The shaping of emergent collectivity has been reduced to our cells. The event, we believe, needs *us* to continue. A new kind of "personal is political" emerges in this intense constellation where the edges where politics and life and art and philosophy co-compose are overridden by a sense of breathless engagement: the state of emergency overcomes us.

The stakes are enormous, and many of us feel them today. Avoca's fabulation did not have these stakes, but the concurrent event of Michael Brown's death did, and we felt it. Urgency was not misplaced. The weight of the world we compose with, a world of austerity and neoliberalism and racism and exclusion which every day undervalues what collective living can be, is a heavy burden to bear. Many of us wake daily with an almost hopeless feeling of urgency, the body poised in a state of acute tension. As months (and centuries) of attacks against black life continue, as more gun violence erupts and wars are fought, as austerity measures undermine our everyday existences and climate change threatens to foreclose the future, as settler-colonialism persists, as we continue to watch the horrifying accounts of refugees streaming across borders looking for a safe landing, how does collective experimentation make any kind of difference?

This is a question SenseLab struggles with. But whenever we come face to face with it (again) we remind each other that collective experimentation is not a choice. It's a mode of survival. For it is experimentation around techniques for group subjectivity that provides ways to reenter the political from another angle. A politics of fabulation seems important in this context. Political events are often lived in the time span of media events – acutely here and then completely gone. The political is lived as staccato rather than as durational, one violent act overshadowing the next. But as all activists will attest to, the work continues even when the attention wanes, and it is often in the waning that the exhaustion settles in, despondency taking over as the status quo returns.

How the collective makes a difference is often not part of the telling. What is told is told in the sound bites of new myth-making strategies, the complexity of fabulation too unwieldy for the Facebook like. But the fabulations are there – the work is to draw them out. What kinds of techniques might be invented to assist us in orienting urgency away from a constant state of emergency? How might we bend our practices toward the desynchronous time of fabulation, even while we are living the emergency? What might emergent collectivity be capable of in this context? What kind of acts are called for? What can we do collectively so that the merest of existences also make themselves felt?

The primacy of action has been rightly criticized as connected to capital, as tending to operate in tandem with the accelerated time of capital's constant need to forecast the newest new.[15] SenseLab asks: what other modes of activity are alive in the act? What kind of telling accompanies what Massumi calls bare activity, activity not simply understood in terms of its spatial extension but in its intensive magnitude?[16] Can we attune to the zigzag movement that cuts across the front line and create with the intensity of a side line? Is there a way to rally across different qualities of line? Can we make the line a field?

A durational field is always immediating. The question of how to compose with the capacitation of the field in act is the one the SenseLab most contends with. How to know when our bodies need to be counted (which lines actually need us to be standing there, numbered amongst those also marking the occasion)? How to know where subtraction is more important, where our presence must be backgrounded in lieu of other qualities of action? How, in the mix, to always foreground the more-than human? How to live the modulation of the act such that we don't simply fall prey to capital's mandate that we do more, be more, bending to capital's infinite need for surplus and accumulation? How to keep the enthusiasm of the body transversal, beyond capture? How to compose with altereconomies in ways that do their work through the creative fissures of capital's leakages without turning these acts into moral imperatives? How to create time for emergent collectivity in a world that asks so much of our time, of our too-human time?

Emergent collectivities are series. There is never *one* emergent collectivity. The work of group subjectivity involves a sensitivity to transversality, to the schizz that cuts across the now of experience in the making. Schizoanalytic techniques are necessary, and they have to be invented each time anew, cutting across lines where they form, inflecting them, redrawing them, thickening them. What kinds of collective practices can we invent that complicate participation across this seriality?

SenseLab seeks to immediate where lines are composed, where they cross, where they perish. Free radicals are key: activated in the telling, in the relation, motivated by the power of the false, the free radical exposes the variability in experience, replacing and superseding "the form of the true," by making felt "the simultaneity of incompossible presents," "the coexistence of not-necessarily true pasts" (Deleuze 1989: 131).

To create openings for free radicality, techniques will always need to be invented that are capable of creating the conditions, in the event, for the activation of its fabulatory tendencies. This will mean attending to the pulse of immediation. By making palpable the durational field that catches futurity in the making, the anarchic share of the event's persistence in the fold of time will become operational.

Emergency lives in the urgency of now, *this time*, this only time. No practice can function always in the state of emergency. The work of the free radical is to supplement the necessary pull of emergency, to compose with the complex time differential of the act. Emergency is with us, and it is here to stay.[17] How to work with the doubling of time this calls forth – the time of the now and the time of sustained action? How to make sustainable, in a more-than human register, the acute sense that all is in the balance? How to not become rigidified by the tension that comes with the sense that there can never be enough action to turn the tides? All scales of action are present in the flash of tigritude. How can the act of activism produce an enthusiasm of the body that carries, in a flash, all these scales, all these durations?

Perhaps the first step is to recall that the flash is transductive: it is not that the child becomes a tiger, or that the child imitates a tiger. It is that the child immediatingly connects to the dynamism of the tiger's enthusiasm of the body: the child activates the form of life of tigritude.

A politics of fabulation does nothing less. It composes at all scales of existence, activating the dynamism of experience in the making. Cutting across more normative tellings, it transversalizes experience. It invents it. And in so doing, it allows the edges of the political to resonate differently, collectively, durationally.

The force of immediation in a politics of fabulation does this: it takes us out of the centre. It opens the present to its schizz. And it teaches us not only that "I" is another, but that the event is not me (Deleuze 1989: 153).

SenseLab has appetite. It creates itself around practices that tune toward an affinity for the interstices that compose across art, politics and philosophy. It wants to be nomadic. It wants to activate the transversal contours of a life in the making, a mode of existence that can only know itself through the falsifications it will become allied to and will then leave behind. This coming and going takes continual work, especially the going. We have to learn, again and again, how to subtract ourselves, how to do this work without becoming subsumed by it. How a practice does its work, how a practice creates the conditions for an emergent collectivity, has to be reinvented each time anew, and with this, our role in it, our place in it has to reinvented as well. It can never be solely about how we did it before. And it can never really be about us. This does not mean that what has come before has no importance. It means that we work from a beginning always rich with inheritances that remain open to deviation.

Experimenting immediation is shape-shifting: tigeresque. Free radical intercession produces an enthusiasm of the body. We are not the centre of experience, tigritude is, vitality affects are. It is here that we must begin, shifting from our belief that we are the center, composing instead with other scales and tempos, with the minor gestures of geological time, affective time, event-time.

To know time differently is to feel how the more-than of existence composes us, composes with us. The political is never within reach. To have reached it is to have organized it into myth. To be politically engaged, to open up fields of emergent collectivity is not to have willed them into existence, but to have been moved by them, to have been composed by them. Our task: to become schizoanalytic experimentors at the edges of experience where the intercession of the free radical unbinds linear narration, freeing the bonds of time prescribed. Our task: to become sensitive to a composing-with that will never tell the true story of how emergent collectivity briefly came to expression. Our task: to move at the rhythm of free radicals who affirm the schizz of immediation. Our task: to destroy, with all the force of the free radical, that which too easily conforms to our image, to our need to recognize ourselves in the work we do.

Notes

1. Our first "home" was Sha Xin Wei's Topological Media Lab at Concordia University (2004-2005). From there we moved to the Montreal-based Society for Art and Technology (2005-2008).
2. For an account of the concept of the power of the false, see Gilles Deleuze. *Cinema 2: The Time-Image*. Trans. Hugh Tomlinson and Robert Galeta. (Minneapolis: Minnesota UP, 1989).
3. Brian Massumi and I have written at length about the event both in its organization and in its aftermath in *Thought in the Act: Passages in the Ecology of Experience* (Minnesota UP, 2014).
4. Brian Massumi and I discuss *Generating the Impossible* in detail in our description of SenseLab techniques and enabling constraints in *Thought in the Act: Passages in the Ecology of Experience* (Minnesota UP, 2014).
5. Deleuze's concept of the intercessor has been badly translated as "mediator." The intercessor, as outlined throughout, does very different work than the mediator. For the full text, see http://eng7007.pbworks.com/w/page/18931080/DeleuzeMediators
6. Our approach is one of immanent critique. For more on the concept, see Erin Manning *The Minor Gesture* (Duke UP, 2016).
7. For a more thorough account of a politics of affirmation see "Affirmation Beyond Credit" in *The Minor Gesture* (Duke UP, 2016).
8. The first series was entitled *Technologies of Lived Abstraction*. Four events are tied to this series: Dancing the Virtual (2005), Housing the Body; Dressing the Environment (2007), Society of Molecules (2009) and Generating the Impossible (2012). A book series of the same name was edited by Erin Manning and Brian Massumi at MIT Press (2006-2016).
9. In the English translation, fabulation is mistranslated as story-telling. While fabulation is a kind of story-telling, it is vital to the understanding of the concept that it be understood as a deviation from mythologization forms of narration.
10. See Alfred North Whitehead *Adventures of Ideas* (New York: Free Press, 1967).

11. For more on the Avoca Project and Watford House, see http://www.fusion-journal.com/issue/004-fusion-the-town-and-the-city/lyndal-jones-climate-change-performance-and-the-avoca-project/]

12. email correspondence, October 2015.

13. http://www.rmit.com/news/all-news/2015/february/chinese-garden-creates-inspiring-public-space/ viewed March 15 2015

14. The lead artist for the garden was Chinese-Australian artist Lindy Lee, the designer and project manager was landscape artist Mel Ogden from Taiwan and gardener, Martin Wynne was the soil expert. Partners in the project included land owners Harvey and Carol Wilkins, the Bendigo Chinese Museum, the Pyrenees Shire, Avoca Primary School and Avoca Business and Tourism Committee. http://www.rmit.com/news/all-news/2015/february/chinese-garden-creates-inspiring-public-space/

15. Many versions of this critique exist, including writing by Franco (Bifo) Berardi, Giorgio Agamben, Steven Shaviro and Gerald Raunig, amongst others. For a compelling read that takes the question further, see Stefano Harney, "Hapticality in the Undercommons or From Operations Management to Black Ops" in Cumma Papers #9 https://cummastudies.files.wordpress.com/2013/08/cumma-papers-9.pdf

16. On bare activity, see Brian Massumi *Semblance and Event: Activist Philosophy and the Occurrent Arts* (MIT Press, 2011).

17. For work on social emergency, see the important work of the Design Studio for Social Intervention. They write: In 2017, we created Social Emergency Response Centers (SERCs) to help people understand the moment we're in, from all different perspectives. Co-created with activists, artists and community members, SERCs are temporary, pop-up spaces that help us move from rage and despair into collective, radical action. SERCs are continuing and growing—a people-led public infrastructure sweeping the country from Utica, MS to Atlanta, Albuquerque, Washington DC, Chicago, Orange, NJ, Hartford, CT, etc. They are popping up in homes, community centers, schools, churches and conferences. SERCs function as both an artistic gesture and a practical solution. As such, they aim to find the balance between the two, answering questions like: How will we feed people--and their hunger for justice? How will we create a shelter--where it's safe to bring your whole damn self? What will reconstruction--of civil society--look like? http://www.ds4si.org/interventions/serc

Fifth Movement

Becoming-Bodies

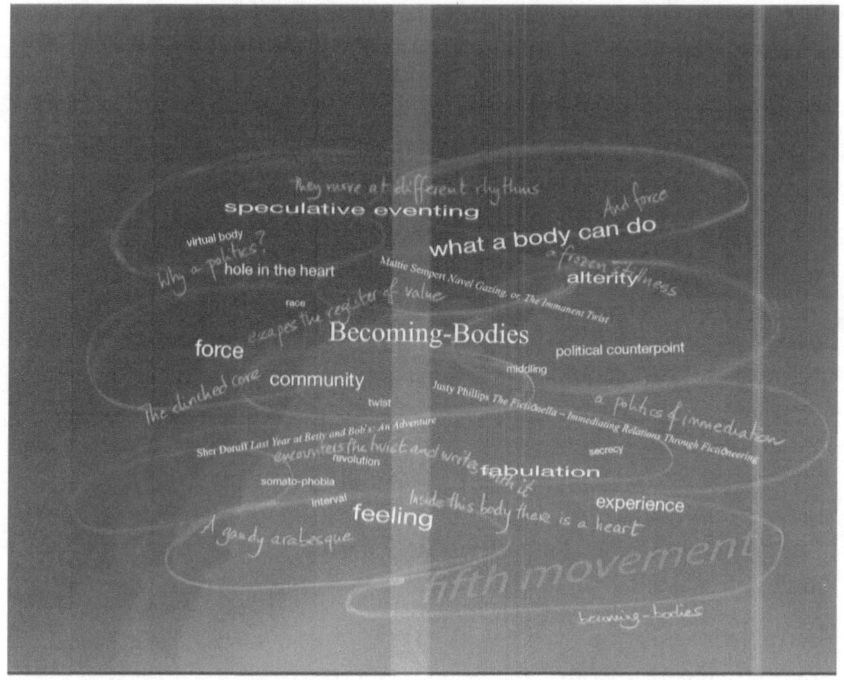

Erin Manning

Prelude

They move at different rhythms. Three times at different speeds, in different durations, the first in conversation, capricious in the bordering of a ficto-critical genre, the second alive with the flash of the unruly that comes when dialogue finds its own pace, narrating across a border that is both character and more-than character, schizo-personal, the third a propositional genre that crosses the fictiō and the novella, a fictiōnella that refuses to recount even as it plays in time, with time.

To cross the genre, to move across what philosophy can do in the interstices of a fabulation, true or not, is a practice of immediation. Deviations from mediatory impulses are necessary to think across and capture not the explanation of a feeling, but the force of its arising. "Most people watch the ceiling as I probe their bellies. But this young woman hasn't taken her eyes off me. A fixed, wide-eyed stare bores into the side of my face. I sense a frozen stillness as my hand rests over her taut navel. She stops breathing. The deer is hiding in a grove of trees, holding dead still until the bear lumbers past" (Sempert, Immediation II, 402).

This force is told in the interval, Justy Phillips might say, felt in the lag where the telling unknows itself. Each story, each text, encounters the lag differently, its rhythm activating the quality of what survives into the telling. While Mattie Sempert participates in an encounter with the twist of the acupuncture needle and the icy toes, Phillips probes the complex passage between feeling and felt where past moves toward an experiencing of the present, "a processual engagement with the eventing of everyday life" (Phillips, Immediation II, 432). Two rhythms co-composing. A qualitative difference is felt here in the force of what can be heard and what must be said. For Sempert, the needle does the saying in a way that always shifts the conditions of what can and must be said. A schism of time is also at stake: the acupuncture needle is always felt before the feeling, its promised zing an agitation before the twist. The story encounters the twist and writes with it, time captivated by the dynamic force of a homeostasis undone.

Sher Doruff works at the nerve end of the erratic edge of all systems. "Immediate!" White Betty yelled. "Diagram goddamn it!" "Bacon it!" "Or Vega-bacon it." (Doruff, Immediation II, 425). This time, the force of immediation not between times lingering on the edge of their overlapping, but immediation activating the overlappings of simultaneities, paradoxes. Time as the haphazard quality of the oversaying in the saying. What we hear in Doruff's narrative is heard in the scramble of many voices speaking at once. "The air in their shared warehouse studio was thick with imploding drama. They all felt it but were reluctant to name it. RED. Gone. BLUE missing. GREEN empty. Left without the foundational RGB they were conceptually, scientifically, politically and philosophically bereft. Voided. Limp" (Doruff, Immediation II, 424).

Rhythm and immediation co-compose. Rhythm activates the fabulatory share that allows immediation to make its work felt. For immediation cannot be described, or defined. It can only be activated, changing the conditions of the fields it brings into relation. Language is not always its favourite tool—it can impose mediatory tendencies hard to discard. Immediation does its work best when language bends.

Fabulation's telling is an event. This event is an attunement to the divergent forces that refuse to be bent into shape. The telling does not straighten them: it foregrounds their capacity to shapeshift.

A protopolitics lingers here, in the different rhythms for the telling. This is a politics of immediation, a politics that gathers in the turbulent unsayings of immediated tellings. This is a politics of the sayings in the said that can barely be heard but are nonetheless felt. A politics of the becoming-body, a bodying always in transition, worlding through the rhythm-events that populate the lines. Why a politics? Because immediation alters the conditions of existence, making palpable what otherwise escapes the register of value. It matters, these stories say, it matters that you learn to listen to what remains unsayable in the said. It matters that the transversal lines trouble the orientation to knowing. Immediation matters, and its materiality, how it comes to expression, also matters.

Mattie Sempert, Justy Phillips and Sher Doruff take us into the mattering. They take us to the uneasy site of language's composition where an encounter can be felt between meaning and quality of tone, where what is said and how it is heard work together to create the force of an account, here, now. This is the practice of immediation, this ability to make felt, in the event, how words create worlds. When worlds resist mediation, when language really does the work of creating a field of expression, a force for the telling emerges that shifts the conditions of experience toward worlds as yet unfelt. It is here, in the event that refuses to script experience, that a politics of immediation most intensively does its work.

Mattie Sempert

Navel Gazing, or, The Immanent Twist

> You never reach the Body without Organs, you can't reach it, you are forever attaining it, it is a limit. People ask, So what is this BwO?—But you're already on it, scurrying like vermin, groping like a blind person, or running like a lunatic: desert traveller and nomad of the steppes. On it we sleep, live our waking lives, fight—fight and are fought—seek our place, experience untold happiness and fabulous defeats; on it we penetrate and are penetrated; on it we love
>
> *Deleuze and Guattari (1987: 150)*

A friend told me recently that she's kept the desiccated cords of her three children.

In a hidden shoebox? I forgot to ask.

What happened to my umbilical cord will always be a mystery. Most likely my mother bundled it into my dirty nappy. Her farm girl pragmatism wouldn't have allowed any sentiment over our shared remnant.

However, I do know that during my birth, my mother, out of it on gas, recalled meeting St. Peter at the Pearly Gates. He was very pleasant and welcoming, she'd say, recycling the story over the years. But while she was conversing with St. Pete I made my way out of her yawning vagina, stretched to the point of tearing. Forceps must have gripped my soft temporal bones. I can still feel a dent above my left temple.

Is that original shock, the violent separation, held, like a miasma, inside our navels?

"The becoming-body," writes Erin Manning, "has no fixed form. It is an exfoliating body" (2009a: 124). Perhaps like the suspended state of becoming-snake, when it is in-between skins. One has been sloughed off and the re-assembling of another has not yet emerged. The snake, between skins, has lost its form. The becoming-body is a virtual body. It is de-territorialized, "free of the fixed relations that contain a body all the while exposing it to new organizations" (2005: 67). Becoming-bodies are re-assembling all the time, in process and in relationship with other assemblages. Exfoliating is a doing, a verbing, an action. To shed the restrictive skin of a binary allows for becomings to unfold. Movement and rhythm exfoliate, says Manning. And for total exfoliation: laughter (2009a: 21).

Most people watch the ceiling as I probe their bellies. But this young woman hasn't taken her eyes off me. A fixed, wide-eyed stare bores into the side of my face. I sense a frozen stillness as my hand rests over her taut navel. She stops breathing. The deer is hiding in a grove of trees, holding dead still until the bear lumbers past.

I glance over at her deep red stockings draped over the side of the chair that still hold the shape of her feet. More of a venous shade of red, I decide. There's a hint of blue. It was only ten minutes ago that I passed her standing at the reception desk, her long red legs capped by a vinyl black mini-skirt, feet planted in ankle high black boots with severe zippers on the side.

I remove my hand from her navel and do the rest of my information gathering over her abdomen. Temperature. Tone. Areas of tension. Skin texture. No scars, moles, or other irregularities. Only a few scattered freckles. Her ribcage is on the narrow side, indicating a relatively weak constitution. My hand moves with a sure, swift touch, conveying confidence born from exploring hundreds of bellies over the years.

Her chief complaint is tight shoulders. Too much computer work, she tells me. But I know it comes from a deeper tension, a deeper source.

When I move away from her navel, she relaxes. Move it back over, and she tenses up again. Like the tree falling in the woods, does her navel relax when no one is probing? Judging from her taut musculature, including her neck muscles stretched like guy-wires to the point of snapping, I don't think so.

Her middle is clenched. Tight.

When I remove my hand, the side of my face relaxes. The deer comes out of hiding and watches the bear shrink in the distance.

She's here for her tight shoulder muscles, not her belly. I move up towards her head and press my fingers into the muscles on the top of her shoulders. Cement.

"In this Japanese style of acupuncture we treat your whole body starting from your abdomen," I say, as I move around to the other side of the table to check the top of her other shoulder, which is also hard as cement. I press my fingers in again.

"We see a connection between your tight shoulders and the tension in your belly."

I notice a thin layer of foundation on her face, discretely blended into her neck. A tiny crater, left by an absent nose ring, stands out. Her black eyebrows nearly meet at a crease in the middle. Long earlobes. A sign of longevity, according to the Chinese.

As she follows my face, the fear-bulge appears again. My cheek tenses. I look square at her, into the stunned stare. The carefully applied make-up suddenly makes her more vulnerable to me. Removing my hand, I make sure my face and voice are soft.

"We need to free up your belly in order for your shoulders to loosen."

She gives a little quick nod, but I don't think she has any idea what I mean.

Her body is like a gated community surrounded with razor wire and sirens. I move away to jot down my findings in her fresh folder. And consider a way in. Maybe I should take the steering wheel and drive straight for the barbed-wired barricade, headfirst into her fear. Or make the white-coated decision of The Expert and disregard her frightened state, her naked vulnerability, however much she's tried to conceal it.

And what of informed consent? I've witnessed plenty of tears over the years, the moment of sweet relief when held-back feelings give way to a rupture. And several times the unrestrained sobs on the treatment table when a belly's come unbuttoned, when the clenched fist opens and blood floods back to the source. The disoriented stupor of having finally let go, but not knowing how to fill up all the fresh free space. I do know this: too much energy is bound up in watching, in holding it all together, in concealment.

The clinched core. Fisted feelings. Anxiety circling a small room looking for a way out.

Without the oppositional tensions of a binary to keep it intact, when skin is neither on *nor* off, what can the becoming-body *do*? Deleuze took up Spinoza's idea of immanence: Not only don't we know what a body can do; we don't know what our bodies will do from moment to moment. "Spinoza never ceases to be astonished by the body: not of having a body, but at what the body is capable of. Bodies are defined not by their genus and species, nor by their origins and functions, but by what they can do, the affects they are capable of, in passion as in action" (Deleuze and Parnet 1987: 74). By rebuking binaries, possibilities open up. Becomings are potentiated by the rub of difference, juxtaposition and paradox, and aspire to ambiguity. Difference is affirmed, celebrated even. Elizabeth Grosz, a philosopher devoted to re-thinking the body, notes that Deleuze and Guattari's "notion of the body as a discontinuous, nontotalizable series of processes, organs, flows, energies, corporeal substances and incorporeal events, speeds and durations, may be of great value to feminists attempting to reconceive bodies outside the binary oppositions imposed on the body by the mind/body, nature/culture, subject/object and interior/exterior oppositions" (1994: 164). By taking up the challenge to contest binaries, such as the Western habit of privileging the mind over the body, somato-phobia—or fear of the body—can be looked at square in the face. This could be an antidote for the centuries-old splitting Cartesian headache: to step into Deleuze and Guattari's world, made up of thousands of wide-open undulating plateaus where the body and the mind can roam, aimless, together as one.

Our umbilicus. The site where the original lifeline, the chewy cord, connected to mother. The odd pucker of dense tissue left over once the shrivelled-up lifeless cord falls off like a withered leaf falls off a tree.

Maybe the wail of a newborn baby comes out as a grieving protest to getting cast from the Mother ship. The shocking finality of the lifeline's snip, never to return. I recall the nightmare I had as a child after watching *2001: A Space Odyssey* (1968): that astronaut floating, forever alone, into deep space, into infinity. The cold sweat of horror turning quickly into dread, which is still not far away inside me.

Could it be that our navels hold that memory? The shock of the snip leaving the trace of our first unforgivable wounding? Could that be why so many people have an aversion to having their navels touched?

Belly button. Our belly's button.

Push a button. Don't push my buttons.

A button gathers and holds two surfaces together.

Deleuze and Guattari took up the term Body Without Organs from Antonin Artaud, another Spinozist, who invented the term as a means to free himself from the disgust and hatred he held for his own body. "Man is sick because he is badly constructed [...] when you have made him a body without organs, then you have delivered him from all his automatic reactions and restored him his true freedom." (Artaud 1988: 79). Deleuze and Guattari folded Artaud's term into their philosophy, having the BwO insinuate a deeper, hidden reality. For them, the BwO embodies a virtual space outside the hard edges of well-formed wholes constructed from functioning parts. "Then," says Artaud, with the conceptual evisceration complete, "you will teach him to dance wrong side out as in the frenzy of dance halls and this wrong side out will be his real place" (1988: 570-571).

But to "dance wrong side out" isn't enough, suggests Rosi Braidotti: "To switch to Spinoza is a switch to the radical materiality of the body: the entire body thinks. You don't think with the mind, you think with the entire fleshed existence." Therein lays the inescapable human rub, the same one from which Artaud sought freedom: "You cannot step outside the slab of matter that you inhabit," adds Braidotti (Vermeulen and Braidotti 2014).

"How's your sleep?" I ask as I move over to the treatment cart. Time to get the flow started.

"Is it going to hurt?" Her voice is pinched, small.

I head towards her feet with a packet of pins.

"Not really, they're so fine and thin," I say. To tell her there's no pain isn't the truth. Sometimes the *zing* can be felt as pain. I start to peel the packet open.

"It's a shame they're called needles because it conjures up injections."

Anticipation thickens the air in the room.

"If it makes you feel any better, when I was little I was terrified of getting my shots. And now I'm an acupuncturist." Most people respond with a surprised *really?* She says nothing.

I touch her toes. Icy. I also notice her feet aren't flopping out at a relaxed angle from her hips. Hip joints can often mirror shoulder joints. Both are holding on tight in this client. Her glute muscles are probably also clenched.

"I wouldn't say it hurts, but you can feel a little tingly sensation. Acupuncture is about getting things flowing again, like flicking little switches, and..."

"You're not going to put one in my stomach are you?" Her voice cuts through the thickness, taking up space. The air moves. Good. She's got spunk.

I press my warm hands into her icy arches, pulling her attention down to her feet. Better not head for the barricade, at least not today. Do I risk another rattled meltdown? And what of informed consent? Tell her: Sorry, but there's a chance you'll have a sobbing attack if I go straight to your clenched navel. Are you up for that? Unbutton it and underneath is access to another land of possibility. The unblinking grip of your implosion-habit is a familiar, steady presence. Exhausting, but familiar. Keep it all contained, quiet, camouflaged.

Anxiety circles the room faster, faster. Frantic. Got to be a way out.

Forces are always at play, even in stasis, in stillness. Another way of putting it, says Brian Massumi, is that "positionality is an emergent quality of movement. The distinction between stasis and motion that replaces the opposition between literal and figurative from this perspective is not a logical binarism. It follows the modes by which realities pass into each other. 'Passing into' is not a binarism. They are dynamic unities" (2002: 8). Moving forces- earthbound and material, animate and inanimate, human and inhuman—rub, crash, scrape, caress, explode, and fuse, as dynamic unities. The swirl of forces on and against surfaces pass into each other.

The new materialists conceptualize "traversing the fluxes" (Dolphijn and van der Tuin 2012: 86) as a strategic move away from dualisms. Grosz comments on Deleuze and Guattari's elemental—or *molecular* in their terminology—conception of the body, which "implies a clear move toward imperceptibility [...] their work is like an acidic dissolution of the body, and the subject along with it" (Kaufman 2012: 52). Cartesian thinking has benignly neglected matter with its preoccupation with the mind. As a relational ontology, the perspective of the new materialists allows for the immanent enfolding of matter and meaning (Dolphijn, van der Tuin 2012: 48). This re-conception of matter tolerates, encourages even, an apparent oxymoron, such as movement in stasis. The endless possibilities of becoming create a power so potent it is capable of defying the classical laws of physics.

The forces created by the actions of multiplicities can yank free of binary constraints by twisting around into the middle, and *pass into* each other.

I gently prod a spot on the inside of her ankle, a particular spot on the body that can manifest the fear-bulge. The long held fixed stare.

"Is this tender?"

She goes frozen again, and winces. Just the feedback I need. But I want her to acknowledge it more directly.

"Does it feel sharp when I press it? Or more like a bruise?" I press it again.

"Sharp."

"And this spot?" I reach over and press into the same spot on her left ankle.

"Ow. That's worse."

Swiftly, I tap a needle into one of the ankle spots.

"There, it's in. Did that hurt?"

Silence. The air in the room circulates again.

"Is *that* it?" Her tone is incredulous, on the edge of a laugh.

"Yep, that's it. Now, remember how I said acupuncture is like flicking little switches and getting things flowing better?"

The pinched voice reappears: "Ah, huh."

"Just let me know when you feel a tingly sensation." Very, oh so very gently I give the needle a minuscule twirl, barely a whisper.

"Ew! I felt it down to my big toe. Like a tingle of electricity."

"Yes. That's the switch getting flicked on."

I've already moved to her other foot and tap another in. I don't bother tweaking the second spot. One zing is enough to start the shift, to initiate the drop.

I move up to the head-end of the treatment table. She's looking at the ceiling. Trillions of cells in her body are starting to hum and head towards equilibrium, like bees reforming a hive. The fear-bulge disappears.

"How're you doing?"

"Good. I feel really... good," she responds, dropping down into free flow. Dynamic homeostasis is just around the corner. She closes her eyes.

I place my hand just under her navel. She doesn't flinch.

"Take in a big breath, and fill up my hand."

She does, with surprising ease.

"And keep doing it several times, okay?"

Once free of the dualist structure of oppositional thinking, territorialized bodies—the literal body, as well as social, economic, political bodies—can find ways to challenge power disequilibrium. With the binary straightjacket removed, we can find out what our becoming-bodies are capable of doing. One option is to leave the stuffy, preoccupied interiors of psychoanalysis, and roam on the surfaces of our intermingling, (organ)less assemblages. We can contest Freud's phallocentrism. And the pinched negativity of desire understood as an insatiable *lack*. Desire as something missing. Instead, desire, according to Deleuze and Guattari, is defined as a "process of production without reference to any exterior agency; desire is a process of experimentation on a plane of immanence" (Deleuze 2005: 63). Their philosophy is one of affirmation: desire is reconceived as abundance, as excess. A plentitude. Our assemblages are in movement, in action, in processes of making. Not looking to fill a hole. "The BwO is never yours or mine. It is always *a* body" (1987: 164).

No external agent: the BwO refuses to be owned.

Birth is shocking, simple enough. Once outside the womb the air pressure changes, forcing the tiny heart flap to snap shut. In the time it takes for the lungs to inflate, the mysterious morphing from amphibious creature to land mammal takes place.

Cast out into a sea of blue scrubs, machines bleeping, the perilous journey outside the womb begins. The unnecessary slap on the bottom that was done in the old days. Vernix, like a thin smear of wet scrambled eggs, gets rubbed off by a scratchy towel. A needle prick on the base of a fresh heel. Add blinding lights, the cold embrace of metal, and this beginning outside the womb is enough for any creature to want to turn around and crawl back inside the Mother ship.

But to return inside is impossible. Docking to the breast is the next best option.

Deleuze returns to the middle as a source of becoming: "It is in the middle where one finds the becoming, the movement, the velocity, the vortex. The middle is not the mean, but on the contrary, an excess. It is by the middle that things push" (1993: 208). Events pass through the middle, in transit, neither here nor there.

Activist-philosophers of change, Manning and Massumi, say that each centre-point of movement, also known as the any-point, "twists around into the middle. In the middle, the immanent limits are in abstract superposition" (2014: 42).

Midway, betwixt and between. The middle holds it together, just.

"Touch resets the any-point of movement," they add (54).

"Your hand is really hot."

I snap back into the room.

"Yeah, they do warm up."

My left index finger marks a spot a couple of inches below her navel.

"How about I tap one in here?"

"Okay," she says, hardly hesitating.

Several thousand years ago, the ancient Chinese scanned the night sky for the North Pole Star, the prominent constellation used as a coordinate to chart the heavens. They considered it the fixed point around which everything orbited. *As it is above, so it is below,* they said, extending the celestial guidepost into the body, fixing it in the space just below the navel.

As long as we can locate our Pole Star, it doesn't matter how far we venture across the horizon. But if we lose our way, by a tangle of fear or a flare of rage, a few calm, focused belly-breaths will lead us to back to the hub—our body's night sky. Yes, there it is. Homeward bound, back to our source.

Perhaps touch, in resetting the any-point of movement, also resets potential? "Potential is abstract by nature," Manning and Massumi continue, "in the sense of not yet being this or that, here nor there. What is abstract feeling, if not thought?" (2014: 41). Perhaps, also, *home* is found "in the immanent twist" (41). In one moment, one breath.

One touch—one twirl of a needle—immediating the forces at work: in the middling.

My left finger continues to mark the way in, easily found on the south side of the small rise in the flesh below her navel. This fleshy gateway into the Pole Star is always there, no matter if the surface terrain is a large mound or flattened surface. A pale freckle, like a faint nebula, sits next to her entrance.

Placing the metal guide tube on the spot, I give the top of the needle a quick tap. It pierces the skin, and the portal opens. The needle sinks just under the surface. A few gentle twirls send down slow ripples. I feel a tiny tug. Contact.

Returning to the desk to light the moxa, I hold the tip of the cigar-shaped stick over the candle flame waiting for the dense punk to smoulder. Her breathing is slow. The flame's wobble is mesmerising.

My mother, while giving birth to me, possibly had either a profound, drug-induced dissociative episode or a near-death experience. Did the experience also get embedded in me? Maybe it helps to explain my love of flying, of watching clouds, or my phobic terror of tight spaces. Does my navel hold that memory? Maybe that's why my friend saved her babies' shrivelled cords to secretly hold like a talisman, preserving the connection. The pain and the ecstasy, forever mummified, hidden in a shoebox.

For my becomings to become becomings requires my "series of assemblages"—me, that is, in Deleuze's terminology—to relate with other assemblages—human, animate or inanimate—whereby my molecules affectively morph with whatever it is I'm in the process of becoming. As I think-feel into the density of flesh, through the gooey interstitial tissue, I listen for an opening. I refuse to collude with this *or* that thinking, side-stepping the binary pothole. My sense-perceptions stay focussed, attuned. My listening finger is becoming-needle. Like how a painter think-feels through colour, or how a dancer think-feels through movement. My becoming-needle think-feels through flesh. I find the grain of things through the movement of feeling-forward.

Exfoliating on the cutting edge of a skin's assemblage, I twirl internal whirls and alter the surface, alter the flow within.

Our realities pass into each other by twisting into the middle.

Her feet are flopped out, relaxed. She sinks deeper onto the table. Trillions of cells are happily humming as yin and yang doe-see-doe around her Pole Star.

Blowing on the moxa pole's cherry-red ember, I move back to the table and hold the burning stick an inch or so over her skin around where the needle is planted. She hardly stirs.

"You'll feel some warmth below your navel," I say. She exhales, lets out a barely audible moan. The guy-wires on her neck go slack. Her head slumps slightly to the side.

As the heat is conducted down the needle, it sends her source a strong reminder: Burn bright, hold fast, keep her oriented. As the heat seeps deeper, a message orbits back to her: Here's your energetic core, located under your umbilicus-stem, its coals smouldering, providing the light whenever you need to find your way home.

My thoughts return earthbound: Will you feel lost unclenched? Are you ready to spill from your middling in your immanent twist?

Deleuze and Guattari offer a prescription for healthy BwO:

This is how it should be done. Lodge yourself on a stratum, experiment with the opportunities it offers, find an advantageous place on it, find potential movements of deterritorialization, possible lines of flight, experience them, produce flow conjunctions here and there, try out continua of intensities segment by segment, have a small plot of new land at all times. It is through a meticulous relation with the strata that one succeeds in freeing lines of flight, causing conjugated flows to pass and escape and bringing forth continuous intensities for a BwO (1987:161).

Hovering my open palm over her skin, I feel the warm glow coming from underneath. Enough moxa. Just a few more minutes and I'll take out the needles.

A few gurgles, a tell-tale sound of relaxation, come from her belly.

After placing the moxa back on the treatment cart, I sit to finish my notes.

More gurgles emerge, sounding like a long line of trapped air bubbles finally freed, rush to the surface.

"The BwO is permeated by unformed, unstable matter, by flows of all directions, by free intensities or nomadic singularities, by mad or transitory particles" (1987: 40), they reassure us.

The stockings sag. The foot's shape is gone.

Sher Doruff

Last Year at Betty and Bob's: An Adventure

Part One

1. TAP Netting

Delicate neon signage snaked a curvilinear path over the archway entrance. The fluorescent, mercury blue script read – *The Arcades Project*. Once through the Romanesque passageway, the interior sphere of the brick and mortar high-rise was straight out of Blade Runner. The cavernous central vestibule had the excavated feeling of a gaping hole. Seventy vertiginous meters overhead, a filthy skylight dribbled patches of bright to the atrium below. Like other vertical shopping complexes of this type, boutiques, service centers and dining establishments lined the stacked walkways of browsing floors. Unlike other malls, this place was un-littered with potted palms, fast food kiosks and inflatable kiddie castles. Bob craned his neck to see a riot of drab looming up, down and sideways.

A gaudy arabesque of rusting iron railing decorated the perimeter of each floor. The only means of transport between levels required scrambling. Huge sways of gritty cargo netting hung from the rafters of the corniced ceiling to the ground floor. Rope ladders of various widths dangled between the bannisters. An entrepreneurial climbing center had scattered colourful bolt-on handholds along the large structural pillars and southwest wall for patrons preferring even more precarious ascents and descents. Rappelling from the top floor for a speedy departure was an option. Gazing upwards from the central commons tended to upset Bob's gastric juices. The pukey sensation only lasted a few seconds. He closed his eyes momentarily to regain his equilibrium.

Shopping or dining in *The Arcades Project* or TAP as it was called by patrons and critics alike, required guts, patience, agility and, most importantly, commitment. All emphasis was on the 'getting there' rather than the 'got.' During the 90c 'netting' transits, visitors carried personals and purchases on their backs, tied around their waists or in small bags held between their molars. A single industrial elevator, reserved for the transportation of commodities only, purred and clanked as the building's ubiquitous soundtrack. The monotony of its rattle as products moved with little effort from supplier to vendor amidst the stench of human sweat was reminiscent of assembly line reek in ancient Fordist factories. In the four corners of this formidable deco cum gothic interior shaft, Bob watched with mantra-like concentration the mechanical transport of heavy boxes and crates of consumables as his fellow bipeds enacted a sardonic politics of verticality.

This was TAP's wacko marketing plan.

Advertised as *the* antidote to online shopping and accelerated lifestyles, 'netting' at TAP had become a spectacular symbol of resistance to mindless consumerism, a bio-friendly alternative to heedless consumption. TAP was a flâneur mecca, flaunting perusal and barter over buying and selling; soft voyeurism over hard commerce. The retailers assembled here were necessarily quirky. Mom and pop establishments, antique stores, craft boutiques, tailoring services, shoe repair shops and soda fountains found their place among the bespoke app makers, solar cell service centers and kinky lingerie shops. Franchise establishments were prohibited.

Curiosity cabinets had been the rage for the past six months. Entrepreneurial merchants enthusiastically hoofed one-off aka 'unique' items as a balm for a surplus saturated public. Vision enhancing devices such as magnifying lenses, kaleidoscopes, diffractive pince-nez and scalable (1x200) monocles were peddled as must-have Idler Implements for the window watcher's toolbox. For a tide had turned. Even outside TAP's fortress exterior, on chic-encrusted high street, value and its objects were in a far from equilibrium state.

The Society of the Spectral

Bob had come to the TAP to lunch with the ladies at Walter's, a fourth floor slowfood joint that boasted the best pea shoot salads in town. As advertised, heart-pumping exhilaration upon arrival would intensify the epicurean experience. Bob reached the balustrade of the restaurant damp with expectation, his taste buds aroused and ready.

The ladies in question were a feral feminist artist group he'd associated with for many years. They called themselves *The Bettys*. As yet the only male member, he often functioned as querulous pet and scapegoat. He'd long enjoyed the lively irreverent conversation from this cadre of distinctive voices, a mix of generations, ethnic backgrounds, skillsets and interests. He was demurely proud of his long-term acceptance in their sect.

Bob had survived the Betty's lesbian separatist phase as a mute cross-dresser, sneaking chameleon-like into women only festivals and public toilets, fastidiously covering his prominent adam's apple with a turtleneck dickey. The Bettys felt a rush of subversive naughtiness during that time, disobeying their own strident political rulebook by harbouring straight male flesh in their perfectly idiomatic, crudely graffittied Volkswagon bus. Though Bob's African-American heritage and performance artist temperament helped to assuage his acceptance in this particular flock of agitators, his sex betrayed him on numerous occasions. The details of these anecdotes remain undisclosed. Lady Luck on their side, the B's + Bob soldiered on unscathed through the turbulent waters of second wave feminist politics.

That was then. As the teeming walls of TAP attest, women had long since taken the reins of attitude between their teeth with the diligence of worker ants. The Betty's carpe diem tactics seized the opportunity this location offered. Hip to the prog politics of TAP's 'un-management,' they embraced a cheerleader role in perpetuating the unfathomable by upending the phrase once pejoratively associated with the hunting/gathering habits of the second sex. Having done what they do, a large banner, black capital letters on a commie red cloth, hangs like an altarpiece from the upper esplanade of the Arcade.

The Bs played their role in setting the ironic yet zealously affirmative tone that had come to exemplify this strange place. Like their Situationist ancestors, they were inclined to display their worldview on posters, graffiti, banners and street art. Ritually lunching every year on the anniversary of the STYD banner installation, they discussed the pervasive long-term effects of their whimsy; the palpable change in consumer habits, the heartbreaking collateral damage. And each year, as they amassed to celebrate, the getting there proved perilously s-l-o-w-e-r. But that was the thrill of it. The risk. The high stakes of political counterpoint. The manifestation of the manifesto. As the years rolled by, these annual displays of self-congratulation always included the scouting of dining options on more easily accessible floors.

*

They lunched heartily, savouring the fresh vegetables, lubricants and animated conversation. On this occasion Bob sat between Yellow Betty the younger and White Betty the elder who, dressed in a sweat-drenched pink jogging outfit, exclaimed during the prosecco toast that this was most definitely her final appearance at TAP. "I can't get it up anymore" she roared while dusting her kale and carrot salad with marinated sesame seeds. Sitting across the table from Bob were Violet, Orange and Red Betty respectively. Devoted to their anonymity, RB and OB wore form-fitting latex rat masks with supple mouth holes.

Dongles, dangles and dinner

Leaning across the table in rapt attention, Bob jostled the glasses, plates and utensils in his peripersonal space. On his right arm he wore seven layers of brightly coloured bakelite bracelets, his recurring fashion statement at Betty happenings. Though a poised and gesturally articulate man, managing this dangly obtrusive presence while dining was a feat he'd yet to master. Absorbed in a Red Betty anecdote about her younger brother's target practice on wild bunnies, he toppled his wine glass. A smooth Pinot Noir with a cranberry aftertaste trickled from the table to the floor.

"Shit. Sorry about that. I, I didn't notice the... damn, well anyway..." Bob sopped up the spilled wine with a napkin. "Please go on, you were talking about the gauge of the gun..." "It's OK Betty Bob, the wine, there's more,... Yeah, the gauge of those pellets, I remember this factoid and I have no idea why. 4.4 mm." Red Betty demonstrated the size of the pellet by mapping a tiny space between her thumb and index finger. "On the big side for BB's" she said. "On the tiny side for rabbit shit" Yellow Betty added. "My little bro never killed an animal but he sure did serve out some pain to more than a few. There was this one gray bunny, we called him Harvey coz he would just appear and disappear. Poof! Like that. My brother would draw a bead on him from feet or so and then Poof! he was gone. I saw this with my own eyes more than once. I told my brother, 'Bobby,' I said, 'this is a sign.' I told him the rabbits were sentient beings and he should shoot at beer bottles or coke cans, something with a logo on it but not bunnies and toads. He was never very good at listening to advice when he was ten. A real brat he was then. Anyway..." On a roll, RB took a dramatically timed sip from her wine glass and continued. "...one fine spring day, Harvey hopped into the yard and up on to the porch where Bobby was playing checkers with himself. He was unarmed coz his pet Daisy Red Ryder BB Repeater rifle was propped in a corner of the toolshed out back. Harvey hopped right on to his boots and sat there all Buddha like. It was crazy. My brother didn't move a muscle. Couldn't. The wind stopped ... dead silence ... and then, after maybe two minutes, ten minutes, Poof! as usual, Harvey vanished. Presto! Just like in a magician's trick.... but for real you know what I mean...?"

Bob was attentive as he traced a dribble of red wine on the white tablecloth with his pinky. "Wow. Impressive. You sure?" He cynically added, "Was there a puff of smoke?"

Red Betty hesitated a moment, ignoring his incredulity. "We've talked about this many times since, me and Bobby, and we both remember it almost the same. He talks about the weight of the rabbit on his feet. Heavy. I couldn't feel that, the cement-like plop of this rabbit presence, but I looked into Harvey's eyes, riveted. Yeah, riveted to my seat. I swear I had one of those epiphanic moments. You know, like seeing god or all of a sudden understanding something that's not supposed to be understandable. Like love or death or intuition." "Or prehension." White Betty sullenly piped in.

Bob's scepticism was percolating like his grandmother's coffeepot. "Yeah, OK... and what exactly did it *feel* like, this, uh, spiritual moment? This revelation?"

Red Betty let out a long breath as her lips flubbered.

"It felt like Nothing escaping."

Bam-ba-lam

Bob oscillated between two tags. At the Bettys' inception he made the obvious choice of the nom de guerre 'Black Betty' but it stuck like a lump in his throat. Long since released from the gender ruse, he was assuredly male - handsome, lusty, impeccably tailored in peculiarly artful layers of mismatch. His appearance was an ongoing performance. The others casually referred to him as Betty Bob. This twist had a certain twang to it they all thought hilarious but he felt the accented nick simultaneously marginalized his gender *and* mocked his ancestral past. He took this jibe in relative good humour but the ongoing debate over his inclusion in 'The Palette' still irked him. Indeed, black as a color sits outside the chromatic spectrum. It's either All or Nothing, void or unity. An art school graduate he knew just enough about the additive and subtractive color systems to be disoriented by the contradictory functions of black and white.

Back in the day when the Bs first initiated their color tags, Bob could have chosen Green as his identifier, a central component in the spectrum, but it required a bold commitment to a political affiliation that had not yet captured his interest. Blue, his favourite colour, was appropriated by a Betty now missing in action; disappeared. Her history with the group was vaguely lit though she had inspired a percentile bump in global veganism several years back. Something about an earworm jingle she'd penned for an ad campaign. This feat was considered a triumph in an off year for the Bettys. Though they held hope for Blue's return, like a super athlete's numbered jersey, the color was retired in her memory. Through the years, numerous interns had dibs on the in-betweens. Turquoise. Pink. Chartreuse. Mauve. Vermillion. They all concurred that subjective specificity across the visible spectrum yields plenty; a Zeno's arrow of Color, infinite perceptual divisibility between hues. A recent digital artist recruit insisted on breaking the B's own boundaries by going Infrared. Her request was in equal parts annoying and exhilarating, a mutational gesture bursting with a prescience that insured the group's survival in the long term. They awaited an Ultraviolet. Perhaps a millennial would venture into the outer reaches of the electromagnetic spectrum, breaching the constraints of color altogether, going Radio, X-Ray, Micro, Cosmic.

Bob, the reluctant Black Betty, had thoroughly researched the secondary historical connotations his name carried – musket, liquor bottle, bullwhip, woman, prostitute, prison wagon – allusions carved into folklore by Lead Belly's chain gang work song. (Jump steady Black Betty bam-ba-lam. Whoa Black Betty bam-ba-lam.) An object of serious anthropological study, this immortalized 'Black Betty' was indefinitely writ. No hermeneutic consensus had been struck on her account. Thus, both his formal and informal tags, 'Black Betty' and 'Betty Bob' unremittingly referred to a troubled *disposif.*

He could work this angle surely. Race. Alterity. Inequality. Bias. Hatred. Slavery. Life experience had primed him slick for nuanced argument. He had a gift for persuasive oratory when dressed for the occasion. Left to his own imaginings however, his thoughts usually wandered into abstract, flighty terrain. A sober if dreamy man, Bob preferred plumbing the physics of light and metaphysics of color to unfurling the polemics of decolonial relations between black, brown, red, yellow and white. The rainbow flag was too literal for his taste. Even as he tended to his philosophical tendencies there was little escape from the magnetic pull of his fugitive legend. The Bettys urged him to get his priorities in order.

At home, a wall near his bed hosted a material witness of his existential dilemmas. Here hung a hand-painted 'Black is Beautiful' poster he'd inherited from his great-grandmother of the extinct Panther tribe. The tension between the brilliant simplicity of its message and its convoluted legacy haunted him. Holding its fading, fragile countenance nakedly in his hands had overtaxed his sensations so he'd carefully covered the dog-eared construction paper in two full rolls of kitchen plastic wrap. The unwavering calligraphy of the three adamant words refracted through the bundle of transparent layers, now nearly unreadable, obscured and buried beneath stratums of light.

Manifesto Epitaph

Following the lively reunion meal the Bs hugged, high-fived and mentally prepared for their departure with one minute of huddled silent concentration. This custom had been Blue Betty's initiative, an impulsive semi-terrified gesture concluding their first celebratory TAP meal many years past. The surviving Bettys continued the tradition, partially in Blue's honour, partially because it was a damn good idea to take a deep breath before committing one's body to the task. Team sport had got this ritual right.

As any seasoned sailor will tell you rope descents can be deceptively difficult, especially on cargo net constructions that flex on every foot and handhold. Gravity's insistence, an obstacle on the way up, is just as hostile on the way down. Many opt to rappel at TAP as it's a quick descent and the pelvic harness has its unquestionably kinky allure. Single rope journeys require another type of skill. Legs wrapped around a wobbly strand of hemp or a swath of aerial silk, one foot threaded to support the body's ascent and slow its descent, this procedure is popular with firemen, pole dancers, acrobats and young boys. Negotiating the knotted, fluctuating instability of the communal Netting is more dangerous in its unpredictability. It requires a certain spidery athletic finesse but more importantly, it demands a versatile response-ability to contingent conditions. The Netting is always otherwise, like the Nasdaq or the weather on K2. Networking techniques are often hard won. Trust functions instrumentally. Red, Violet, Yellow, Orange, Black Betty and the in-betweens have always preferred this, some would say, more challenging collaborative route.

In their farewell huddle, OB broke the solemn mood with a hearty, horribly clichéd "You go grrls!" They groaned then whooped in unison as they began their return to ground level, butt-skimming the waist high railing, one leg secured on the safe side, the other dangling the void. Carefully finding toeholds on the unstable rope, they hoisted their aging bodies over the barrier. Affable Red Betty was as always, wearing her rat mask and infectiously pos attitude. In one enthusiastic move, following a bravada wave to Yellow Betty carefully descending to her right, her left foot missed a notch in the netting. Having elected to wear her new stilettos, thinking the heel would hook securely around the hemp thongs like a boot in a stirrup, she had neglected to factor in the slick danger of her stylish footwear's polished soles.

She slipped one meter, then eighteen.

2. Red Betty's Black/Whiteout

It took approximately 1.83 seconds for Red Betty to break apart on the cold marble floor of TAP's interior vestibule. She dropped silently, her scream resounding internally, throughout the soft tissue of her imperceptibly accelerating body. A lot can happen in 1.83 seconds at an average falling speed of 17kph/40mph. The accumulated light and dark of her forty-two years flashed in stroboscopic flurry.

"Bets, get in here and do the dishes."

"Sis, you seen my BB gun?"

"Mmmm, I love you darling."

"Don't stop..."

"Happy New Year!"

"Help me!"

"God, no!"

"Congratulations ma'am, it's a …."

"Harvey!"

Blackout.

Whiteout.

Umwelt Ticks

It's doubtful any pair of eyes saw the tick from 286 to 287 as Red Betty's statistical moment was calculated.

The Arcades Project hosted a real-time line item on the dynamic Umwelt that is the Worldometers homepage. On this stroboscopic seizure-inducing multi-ticker array of faux coordinates and unadulterated portend, TAP held its place as a near static three-digit antidote to the ruthless advance of advance. Nestled alongside the global update of births and deaths, military expenditure, energy consumed and forests lost, TAP's digital counter recorded the on-site demise of its patrons. Accumulating at a creep, TAP's incrementally slow pace was nonetheless chilling, a reminder of desperate conviction clamouring for air in the throes of an anthropocene death spiral.

The mesmerizing worldometer beat of environmental and demographic data appeals to news junkies with entangled interests: a longing for homeostasis on the one hand and a desire for an exhilarating far from equilibrium rush on the other. TAP ticker-watchers are harder to pigeonhole. Catastrophe addicts, conspiracy theorists, rubberneckers, anti-consumerists, rock climbers, rock stars, queers, artists, Betty groupies, greenies, vegans, economists, socialists, stockbrokers, fifth wave feminists, neo-futurists, eulogy hobbyists, undercommoners, gamblers - the gamut. TAP's own website hosted 'In Memorium' pages of dropped shoppers, those who risked their lives for an untenable cause, for the transcendental displacement of capitalist hegemony everywhere. Here, martyr videos of the desperate and the doomed were posted alongside photo archives of the accidentally dropped ones, those for whom conviction proved fatal. This digital graveyard proliferated with affirming life images uploaded by family and friends. The Dylan riff "She knows there's no success like failure and that failure's no success at all" was popular. Many offered eulogistic banalities. "May she rest in peace" was by far the most common and the most 'unliked.' Red Betty, when once a living, breathing eulogist herself, preferred more creative adages. Her "RIP & DIFFRACT" gif went viral upon her passing.

She'd been an avid worldometer observer, hypnotized by the insistence of the counter's progress. The tockless tick, tick, tick, tick, tick. She had no idea what exactly to do with this barrage of accumulating data. She'd tweeted *"Whoa horsey, slow the fuck down. I wanna smell what remains of the roadkill"* to hysterical confusion among her followers at #popupworld. As her color boldly announced, her leftwing leanings literally left her a misplaced contemporary on a planet where the horizontal political spectrum no longer held traction, left and right convolving into a meaningless ideological stalemate. The once well-defined, color-coded political spectrum had dissipated, exemplified by the co-opting of Revolutionary Red by neoliberal political parties. Resistance would require encryption.

Once upon a time as a younger activist, RB's political response to governmental and institutional horrors was straightforward though admittedly ineffective. She collectivized, marched, threw stones (sometimes), resisted arrest (always), spent a day or two in lock-up then got bailed. At candlelit rallies she cried together with friends over a slew of injustices: the gross indecency of the distribution of wealth, dominant nation war mongering atrocities, genocide, vivisection and the stubborn persistence of racial hegemony. Micro-political activists cut from the same cloth as Red Betty threw their bodies into the polemic. Resistance was a tactilely felt force. Two days before her fall she'd tweeted: *"I feel failure in my fingertips every time I click the submit button on Avaaz petitions"* #popupworld.

Shaz Dada Blog Bits

Arts and Politics journalist Shaz Dada's remarks on the drop of Red Betty. First published in Dada's blog, Situations.

20 April

On Falling, Failing and Flying

It must be said today that as a community we are again confronted with expressing an unambiguous feeling of loss in the face of ambiguous success and fulfillment. Deeply saddened by the passing of Red Betty of the notorious art propagandists *The Bettys*, we nonetheless, according to her own wishes, joyfully observe her adventurous life. Red Betty consistently walked the talk, inspiring generations of ethically vibrant artists, activists, theorists and precarity workers of all stripes, patterns and colours. We have the Bettys to thank for the anti-neocon-consumerist approach to daily shopping and of course the twisted *Shop Til You Drop* slogan among other memorable idioms. 'Cleavage Rules' is my personal favourite. When Red Betty dropped to her demise at TAP on 15 April she was, like so many courageous and vigilant predecessors, *cleaving* her artmaking to her life and death.

Until her untimely passing, Red Betty had been an aggressive advocate of the non-monetary exchange of services and goods. Her strong teeth and broad back had carried more than her body weight in perishables and necessary toiletries over the years. While the others have opted to play and pay with J-coins, she chose for barter only and the ingenious scrutiny of what she referred to as the 'really free' market. Living healthfully off conspicuous urban food waste, she'd convened a band of rat-masked activists, daily foraging for ample spoils in a gluttonous city. Well fed and well read, her tireless advocacy of a better way had given her iconic status in an urban field fast approaching 22,000,000 inhabitants. Her drop will surely have an effect on the art of dissidence.

I interviewed Red six years ago when Blue Betty first went missing. She was articulate, funny, concerned and unassuming, exuding, like her color, a very powerful aura. Perhaps more than any other Betty, she helped to construct the TAP project as a singular actualization of aesthetic resistance. She made a difference. Arguably, the transactional agency of placemaking that occurs in that arcade is of the profoundest sort. So it is with sadness and muted celebration that I extend my **"RIP & DIFFRACT"** to Red Betty, her friends, family, colleagues, comrades and many admirers.

3. RIP RGB

The air in their shared warehouse studio was thick with imploding drama. They all felt it but were reluctant to name it. RED. Gone. BLUE missing. GREEN empty. Left without the foundational RGB they were conceptually, scientifically, politically and philosophically bereft. Voided. Limp.

Thoroughly shaken by Red Betty's sudden departure, the gaping sinkholes in the Bettys ROYGBV spectrum signalled the imminent collapse of their project. A sense of urgency prevailed in desperate defiance of any tendency to retreat into a sullen depression, a despairing purgatory. Collectively they needed to get back in the saddle. Mottled crew that they now were, unable to address the issue of their insolvency directly, they opted instead for a refreshing dip into the chaosmos. Anon proclaimed *'it was there a horse soon dancing'* so they abided. They partied. Hard.

Waking Finnegan

"Fuck, I'm messed up. Can't handle red wine anymore not to mention scotch and soda." "Partying ain't what it used to be but I still gotta say that being touched by the dark waters of a single malt feels real good right now." "Crank up that tune sweetie, I adore Sonic Youth. Perfect music for an imperfect moment." "Don't ya miss her...Red, I mean? Fuck, I do. She had the best style of us all. Knew how to wear stilettos like a catwalker." "Uuhh, well, hmmm, maybe not...you know... anyway, there's no justice in this goddamn world." "You got a smoke on you?" "Nope." "... crudités?" "... and then this skinny dude with a plastic pen protector in his pocket, no joke, started writing equations on the kitchen tile and...." "Did you see the exoplanet photo that went viral yesterday?" "Kinda." "Speaking of rats, have there been any more updates on that woman with the neon rat scratch? Her name is Betty right, or Bette or Beet, anyway friggin weird." "But hey, everybody, y'all listen up. Personally, and maybe this is just me but (clears throat) I don't think we oughta go to TAP for awhile. We should lay low, you know what I mean? Reconsider our asser(burp)tions." "Fuck no, that's the worst thing we could do for Red, abandon her project like scared little girls." "We gotta go back tomorrow in style. Walk through the archway with quiet dignity. Climb that Netting like ants up a vine." "Immediate!" "Hey, let's barter her ratty mask for twenty vegan dinners for the homeless at Slushy's. She'd like that." "Sounds patronizing to me." "Yeah, me too." "Fuck this shit." "Let's not enter a polemical pit tonight folks. OK? It's time to get wasted on fond memories. Celebrate Red's leaving, cry over Red lost. It's not, I repeat NOT, the moment for politically correct fisticuffs. We got plenty of time for that tomorrow." "Okedoki, White is right as always bam ba lam." "Say that again without irony Betty Bob, pleeeze, for Red's sake..." "Okedoki, White is right as always bam ba lam."

Baconing

Impulsively, amidst the after party chaos of their eulogistic bash, the surviving Bs began redesigning their studio space after Francis Bacon's catastrophe-style atelier. Creating a material shit storm felt like the right thing to do. There was no discussion. This was a moment when years of embattled collective negotiation paid dividends in collective intuition. Spontaneously fastidious, they began fashioning their workspace from hoarder photos of garbage heap rooms. "Shock inertia before it grabs a stranglehold" YB kept muttering.

Following the dead painter's lead they played with a cacophony of perceptual triggers and dissociation mechanisms. This technique would surely horse jump them towards an indeterminate creative intensity, help to alleviate their alarming sense of loss and despair, the affective noise of hyper-stimulated precarity. Orange Betty pointed out that wading through mountains of accumulated debris could backfire on their delicate emotional states but her listless argument was overruled.

They went wild. Playing in a vibrational field of non-attachment, flush with the simultaneity of destruction and creation, they wrestled tumult to a fever pitch. "Immediate!" White Betty yelled. "Diagram goddamn it!" "Bacon it!" "Or Vega-bacon it!" A tactical pro by now at whipping vitality into motion, WB enthusiastically shouted motivational aphorisms through a hand rolled cardboard megaphone. "Infinite entanglement!" she shouted as she slipped on a slime heap of newsprint, vinyl shards and coffee grounds majestically laid out in a logarithmic spiral by VB. Her hipbone flinched in surprise as she hit the concrete floor. Blacks, blues and yellows colonized her haunches.

Soon they were knee deep in debris and images: images of images, junk, tools, objets trouvés, boxes and assorted detritus. The central convivial table in the 200sq meter warehouse loft was strewn with books, magazines, poster scraps, tools (markers, pens, brushes, tablets, tweezers, screwdrivers, spray paint cans, tape, glue, arduino boards, raspberry pi's, wires, transistors, alligator clips) potato chips, donut holes, kale crackers, and displaced dust. Every bare centimeter in the high-ceilinged drafty workspace was soon covered with things and representations of things. Articulated gibberish. One had to wade through an assault on the senses to carve out a still point in the mess. "Do you feel satisfied yet?" YB tentatively whispered to VB as they watched Infrared Betty swipe snow angels in a pile of shredded Cosmology magazine pages mingled with hundreds of poetry shards (among them clippings from Anne Carson's *Autobiography of Red* and Maggie Nelson's *Bluets*). Forging a butterfly pattern in a riot of spectral effervescence technically unavailable to human perception, this mélange of language and Hubble photos, of chaosmos and chiasmus, rendered an invisible universe carnivalesque, a Fellini cosmos in a Wes Anderson palette. IB sang "Come fly with me through *The Verse,* through *The Verse*" to no one in particular.

Attuned to a sighing collective exhaustion, the Betty's caught their breath as they surveyed the scene. The words "Impressive" and "OMG" filled thought bubbles floating over the silence. Even by their own rigorous standards, they'd outdone themselves. For a kaironian moment they felt relieved, marginally content. And then, as if on cue, an unmistakable twinge, an undeniable tendency towards conceptual catharsis infected the semblance of closure. Slowly, they reassembled around the kitchen table. Philosophical conversation usually worked on their metabolisms like a psychedelic drug. "Let's talk Color girls," White Betty slurred as she massaged the ache in her hip. " How bout we sleep on it first," whined OB.

4. Dic cur hiccup

Long a Betty tradition, close reading sessions on topics of shared interest were as comforting as food prepared together. They called these conversations *Dic cur hiccups* after Leibnitz's advice (dic cur hic) to say what's up, what's happening now. Fragments of feminist, queer and decolonial theory convolved with continental philosophies and approaches to artistic practice. Heady and happy, Whitehead tended to rule. Often, without formally beginning, disparate banter slowly dribbled into a kind of coherence. Provocations and questions littered with anecdotes and nonsensical tangents settled into focused concentration.

The morning-after Red's bash, copious amounts of coffee and green tea were consumed from stained jelly jars as they tried to rectify their hangovers with caffeine. At the crack of dawn teetotaler Ochre Betty pulled Wittgenstein's *Remarks on Colour* from the library rubble. She printed out Part I pages 2-14 for the groups perusal. Amidst the cacophonous distraction of their 'baconing,' the B's struggled with the text at hand. One hour into the discussion Ludwig's proposition 52 was generating animated argument:

52. White as a colour of substances (in the sense in which we say snow is white) is lighter than any other substance-colour; black darker. Here colour is a darkening, and if all such is removed from the substance, white remains, and for this reason we can call it "colourless".

Orange Betty: What bullshit is this? Why are we even talking about substances? And a substance colour? Passé dogdoo...

Brown Betty: Do you think he means materiality?

White Betty: Personally, I don't get it either. Is he saying that white is colourless in uhh, essence? Or that essence is colourless? You know I don't think this way and I have the most at stake here since, well, you know, I am White Betty... or I thought I was but then, aah, aah, maybe this can work for me in terms of eradicating identity politics altogether. I'm kinda confused... Or is he saying all substance is white with variable degrees of darkening? That I could live with. Or...no... it's still confusing, objectionable.

Violet Betty: Well, it's easier to grasp if we think about uhm, appearances, right? I don't know, I never studied philosophy, but anyway, a rose is a rose is a rose is sometimes red. Snow, when a dog hasn't pissed on it looks white. Isn't that what he means? Substance is colour or colour is substance or something like that?

Orange Betty: Uh uh, I don't think so. There's more going on here. I smell a rat.

Infrared Betty: Hey OB, you've always been paranoid.

White Betty: Hang on darlings. Let's get back to the text. That's our task here after all.

Orange Betty: What do we do with this?

Brown Betty: (head dangling) I'm sorry, can we deal with this at another session. I can't think straight today.

Vermillion Betty: (chuckles) I can't think queer today.

White Betty: OK, let's skip that bit for now. One last try (reading aloud):

68. When we're asked "What do the words 'red', 'blue', 'black', 'white' mean?" we can, of course, immediately point to things which have these colours, -- but our ability to explain the meanings of these words goes no further! For the rest, we have either no idea at all of their use, or a very rough and to some extent false one.

White Betty: We can all agree with that right?

Orange Betty: (murmuring) In principle I want to disagree with anything he says.

Vermillion Betty: In principle I want to agree to disagree.

White Betty: But this goes straight to the heart of our problematics. Our tags, our post-identity politics, the work we make. No?

Violet Betty: The limits of language. That's the point right? And actually, I think that's a cool concept. You know, what we can't say. What we can't know.

Orange Betty: But...

Black Betty: (excited) But ... sorry ... I'm just riffing ... backing up ... if color is a darkening like he says in 52 then he's playing his language games in the subtractive field. White is originating. He's taking a side, flipped to a specific system of reference, of belief.

Orange Betty: Huh?

Ochre Betty: So what?

Mauve Betty: (sifting through loose images on the table) Hey, check this out, a snap of one half of Ronald Reagan. It's hilarious. "Where's the rest of me?"

Violet Betty: (undistracted) Yeah, continue, whatch you on about Betty Bob?

Black Betty: You know, this theory I'm working on about the relational difference between dual systems of color, additive and subtractive. The additive system, RGB, you know, all prismatic color in white light and the 'other' one, the subtractive, CYM, all color absorbed in black.

White Betty: As usual, you're obfuscating ... I want to understand the significance of this but you're always soooo opaque.

Black Betty: Yes, yes that's it you see...

Brown Betty: I'll look for a blackboard and chalk. Must be something around here... you could draw it for us...

Violet Betty: (glaring at Black Betty) Can we not talk about your pet project now and focus on the text please.

Black Betty: (demurring) Yeah OK, sorry... it's just...

White Betty: (sighing) maybe later Betty Bob. I'm interested.

Orange Betty: But hey, are we really talking language games here or are we enmeshed in something other? I always thought this analytic perspective carved out a suffocating system. I just, uhh, I just don't like it. I instinctively prefer the process thinkers, not the logicians.

Infrared Betty: And for the record, sorry I got to interject, can we also talk about Pink or Beige or Gray for fuck's sake? Don't y'all get sick of the primaries after awhile?

Brown Betty: You got that right.

Mauve Betty: Oh my god, you gotta see this!

And so it went...

As a coda to the loud, heated, inconclusive discussion punctuated by tangential remarks, Violet Betty recited a passage from Derek Jarman's *Chroma* to sober the escalating din – *"Red is a moment in time. Blue constant. Red is quickly spent. An explosion of intensity. It hums itself. Disappears like fiery sparks into the gathering shadow."* "Voila" she concluded.

5. Whoa Black Bessie

A black man and a Betty, Bob was often off-balance. He took his politics and his philosophy seriously as did the other B's but he was an exception to their rule in oh so many ways.

Both-neither.

And...and...

He'd bonded with Red and missed her. She'd been his link to collaboration, to mixing it up with others. He felt the scissor cut of the sever, the cleave, now that she was dust in the wind. He was on his own, no matter how crazy comfortable the Betty gatherings felt. Red's fall jolted his temperament.

"I have this funny feeling" Bob whispered to IB. He'd fallen hard for her since she'd joined the group. It wasn't her toned bod (he told himself) or her enthusiasm for all things cosmopolitical that grabbed him. "I've got a sinking feeling my concerns... my art ... is wanking bullshit like Yellow always says." IB nodded. Bob couldn't tell if it was a nod of agreement with his doubts or an empathetic gesture. He suspected his infatuation with IB might have something to do with her uncanny likeness to his boyhood heroine, Bessie Coleman. But he might be projecting. The remembered warmth of his grandmother's stories flooded his dreaming with the thrill of adventure, the twinkle of starlight in a pitchblack sky, the waning blue of the vanishing point on an ocean's horizon. This was the stuff of his future perfects, his will have beens.

Next to the cellophaned Panther poster on his bedroom wall he'd pinned up several photos of the aviator that he'd cut from a tattered second hand book he'd found in a Strand dustpile. His grandmother had told him bedtime stories of Bessie's barnstorming exploits, her bravery, her remarkable resistance to racial profiling. "She was the first woman of African-American descent to earn an aviation pilot's license Bobby. She had to go all the way to Paris France to do it coz there was no way she was getting into a pilot's school in the US of A with two strikes against her, that being black and female as she was." "Did she fly around the world Grandma?" he remembered asking. "No Bobby, she died before that was possible. You're maybe thinking of Amelia, but she didn't make it either. Anyway, Bessie died in a senseless way, falling from an old plane she'd bought herself, a tuna fish can with wings. A real aerial acrobat she was. A daredevil flying loop dee loops. Anyway, she didn't have her seatbelt on when her dodgy plane went belly up mid-air, a wrench in the gearbox they said. Sounds like a bad joke but that's the truth of it. She dropped 2000 feet they say."

As a kid, Bob would often dream of Bessie falling through the Floridian air. She always wafted like a skydiver or an angel, seeing things through her goggles no on else had seen, feeling things, remembering things, as if she had all the time in the world to float on a future. This dream always included a bright yellow single propeller plane trailing a metallic banner out its ass, fluttering in the sky like a giant water moccasin waving through prairie grass.

Justy Phillips

The Fictiōnella: Immediating Relations Through Fictiōneering

When you and I catch sight of a Great Tufted Owl in a forest 200 kilometres northwest of Montreal the world splits open once again. Our air-locked hire car splinters in two in five in eight in more. Separates with such devastating force, the nearly from the living.

In the stillness of more-than one. We consume each other. Move-with each others' consuming. You. I.

She. The plumed beast. Aloft.

High in the canopy where cuts are made of ochre light. Organs of sugar soap and air.

In his seminal discussion paper on contemporaneity, philosopher and media theorist, Boris Groys asks: "How does the present manifest itself in our everyday experience—before it begins to be a matter of metaphysical speculation or philosophical critique?" (Groys 2009: 1). As an artist and writer, my life is shaped by the precarious ecology of *fictioneering*—a practice of "speculative eventing" that generates immediations through chance encounter and constructed situations.

Fictiōneering: *To make-with the living experience of events.*

The term "fictioneer" (C19th) is commonly defined as a "writer or inventor of fiction." By activating the Latin root of fiction, *fictiō*, meaning "to make or produce" rather than the more common understanding of *fiction* meaning "the act of feigning or inventing imaginary events" (The New Shorter Oxford English Dictionary 1993: 941), a practice of *fictiōneering* becomes both a relation-producing movement and an active and ongoing, processual engagement with eventing of everyday life (Phillips 2014). The in-act of fictiōneering is not a matter of truth.

Only experience in-the-making. As a fictiōneer, the *present* manifests itself in my everyday experience through imperceptible acts of *telling*.

Fictiōneering is a practice of speculative eventing that embraces chance encounters through techniques of attuning, wandering, distilling and scoring. It can be understood as a bringing into language the living experience of the event. Conceived as a "process of thinking by doing, always with the understanding that concepts are made in and through the event"[1] research-creation is a mode of enquiry that, as artist and philosopher Erin Manning argues, refuses to posit "the terms of its account before the exploration of what the account can do" (2016: 29). Fictiōneering extends this mode of enquiry by drawing into its sphere of relations, what I might propose as the "interval" (Manning 2009a) of *telling*.

In the dark green fields of the north of England. In the throbbing pink flesh of my failing heart. Stretched to the limit. I thought I was looking for my father. But now all I feel is yours.

A conjunctive meeting of "fictiō" and "novella," the fictiō-nella extends the *making* force of fictiō with the novella's unique form of *telling*. Originating in Italy during the Middle Ages, the term "novella," from the Italian word "novella" (meaning *new* or *news*) is widely understood to be the telling of a single, suspenseful event, situation or conflict leading to an unexpected turning point. Often depicting events concerned with real-life people in a real-life setting (hence, the recounting of "news" events), the term "novella" is also used to relay fictive events. The novella, writes literary theorist, S. Trenkner, is "an imaginary story of limited length, intended to entertain, and describing an event in which the interest arises from the change in fortunes of the leading characters or from behaviour characteristic of them" (1957: xiii). In its earliest forms, the novella was an oral tradition, activated and animated through voice alone. To this day, through its commonly published short story form, the essence of the novella continues to be made *felt* in the telling.

I did not bother to check the ocean floor for upturned rocks. I did not think at the time that your grief was my grief. That your life was my living. That I could be of any assistance whatsoever in filling the absence of your loss.

I did not think you might still feel the salt in his hair. Late at night where you lie warm and pulsing in my arms. I did not see how all of this was growing inside me. Because I was looking for my father. And yours was already gone.

Critically, the fictiōnella is a gesture of *experiential* and *imperceptible* telling. But more than this, it is a telling event.

Drawing together as a shared, transversal opening, philosophers, Gilles Deleuze and Félix Guattari's concept of the "novella" and artist and philosopher, Erin Manning's concept of the "interval," I use fictiōneering to *think-feel* a new gesture of imperceptible telling.

Deleuze and Guattari conceive the novella as that which has already happened. It is presented in contrast to the literary genre of the tale, which they define as that which is yet to unfold. Rather than focusing on the dimension of time, however, Deleuze and Guattari define the essence of the novella as its fundamental relation to *secrecy*. In the novella, write Deleuze and Guattari, "you will never know what just happened" (1987: 193). *I know this through experience.* When I feel the hole in my heart, what I feel is never the event. Only its aftermath. I feel weakness in my legs, palpitations in my chest. Aching in my jaw. I feel anxiety. Materiality. An intense and overwhelming sensation of a bodying that could be my own. But for its edges.

The novella, write Deleuze and Guattari;

> has little to do with a memory of the past or an act of reflection; quite to the contrary, it plays upon a fundamental forgetting. It evolves in the element of "what happened" because it places us in relation with something unknowable and imperceptible ... It may even be that nothing happened, but is precisely that nothing that makes us say, 'Whatever could have happened to make me forget where I put my keys, or whether I mailed that letter, etc.? What little blood vessel in my brain could have ruptured? What is this nothing that makes something happen?' (1987: 193).

As blooms of rising damp scale the walls of his small bathroom. My father and I. And seep into the lounge where his television plays in the dark.

Deleuze and Guattari's conception of secrecy, writes philosopher Claire Colebrook, is "not *a* content to be discovered—*the* secret, *the* sense, *the* genesis of relations—so much as relations where no term is exhausted by or through its perception of any other" (2010: 292). Secrecy, Colebrook writes, is "the invisible form that orients perceivers and bodies but that is not itself perceived" (2010: 292). Secrecy as imperceptible, orienting force.

The air is full of blue and white. Flecks of iridescent dancing light in the sweet haze of his home-made cigarette. A symphony of under-stated self-fulfilling neglect. He gets up from his chair momentarily, to make another coffee. Leaves the shape of his body. And then back to the safe upholstery of his refrain. Secreting all the little things we cannot say because we don't know what to say. Because we are afraid.

And all the things you could not say

because of that day. When the ocean swallowed your father. Whole. Knitting his gentle organs into coral reef.

In bringing together the two concepts of fictiō and novella, a new relation is born. The "fictiōnella," is what I will come to define as a formless telling. Rather than finding presence in the layering or joining of their conceptual forms, the fictiōnella creates an opportunity for invention in the conjugating "interval" of the event. Invoking Erin Manning's concept of the "interval," a relational quality of space-time, the fictiōnella is less concerned with coming to "know what just happened" but rather, the proposition *of coming to feel what just happened*. For Manning, "the interval never marks a passage: it creates the potential for a passage that will have come to be" (2009a: 24). Thinking the interval though the event of dancing, Manning writes:

The interval is duration expressed in movement. It is not something I create along, or something I can re-create by myself. It exists in the between of movement. It accompanies my movement yet it is never passive. It activates the next incipient movement. The interval is the metastable quality through which the relation is felt. Many potential intensities populate it. It expresses itself as the shifting axis that connects us. (Manning 2009a: 17)

As the polyphonic interval of fictiō and novella, the fictiōnella might best be understood as an interstitial living organism of body, duration and event.

–

Interval.

Thresholding

Cut

The fictiōnella, through this interval that I have come to define as "experience in the making-already made felt," tells-with the affective, political and material force of speculative eventing.

In the realm of the visible—the discernable—this interval of experience in the making-already made felt is most easily identifiable in already existing artworks. The silhouette of a lame horse on a Tiranan highway (in Anri Sala's, *Time After Time*, 2003). A dead mouse, a mound of basalt, sporadically planted marijuana; plants that affect the psyche, the digestive system, sexual impulse and the brain; upturned tree roots, heaps of cobble stones, a shallow pool of water, mud, a marble sculpture, a bee hive and the intermittent arrival of a dog named Human (in Pierre Huyghe's, *Untilled*, 2012). An unfinished house in the Mexican town of El Rosario (in Justy Phillips', *Event #87: and towards the unknowable,* 2012). The fictiōnella, however, should not be misunderstood as *form—a* mediated object, *a* printed book, *an* assemblage of feathers and rocks, *a* voice, *a* moving body, *a* back-lit video streaming live cross-hemispheric feeds. These are merely the visibles—perishings of that "which gives itself to be perceived while always being more that what is perceived, bearing the potential for further secrecy" (Deleuze and Guattari 1987: 290). This *formless potential—this* is the fictiōnella. *This* is the fictiōnella's imperceptible glory.

Back home, the giant kelp writhes in the depths of the Tasman sea. He could have chosen that place. But I guess this is where he knew you would be.

Such glory demands to be felt. But it is a balancing act of precarious holding. Move too quickly and you'll only ever catch what's in view. Too slowly and the weight of your holding will crush you along with everyone else you know. Don't move at all and you'll perish, relations proliferating beyond and before you. To tell-with the fictiōnella you must allow the fictiōnella to tell-with you. To compose you. Imperceptibly at first. Perhaps without your knowing. Just a feeling that something has happened. Is *happening*. Over and over, the same question in my head: "What happened? Whatever could have happened?" (Deleuze and Guattari 1987: 192).

We're moving forward on a corrugated road when you recognise his eyes in the trees. In the place where a copse of silver birch sheds skin upon skin.

Your

Dad.

It has to be.

The mottled forest kisses him in slippery gills. And the car we are travelling in does not stop in time for you to ask him where he's been. For seventeen years adrift. At sea.

In a concrescent collision of fictiō and novella, the fictiōnella makes-with the affective, political and material force of *telling*. However, unlike the novella, whose primary expression is *narrative*, the fictiōnella is an *experiential* gesture always in-the-making. No tracing. No recounting. In this world everything is new. The fictiōnella is always the first time. The first space. The first wriggling, thresholding fizz.

And first it is you who cannot breathe. And then it is I who cannot breathe. The distance between the car and the verge and the ground and the sun and the broken tree which holds him motionless in this blue. Amphibious weight. A tidal rip cleaves you back into his glory plume. And me, to the sorrow of your Great Barrier Reef. I meet the crabs and the barnacles and the water fleas. Unleash from that day the most spectacular metamorphoses from free-swimming plankton to reef-dwelling

Father

-lost

-at

-sea.

Whilst the fictiōnella may exact details of everyday events, people and places, unlike the novella, these singularities are merely markers of a more complexifying assemblage—an entering into relation with the imaginings, trustings, desires and ineffable lines that score our own lives with the lives of *others*. Perhaps this is the *secrecy* Claire Colebrook marks as "the positive affirmation of an imperceptibility that is created through the proliferation of perceivers" (2010: 292). In other words, the joy of the imperceptible is only created through the proliferation of its perceivers—its voices, its readers, its performers, its partners, its memories, its vibrations. I tentatively ask: *The fictiōnella as perceiver of its own telling?*

As a direct experiencing of living events, the fictiōnella illuminates the perceiver at every turn. The "I." The "You." The apersonal *othering*. These tendencies reveal not only the ability to cut from all directions but perhaps more importantly, the ability to *affect* the cut, deeply. To propel it forward. To dart it with precision. And force.

All our insides are on the outsides. Trailing. Trawling. Hundreds of metres cast from the window on your side of the car. Knotted and tangled they fall away in messy clumps of something once remembered so clean. I put my hand on your knee desperate to anchor this spectacular moment in more than the rivulets of petrified dirt that carve our wheels into all the things relentless summer rains have washed away. But the speed of this extrapolated body catches us both on the run. How badly I want to catch a glimpse. Of your dad looking out from his silvery ocean hide. To trace the gentle tufts of his eyes with mine.

Beyond any given *form*, the fictiōnella extends its living lines towards *formless* expression by moving-with the speculative opening, *experience in the making-already made felt*. This hyphenating interval of "space-time," this is where the fictiōnella composes itself. But more than this. This is *how* the fictiōnella composes *us*. How it gestures and cuts. This is how it *immediates*—by moving us to experience immediation as always beyond perception. But never beyond feeling.

To squeeze into him these years of missing touch.

My father not yours.

To let him feel.

This mass of invertebrate life between us.

Notes

1. SenseLab website www.senselab.ca

Sixth Movement

Paradoxes of Form

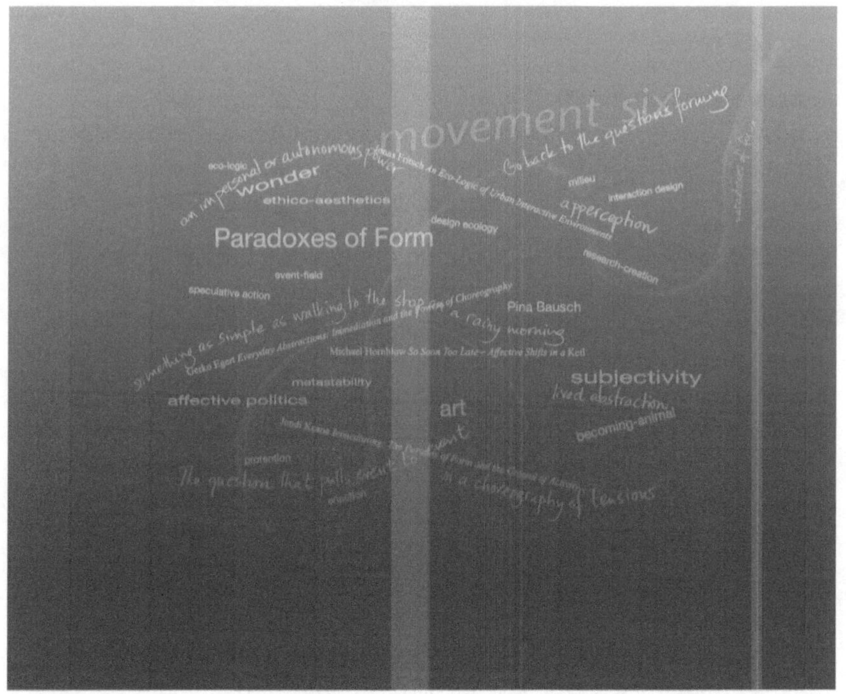

Anna Munster

Prelude

Something as simple as walking to the shop on a rainy morning. Will you: take an umbrella? Tuck jeans into boots? Walk the quickest way, avoiding a downpour? Check RainAlarm on your iPhone? Plans begin to form; shaping movement, ordering time. The walk to the shop can be executed, has a trajectory, acquires a profile.

No! The door blows open and your umbrella sucks the rain inwards drenching the bottom of your pants and, as you lean down, you drop the phone onto the slate step cracking the glass letting in moisture and shutting it down. Swiftly, you plough in to the horizontal storm, throwing the forces of body across those of weather, pavement, traffic. The route is forgotten yet taken up anyway by habit, as you bend to a new mode of tackling the walk, re-orienting and abandoning previous plans. You and the day find a different yet faintly familiar carriage to a morning coffee.

The form of this walk was neither in the prior preparation nor in the chaos ensuing from a sudden change of plan. That walk formed in the middle, in-formed by events unfolding. Form is incessantly emergent and the emergence is shapely. Such in-forming, in the middle, is always at hand yet our capacity to follow and feel its contours fall away to habit. Michael Hornblow lands on a process for elongating such middling. To suspend middling, and so immediating a temporal sequence, is to foreground and value the nonlinear back and forth of thinking and making:

> Thinking back and forth, feeling what just happened, what things have been and are still becoming, as all these emerge together—there are many modes in which an event seems to shift, as if outside of itself, just as this outside is felt within thought. Events are always in the middle of things,

> even as this middling seems far-flung for the Now moment.
> (Hornblow, Immediation II, 456)

A thickening of experience's middle that William James called the specious present—a "vaguely vanishing backward and forward fringe" (James 1950a: 613).

There was no prior form. In that very moment of planning the route to the shop—or the art performance—movement had not ceased but changed form from walking to strategizing. The prior form was already moving in to something else, that "else" moving at a different pace. This paradox of form—that form changes as it tries to inform something not yet formed and so experiences ... a loss of form. But how to get hold of that shift? Not in order to pin it down but to let forces escape and possess themselves of something more....

Go back to the questions forming. The questions were never "about" something else; were never a moment in which form could be hylomophically imposed on what was/is about to happen. As Gerko Egert states: "There are no pre-given bodies, no entities that can be arranged by a person in space and time, only movements interfering with movements" (Egert, Immediation II, 445). Questioning is instead a force that both provokes and abstracts from movement's infinities, cutting across all possible routes, decisions, backtracks, bifurcations, sequences. Egert takes up the question of questioning as a mode of choreographing movement in Pina Bausch's dance, arguing that: "The process of questioning transversally runs as a choreographic force through the dancers' bodies acting *upon* and *with* other movements" (Egert, Immediation II, 445).

It turns out that piling up questions was never going to result in a blueprint for getting to the shops. Questioning is already thought moving—into another thought and/or into action—shaking up the sedimentation of the before and after of form and movement, design and making, theory and practice. Questioning is movement enough to transform practices of dance, performance, even interaction design. In challenging "design" as set-up for planning the "interactivity" of people and digital technologies, Jonas Fritsch develops a different "eco-logic" for interaction practices: "A question also arises around the notion of the events staged by urban interactive environments. One might ask of all the projects; *when* is the event actually taking place—or what is *the event* taking place? And how is the event taken up into other events, from an eco-logical point of view?" (Fritsch, Immediation II, 484).

The question that pulls event to event—changing the unfolding of events and itself changing in each occasion—is (an) *immediation*. Unfolding events never occur according to plan. Their movement can be found in their immediate differencing: does the page open this way or that? How will the fabric fall as it meets a body halfway? How does a meal get cooked and then how is it eaten? Both every day and extraordinary events form in differencing. Differencing that processually generates as each tension and continuity transversally meets, creating novel ways to unfold form. And these processes are also an abstract arc of action that cuts across, pulled through and into all these unfoldings. Or, simultaneously and in difference: " ... the experience of paradox can draw an immediating practice out of lived abstraction," Jondi Keane (Keane, Immediation II, 490).

Gerko Egert

Everyday Abstractions. Immediation and the Powers of Choreography

The Transversal Powers of Questions

Movement is brimming with questions. Movement asks questions, it reacts to questions, it can repeat and retain questions. The only thing it persistently avoids is answering questions. Choreography navigates by questions and with questions. It modulates movement's immanent force, its *questionness*: its *where-ness*, its *who-ness*, its *how-ness*. By articulating questions, choreography produces—and relates to—multiple movements: the technique of questioning is relational and transversal, spanning across different movements. How do the techniques of questioning feed problems from one event to another? How does the immediating power of choreography work?

Choreographer Pina Bausch knew about the question's power and used it as a choreographic technique. In the rehearsal process of *Walzer* (1982) she asked: "How to hold on to someone when you are scared? How does an animal move into a trap? Which body part is your favourite to move? How do you open a boiled egg? How to hold a cigarette?" (Hoghe 1986: 84, 87, my translation). Bausch simply threw these questions into the studio. They were asked in order to start a movement, a scene, a situation. They cut into an ongoing process, altering and modulating an already existing movement. Sometimes they were even just text fragments, or verbal propositions intended to create new events: "building a pyramid. Trick table. Under an apple tree. Look what I've got here" (84, 87, my translation). These questions were not answered with "yes" or "no," they were not to be answered at all. They opened up new possibilities, new movements, new texts. They called for certain material, a specific prop, a song, another question. Three men stand in the studio next to each other. Two others climb on their thighs, a woman balances atop. Where is it best to hold the other person so she does not fall? How much tension do your legs need to carry the other bodies? Where do you need to shift the weight to balance the whole pyramid? In which direction can you fall? How is it safe? How can I get back on the ground?[1] The movements of the dancers articulated questions, which do not long for verification or falsification. These questions present in movement are what Deleuze describes as "essentially problematic events" (Deleuze 1994a: 195). They articulate a difference that can only be resolved by the production of new problems and new questions, and therefore they can never be resolved. The question posed is radically open (i.e. unanswerable), it "animates works of art as much as philosophical thought" (195) and it "alone has an opening coextensive with that which must respond to it and can respond only by retaining, repeating, and continually going over it" (195).

Bausch uses the power of the question to create a choreography in which the various movements take up and repeat the question and thereby retain the question in its openness. Every movement, every action, every word or thing poses the question anew—yet differently. How does an animal move into a trap?—How does a trap move? Who moves into a trap? How to avoid a trap? Where is a trap? Caution!

The powers of the questions posed are strong and manifold: too strong to create a fixed technique simply applied by the choreographer. Too manifold to maintain any hierarchical organized dichotomy of the questioner (choreographer) and the responder (dancer). In addition to the questions' power to create new questions, Deleuze describes two further powers. The first power is the "power of the absurd"—"the question silences all empirical responses which purport to suppress it, in order to force the one response which always continues and maintains it" (Deleuze 1994a: 195). The second power is "of the enigma." It folds back and undermines the position of the questioner: It puts "in play the questioner as much as that which is questioned, and to put itself in question" (195). The third power is "of the philosophical Odyssey." This is: "[T]he revelation of Being as corresponding to the question, reducible neither to the questioned nor to the questioner but that which unites both in the articulation of its own Difference" (196).

The process of collective experimentation in the rehearsal process of *Walzer* choreographs not only the dancer's movements with questions, but the studio itself. The space and the bodies turn into a differential field of asking. They put the dancer as well as the chorographer, the décor as well as the stage designer, the props as well as the technicians "into question" (that is, second power). "How does a pyramid dance?" is not a question posed from the stable position of the choreographer. The act of balancing, of attuning with other movements, other forces, other bodies is also not performed by the subject of a dancer—the act of questioning becomes itself a process of individuation, articulating its own difference. Chorography here becomes the immanent modulation and production of differentiation: a choreography of differential movements and tensions rather than individual bodies.

Choreography as a method of posing questions is an "impersonal" or "autonomous" power, not so much in the content of the questions but in the "how" of the asking. Even though these choreographic techniques are not without a subject they are not yet qualified. They are subjects in the making, or "larval subjects": "rather patients than agents" (Deleuze 2004: 97). Only they are "able to endure the pressure of an internal resonance or the amplitude of an inevitable movement" (97). The larval or moving body can unfold in the dramatizing choreographies and take up the dynamics of the "how," "who," "how much," and "in what way" (98). The absolute intimate and at the same time totally arbitrary common question—How do you open a boiled egg?—addresses neither the dancer's technical abilities nor her individual expression. The process of questioning transversally runs as a choreographic force through the dancers' bodies acting *upon* and *with* other movements. The opening of the egg creates the "how" of the movement moving between the dancers. Neither egg nor dancer was first. The movement's *how-ness*, its question-force "unites [questioner and questioned] in the articulation of its own Difference" (third power) (196). The power activates new questions and new differences reverberating in the studio, the rehearsal process, the choreographer and the dancers, they echo across the stage and the audience, across the video and this text. This choreography is not performed or created by a choreographer but rather the process of the events unfolding (Manning 2013: 76). Many relational movements intermingle with each other and create a space of intense connections. There are no pre-given bodies, no entities that can be arranged by a person in space and time, only movements interfering with movements. In the process of posing questions a tense assemblage of movements emerges and the bodies become knots in a choreography of tensions.[2]

Choreographing Tensions

The questions emerge out of the movements and various actions of the dancer's everyday experiences. They feed the lived experience of the everyday in and though the choreographic process. Questions of power and gender relations as well as the experience of the social and economic tension of a conservative 1980s West Germany created the choreography of *Walzer*. The modulating power intensifies the tensions of the everyday in conjunction with the dancers, Bausch and the audience. Coming out of the midst of everyday experiences each question opens a speculative realm, it becomes the trigger for experimentation in the process of rehearsing. In the rehearsal studio the questions get inflected, they change and transverse. With every proposed movement, scene or gesture they fold back into the concreteness of the dance's experience.[3] Without simply reproducing the given or creating a utopian society, the questions modulate and differentiate the various experiences, bodies and movements. By taking up the differences and tensions of the everyday and differentiating them in the rehearsal, the technique of questioning doesn't provide any answers. The questions keep the strength of differentiation in the act of asking.

Like dance, the everyday is full of movements, full of choreographic powers, and thereby full of new differences and tensions. Think of the everyday movements of cooking: cutting the vegetables, heating the water, mixing the herbs. In the middle of the preparation the phone rings and you need to answer it, so your friend takes over the cooking. Pulled into this differential (and difficult) situation a lot of questions will arise: how long does the rice need to cook? How do the herbs taste with the rest of the meal? How do I continue with the vegetables? The only question she dismisses immediately is: *what* was this supposed to become? *What* was my friend's plan? None of these questions can resolve the situation or reproduce the initial plan (if there was one). These questions take up the process of cooking and modulate it differently—or as Deleuze would say: they dramatize the cooking.[4] By proposing his "method of dramatization" Deleuze calls for a technique that uses "a certain type of question": Instead of asking, "what is this?" Deleuze proposes that we ask "who? how much? how? where? when?" (Deleuze 2004: 94). These questions do not repeat or even resolve the given. They take up the tension of an existing process (like the differential field of a meal in preparation), but instead of eliminating these tensions (by turning off the stove, pausing the cooking, waiting until the friend is back and the cooking can proceed in its "original" way) they inflect the process—they differenciate this already differential situation in a new way.[5] As cooking runs transversally through the ingredients, the stove, the spoon and the multiple cooks, it does not follow a pre-given structure. No cookbook dramaturgy is executed, but a differenciating process happens instead. Cooking does not answer "how to eat this?". Cooking dramatizes food. By bringing in new questions, new ways of preparing emerge, and the food unfolds as a space-time event.

The cooking, as well as the choreographic practices in the rehearsals, take up questions that emerge in the everyday and differenciate them anew. In Bausch's "theatre of multiplicities," (Deleuze 1994: 192)[6] the movements in the studio actualize the tensions, the struggles and the power-relations of the everyday. In both contexts, the human subject is in no way central. The music, the lights, the props, and the space, on the one side, and the boiling of the water, the chopping, the mixing, the frying, on the other side, dramatize the choreographic processes. As an ecological process the method of dramatization "surpasses man on every side.... The inhuman and the superhuman—a thing, an animal or a god—are no less capable of dramatization than a man or his determinations" (Deleuze 2006: 79). By emphasizing the processuality that is "more than human" (Manning 2013: 81) with regards to choreography (of cooking, of dancing), the tensions are in no way reducible to the human body, to its movements or its actions. Cooking and choreography are always dramatizations of the ecology and of the milieu.

Choreographic Materialities

As the method of dramatization is not linked to the human *per se*, questions cannot be reduced to the realm of language. When, in New York in the 1960s, the everyday moved into the studio and onto the dance stage, the questions immediately posed were: "How do you do it?" and "Where does it move to?" The focus on movement was taken over by the question of action. Like Bausch, choreographers such as Yvonne Rainer or Trisha Brown were interested in the movements of the everyday. With their choreographic techniques, they asked: How can one create pragmatic movements on stage? By creating chorographic tasks, the question shifted from the "what" to the "where" of movement. The chart of Rainer's *Parts of Some Sextets*, a choreography for 10 people and 12 mattresses states among other tasks: "One vertical mattress moving back and forth on single layer" (Rainer 1965: 174) or "Move pile to other side" (175). These tasks are full of questions, not only verbal ones: "Where does it move to?" asks the chart. "How and who does it move?" asks the mattress, its floppiness, gravity and the floor. These choreographic techniques consist of more than just verbal questions. The mattresses, the elastic rubber foam, the absence of handles, they all articulate the power of material questions. Like verbal ones, these questions are taken up by the dancers. They are repeated, modulated and reformulated by the movements of the dance. The softness of the material transduces into the wavering and balancing movements of the dancer. The size of the pile of mattresses feeds the where-ness of the arm's stretching. Even though neither Rainer's task nor the mattress articulates *one* particular question, the assemblages of weight, sloppiness, anatomy, gravity etc. create a bunch of interfering questions. In their differential multiplicity, they differenciate and dramatize the act of carrying and moving. Objects do not simply stay objects—in the act of posing questions they themselves become choreographic. "Choreographic Objects"—as choreographer William Forsythe writes—are "an alternative site for the understanding of potential instigation and organization of action to reside" (Forsythe).[7] Coming out of the midst of the everyday, the objects feed the "potential for instigation" into the choreographic process. And by immanently carrying over everyday movements, the object becomes a process of immediation: this is not a question, an action, or a movement nicely packed and sent into the studio; this is the dramatizing force of materiality differentially immediating the field of everyday tensions into dance. Here the object is rather an operational status than an ontological or pregiven entity—it is the result of an event, its "datum" (Whitehead 1967a: 176). Every "occasion arises from relevant objects, and perishes into the status of an object for other occasions" (177). As "datum" the objects feed one occasion into another. By taking up the datum, the new occasion does not ask: what is the datum? The object-datum is itself a question. This question can only be responded to "by retaining, repeating, and continually going over it" (Deleuze 1994a: 195). By *relating* one occasion *into* another one, the question-object does not simply carry-over or repeat a given thing or movement, but proposes and differenciates them anew. In this sense, immediation becomes a *relating-into* (by its question-object-datum), rather than a *transferring-over*. The everyday *relating-into* dance, the mattress *relating-into* choreography.

The performed movements—carrying, lifting, balancing—are immanent to the objects and the related tasks. And at the same time the object's choreographic force modulates these movements from within: The mattresses' weight, its soft material and its size produce the wobbliness of the movement across. The task "move pile to other site" intersects with the dancers' proprioception and navigates the movement's spatial orientations. All these choreographic powers are operating immanently to the movements performed. They are folded into movement. None of them determines the movement's course. They all act as questions that insist on going beyond any proclaimed fulfillment. How does movement take up these powers? Where do these questions open up again? Where do differences emerge anew?

Abstraction

Powers acting upon powers create a field of tensions. As a choreographic diagram they alter the ongoing movements, inflecting them, speeding them up, slowing them down, changing directions and dynamics. They create and change the various relations between them. None of these powers can be attributed simply to *one* movement. Abstractly they run between and through various movements creating a metastable choreography.

To think of dance simply as a field of ongoing movement or a continuous bubbling would neglect the choreographic tensions that make up the field. But thinking of choreography only as a structure of tensions and relations would neglect the force of movement and its penchant for change. This would be a choreography totally saturated in the actual. But tension—as understood here—is more that an actual equilibrium of powers: in its virtuality it is pushing towards change. This choreography of tensions is more than stable—it is metastable (Simondon 1992: 301–302).

Running through the ecology of movement, the powers of choreography create the abstract arc of an action: the carrying of a mattress, the opening of an egg, the move into a trap. This is not the linear arc of suspense in a classical drama but the nonlinear tension of dramatization. Operating right in the middle of the concreteness of movement, action is abstract. "Real and abstract" as Massumi states, "The actual form and the abstract dynamic are two sides of the same experimental coin. They are inseparable" (Massumi 2011: 41). Action cannot be seen without the form of movement, yet action is more (and less) than movement taking form. Abstraction is in the middle of movement: it is "embodied thought" (Massumi 2014: 7). Only in retrospect or speculation can you abstractly "know" the causality leading to the actions' purpose. Only then you can abstract and single out the useful, contributing movements from the rest. At the same time, any abstractions produce effects that open up possible futures. Abstraction is adding new connections, new movements, new lines to the field of movement. In this sense, every question, every task, every object creates new arcs of abstraction: action.[8]

Acting in the everyday you never just move in or with the actual. Bending down to the floor already anticipates the lifting of the mattress and the remembrance of a mattress' weight. The lifting already anticipates the carrying, the experience of your friend's last relocation already anticipates the mattress' wobbliness and the tiredness of your body while carrying anticipates the good night sleep. Arcs leading to arcs leading to arcs. They just don't follow any linear causal order. Lying in the bed you think of the course of action. Retrospectively. Abstractly. While moving, you speculate the course of action. Virtually. Also abstractly. But how sure are you about your good night's sleep? The carrying is causing pain in the back and you lay awake at the new home on the familiar mattress, its dents and softness. Other actions (most likely the repetitive lifting you have done earlier) feed into the arc (causing back pain) and now foregrounding more the "how" than the "where-to" of the lifting.

This is not just movement moving: the object (mattress), the task (moving the mattress to the other house) the question (How to move a mattress?) create a choreography that composes multiple movements, producing the abstract arc of an action. This action contains more than just one or two movements—it runs abstractly through the multiplicity of an ecology of movements. Which movements and relations you experience as important and which you simply ignore (or even deny) and thereby exclude from the course of action are conditioned by the habit of organizing the world in meaningful and causal-functioning ways.

Not everybody changes houses every day. Yet, you move every day—you move in and through an ecology of movements, choreographed by the abstract lines of actions. You move your favourite body parts, you move your least favourite body parts, you show, you look, you smoke, you hold on to somebody. Sometimes you fall into a trap. Sometimes you open a boiled egg. Often you carry things even though they might never arrive at the other side. These actions are neither a subset nor the essence of your everyday movements. As abstract forces they accelerate movement, they change its direction, its rhythm, its intensity. They produce new movements, new differences and new tensions.

By taking these questions, tasks and objects and placing them into the realm of dance, they bend the abstract arc of action into the choreographic process. Without simply staging the action of changing houses or moving into a trap, the powers immanent to these questions produce and choreograph new movements. At the same time that action starts to perform, movement outruns its path and its ends. Other movements take over. New questions emerge. New speculative action. The mattress finds a way. Another way.

Immediation

Nervously the cigarette is wandering between the fingers, from one hand to the other, to the lips and back to the hand. Anxious tremor. Sitting on the chair, waiting, the women does not know what to do or what to say, it feels like everybody is staring at her. Maybe she just does not know how to hold a cigarette. Maybe she is not used to it. Maybe she does not even smoke. Movingly she answers the question: how to hold a cigarette? Movingly she cannot answer. And yet, every movement seems to be a preliminary answer—and the repetition of the question at the same time. She cannot stop moving, she cannot stop answering, she cannot stop re-posing the question. Without the cigarette there would be just hands wandering in front of her chest and her face. With the cigarette she finally can stop. The arc of the cigarette's burning offers an (temporary) end. Another cigarette will follow. The cigarette turned movement into action.

At the same time the choreographic force of the cigarette made movement expressive: you see nervousness, anxiety, and shyness. Abstraction created expression, movement became choreographed. This is not the abstraction of an inner feeling, a subjective emotion articulated through hand gesture. This is movement expressing its choreographic force by posing another question. How is she moving her fingers, where is she moving her hands? It is movement's question-ness—in this case its how-ness and where-ness. The process of abstraction does not simply add meaning on another level. Choreography is no mediation of movement in the realm of signification. Yet, the expression of movement goes beyond the event of movement moving; feeding into another event, another movement, another choreography. This is the immediating power of abstraction. Taking up the choreography of smoking, and forcing it beyond the immediateness of the event, the power of abstraction turns into immediation. By feeding into another nervousness and into another cigarette it creates the arc of reassurance. The always-prolonged arc of a bad habit.

This is not immediation as the opposite of mediation. The "im-" is more the "im-" of immersion, than the "im-" of negation or of "opposition." Immersion and immedation share the power of "pulling into," yet immediation forecloses any total dissolution and envelopment. Immediation is not about an individual entering another sphere but the pulling of an action or experience into another event. Cigarette pulling towards cigarette, pulling towards cigarette. This is the immediation *of* choreography *as* choreographic force.

By taking up the movement's question—How to hold a cigarette?—Bausch rendered the choreography of smoking expressive in a way it wasn't expressive before. Using the question as a choreographic tool she fed the movements of smoking into the practices of the rehearsal space. Immediation never acts in linear fashion and the everyday does not simply serve the choreographic rehearsal. Smoking takes place in the breaks, it forces the rehearsal to stop, it changes the questions—who has a cigarette? Who has a light? The talking continues, new ideas pop up. The rehearsal restarts, the cigarette is still burning. People are tired and hanging around. A new smoke, another cigarette. Are we still rehearsing? Everyday rehearsal.[9] Dance practice and everyday life fold constantly into each other. And in these foldings the forces of choreography create a nonlinear assemblage: Questions of the everyday, feeding into the studio, into new rehearsal sessions, into performances, into writing, and back into the everyday.

After the opening night, you light a cigarette. But your movements have changed. Choreography now foregrounds the how-ness of your movements. Habit starts to struggle with uncertainty. The "aftereffect" of perception makes itself "oddly" felt "like a very faint déjà vu" (Massumi 2011: 166). The experience of the choreography of smoking shifts the way you feel your hand moving, your fingers tremble. "You are consciously experiencing the semblancing of experience—its double order; your double existence—that normally remains in the nonconscious background of everyday life" (166).[10] The power of choreography feeds (back) in the everyday movements, it differenciates them, it shifts the question: immediation.

Everyday Politics

The smoking of a cigarette, the moving of a mattress, the opening of a boiled egg—these immediating choreographies operate between dance and the everyday. By transversally pulling and feeding abstract questions into and out of one event and into another, new questions are raised and new tensions produced. These questions speculatively navigate our movement, our attention and action. These questions also open up new connections, and new movements that relate to one another. Choreographies of smoking are not only made of fingers moving, they interlink with the psychic as much as with the economic, the environmental as much as with the demographic, they are also physical and biological choreography. By acting across all of these different ecologies, the choreographic work articulates the political of the everyday. None of the questions raised in the everyday can be taken as merely personal, private or artistic in nature. Every question addresses the politics of ecology in a Guattarian sense (Guattari 2008), as an ecological question. By taking these questions up in the context of the everyday, choreography foregrounds how every movement effects other movements. Every arc of an action extends into another event and thereby foregrounds its relation with other choreographies (ecological, social, psychic, economic, etc.) By extending the relations, new differences emerge: none of this choreography, nor the interplay of differences, operates in the seamless flux of the logistical imagination. These relations are tensions, forces pulling in multiple directions. It is the power of (everyday) choreography that navigates, disciplines, modulates and creates movement's differential and conflictual interplay. The choreographic process of dramatization relates these manifold forces of movements without simply synchronizing them or bringing them into one coherent form, but creates productive differences and tensions. In the interplay of these various movements, choreography is rather the immediation of tensions: it operates in the difference of the everyday at the same time that it expresses its powers through new questions, new movements and new tensions.

Notes

1. Very little documentation exists on Pina Bausch's rehearsal processes. The descriptions in this article are based on the TV documentary Walzer – 41 Minuten aus den Proben. Pina Bausch und das Wuppertaler Tanztheater April – Mai '82 (1986, Bayrischer Rundfunk Deutschland).

2. The concept of a "choreography of tensions" is in line with Susanne Langer's concept of "dance tensions." According to her, dance is the "interplay of virtual forces of 'space tension' and 'body tensions' and even less specific 'dance tensions' created by music, lights, décor, poetic suggestion, and what not" (Langer 1953: 186).

3. The rehearsal process and the movement experimentation can be described as a speculative (Whitehead) or speculative-pragmatic (Manning and Massumi) activity. In reference to his speculative thinking, Whitehead writes: "The true method of discovery is like the flight of an aeroplane. It starts from the ground of particular observation; it makes a flight in the thin air of imaginative generalization; and it again lands for renewed observation rendered acute by rational interpretation" (Whitehead 1978: 5). Like philosophy, the rehearsal constantly moves between the thin air and the landings of movement's flights. On technique as "speculative pragmatic" see Massumi (2001: 85) and Manning and Massumi (2014: 89–90).

4. In 2013 a group of people from the SenseLab experimented with these questions during the event "Enter Bioscleave." The setting was a camp in the woods, several huts, each equipped with its own kitchen. The propositions were: 1) Go to one kitchen and bring an ingredient for cooking. 2) Cook for 7 minutes. 3) After 7 minutes leave everything as it is and move to another kitchen. 4) Take up the process of the kitchen 5) Start again with 2) This choreographic technique is called "Anarchist Touski."

5. Note that Deleuze differs between the differentiation (with a 't') and differenciation (with a 'c'). He defines the difference as follows: "We call the determination of the virtual content of an Idea differentiation; we call the actualization of that virtuality into species and distinguished parts differenciation" (Deleuze 1994a: 207). In regard to the method of dramatization he concludes: "In short, dramatization is the differenciation of differenciation, at once both qualitative and quantitative" (217).

6. In reference to the theatre of Antonin Artaud and Carmelo Bene, Deleuze develops the concept of a "theatre of multiplicities": It is "a theatre of problems and always open questions which draws spectator, setting and characters into the real movement of an apprenticeship of the entire unconscious, the final elements of which remain the problems themselves" (Deleuze 1994: 192).

7. In her discussion of Forsythe's "Choreographic Objects" Manning links his work to Deleuze's concept of the "objectile": "They extend beyond their object ness to become ecologies for complex environments that propose dynamic constellations of space, time, and movement. These 'objects' are in

fact propositions co-constituted by the environments they make possible. They urge participation. Through the objects, spacetime takes on a resonance, a singularity: it becomes bouncy, it floats, it shadows. The object becomes a missile for experience that inflects a given spacetime with a spirit of experimentation. We could call these objects 'choreographic objectiles' to bring to them the sense of incipient movement their dynamic participation within the relational environment calls forth" (2013: 92). See also Deleuze on the "objectile" (1993: 19).

8. Action, as it is used here must not be confused with the concept of activity Massumi develops in his account of an "activist philosophy" (Massumi 2011: 1). Yet, both terms—action and activity—are closely related and depend on each other. Whereas movement, as I use it here, is more on the side of activity, action is concerned with the question of the abstract arc, its tension and the becoming of its continuity. What is at stake in this essay is nonetheless a non-subjective, non-voluntaristic concept of action, in which action is precisely based on abstraction in the field of "bare activity" (Massumi 2011: 2) and movement. Discussing the concept of abstraction in play in *What Animals Teach Us about Politics*, Massumi describes the "style" of an action between its "execution" and its "dramatization." Yet, "execution" and "dramatization" are no either-or decision but "mutually included" in the act (Massumi 2014: 9, 11). Style is here referred to as the "type of question" (Deleuze 2004: 94), the questioness of movement.

9. Tiredness, sickness and smoking are dominating the atmosphere of the rehearsal process of Waltzer as shown in the documentary Walzer - 41 Minuten aus den Proben. Nonetheless, this atmosphere functions as an affective motor for creating new movements, new scenes and new questions. The scene of a women smoking coming out of the pragmatic question, "Who wants another cigarette?" is articulated in the rehearsal break.

10. In its passage on the immediation of perception Massumi refers to the sensation of a John Irvine art installation and its force as felt during a walk down the street afterwards. "You are aware of thinking-feeling the depths of the city as you walk and look" (Massumi 2011: 166).

Michael Hornblow

So Soon Too Late: Affective Shifts in a *Ketl*[1]

Thinking back and forth, feeling what just happened, what things have been and are still becoming, as all these emerge together – there are many modes in which an event seems to shift, as if outside of itself, just as this outside is felt within thought. Events are always in the middle of things, even as this middling seems far-flung for the "now" moment.

Drawing on systems-based and philosophical approaches to affect and situated cognition, I discuss a media performance project called *Ketl* to consider how media may be seen to open (and withhold) relational processes of collective creation. I want to define media quite broadly, for both this work and its writing—to include physical objects, digital interfaces, site-specific elements, and their modes of description; where it's not just specific kinds of media, but the speeds and slowness they allow in modulating affective tonalities for bodies and persons.[2] If the immediacy of the event is already a "specious present" that's blurred and smudged across untimely modes of attention (Varela 2000), then perhaps media do not so much mediate our experience of the world, as enact an ecology of thought that includes human and nonhuman agents.

This allows us to think about media in the manner of immediation, a term that lends itself to strange middlings. Immediation marks its own disjunctive coherence when we pull the term apart to find those that comprise or decompose it – immediacy and mediation. Our tendency may be to immediately suspect mediation because it suggests a position of representation, a mode of presentation or of resolution. We may feel more in favour of immediacy because it seems to deliver the pure event to us as a singular moment in time. I aim to trouble these oppositions, to open instead a productive disjunction in terms, where immediation may offer a more immanent and shifting relation across immediacy and mediation. I seek to show how immediacy and mediation shift through various practices of thinking and making in the development of a project. This has an affective dimension that becomes useful for understanding collective dynamics within collaboration and participation, especially at different scales of relation.

In doing so, the art making process may also reveal underlying conditions within a given milieu, to offer a critical perspective on social mechanisms of control and agency, even as these conditions become generative constraints drawn through the aesthetic logic of a work. For *Ketl*, I aim to demonstrate how online geospatial interfaces are embodied through affective states of withdrawal and openness across a broad set of registers. Here I identify formative points and critical shifts, where particular techniques emerge in the process as ways of approaching affective immediation in media performance practice. These move through collaboration and creative development, to audience spectatorship and participation, where affective and emotional tonalities are complicit with analogue and digital elements.

Ketl—in the time of writing

These shifting relations are also immanent to the practice of writing itself. In the back and forth of writing both for and about performance, this essay becomes another site for immediation, where problems of description trouble the boundary of thought and materiality. Immediation offers a concept at the intersection of writing and art practice, where description is inflected by the fabulatory impetus of media entities, such that writing may feel the aesthetic quality in which these entities are coordinated.

Ketl is part of a continuing project that has involved workshops, research-creation events and exhibitions – with performance, video, and participatory actions, using mobile, locative and interactive media. This essay focuses on one iteration – *Ketl* at FOFA Gallery in Montreal (Hornblow and Sans 2015).[3] The problem with describing the work is that it's already a long and variable series and I'm still in the middle of everything. At the time of writing (July 2015), we've just completed the performance at FOFA Gallery, and I'm now preparing two presentations for the International Symposium on Electronic Art, to be followed by a work at the Affect Theory Conference in Lancaster Pennsylvania.[4] Being caught in the middle of things can be a source of much anxiety, but just

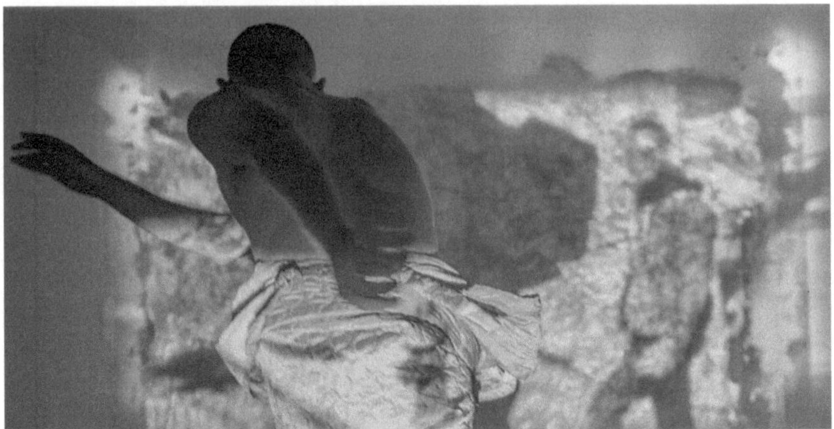

Figure 48: *Ketl* 2015, Hornblow and Sans, 2015. Image: Kinga Michalska

as deadlines loom large they also allow new forms of life to appear. To say "at the time of writing" may then become a matter of foregrounding the time of writing itself. Where immediacies shift across multiple durations and scales of action, we may feel many speeds and durations in which things already describe themselves somehow, and where media come to enact processes of thinking and making in the back-and-forth of our own descriptions. If writing may describe a work, it is through singular, untimely and distributed processes of immediation where multiple media shift in tonality, opening and withdrawing, with and from one another.

> *"So I've been thinking about*
> *withdrawal and opacity*
> *transparency and openness*
>
> *how they seem to go in a loop*
> *or get folded through in a way"*
> *Ketl* (Hornblow and Sans 2015)

Flashback to the FOFA performance/event – the opening lines for *Ketl* are repeated over and over as I bounce up and down on the spot. People enter the space and spread tentatively around the perimeter, finding a place to land while I shift position with each repetition, framing their movement in-between short, improvised dance sketches. The bouncing is a warm-up exercise borrowed from dancer/choreographer Yumiko Yoshioka – a good way to ground yourself and get into a dancing body, which is useful for me now as I'm feeling nervous about how things might work out. A warm-up exercise is not always the best choreographic gesture to begin with, but it suits the text. With each repetition the words get mixed up a little, finding strange loops, as if I'm not quite sure which way round things should be. The bouncing and framing gradually opens into more extended movement and vocal phrases, as the grounding effect amplifies my expression on different levels across the floor, displaced, all the while, with broken gestures to lend the text an open uncertainty.

First Formative Point—Impossible Indifference

I've been feeling and thinking about withdrawal and openness for some time, but it was only in the intimate immediacy and mediation of working closely with another person that this became something to work with. We had met just recently through a mutual friend, had nothing much to go on – Sans and I – except a feeling of shared sensibility, and a curiosity around affective states in the creative process. Sans sent me a YouTube link to a lecture by Catherine Malabou on the possibilities of new forms of withdrawal, after reading my paper for ISEA (Hornblow 2015b). In "From Sorrow to Indifference" Malabou challenges Deleuze's reading of Spinoza, suggesting that each of them disavows a total lack of affection for wonder in human experience (Malabou 2013). Drawing on contemporary developments in neurobiology, Malabou argues instead for the possibility of total withdrawal, and that "inspiring indifference" – rather than "inspiring sad passions" (as in Spinoza) – has become "necessary for the exercise of power" in contemporary political spheres.[5]

This isn't something I want to deal with right now, or at least not yet. It's still too soon for indifference – except to say that withdrawing from the question allows for the possibility of drawing with-and-from what becomes delayed so it may enter untimely relays with other things. For now, I'm more concerned with how the serial immediacies of this process and its enactive mediation may find a disjunctive quality of immediation. In the middling of withdrawal and openness, transparency and opacity, immediation moves as an affective shift; as I came to wonder during the *Ketl* performance – "how they seem to go in a loop or get folded through in a way" (Hornblow and Sans 2015).

Second formative point—screen / display

Collaborations are never without difficulty. It's hard to know in advance what the outcomes may be and how they might land. Especially with new work, iterations or partnerships, there's a delicate search for formal coherence, while allowing all entities in the process to have their autonomy and potential - as much as these are already relational and with context. After several discussions we are finally in the gallery, which doubles as an open studio for a group show seeking to foreground process and collaboration through a series of "visitations." We're trying to define how my video-art and performance elements may work together with Sans' contribution using 3D animation and face recognition through the real-time software environment Processing. There are a lot of things on either side, with many constraints beyond the technical - conceptual, spatio-temporal, compositional, performative. We sit around a laptop considering different scenarios for the interactive media, but keep hitting a wall. The speculative nature of the project makes it difficult to anticipate how technical objects might sit alongside everything else, without actually testing them. But we don't have a lot of time, and each task requires a series of steps, the linearity of which limits adaptation to changes in process. So we bounce around a frustrating *mise-en-abyme* of projected ideas that don't seem to land in any future, only collapsing in a proliferation of possibilities that seem to withdraw on themselves.

Realizing that half the problem is being locked in a screen world, we move into the concourse beside the gallery to consider the space where

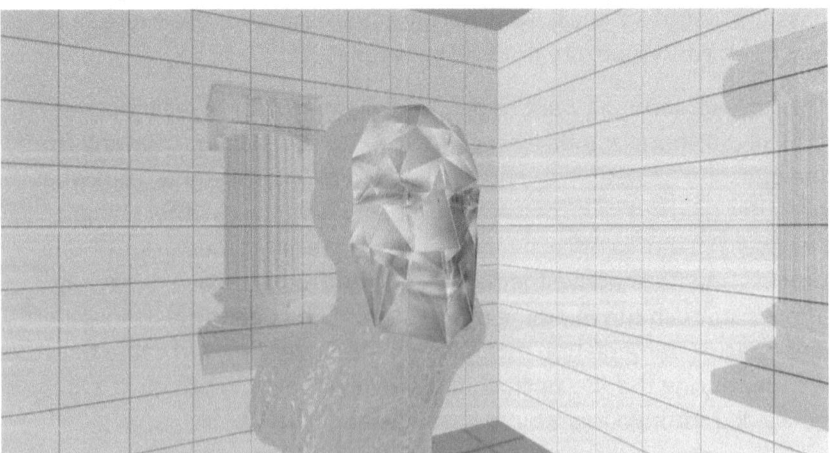

Figure 49. *Ketl*, Processing screenshot, Hornblow and Sans, 2015

the work is to be installed – a long narrow display area known as the vitrines. Suddenly everything shifts. Now that we have a real wall to bounce off and a real window to look through (rather than a digital one), the dead ends open up as the conversation moves through our bodies with each scenario placed *in situ*. We reach a brief impasse for deciding which options should be pursued and how, but the shift has opened enough of a middle ground for charting a way forward. Now media has moved from its usual place in technological interfaces to include the wall and the space it enacts, a move that arrives with an accompanying shift in affective tonality.

Slippage and Appearance—Affective Tonality

The screen/display experience indicates how states of openness and withdrawal move as a speculative horizon that extends or recedes, even collapses, drawing with-and-from the media (materials, spaces, devices) in which we situate our attention. External elements do not so much mediate our experience, just as mediation is never only a site of communication and negotiation. Instead, such elements enact speeds and slowness for which their immediacy is variable and distributed. The movement from screen to vitrines seems to offer a technique that has something to do with shifting scale and/or mode of attention – but there's something more slippery going on that eludes individual agency. To account for a strange middling, the shift may be found in that slippage where the now moment seems to both elude our attention and enact the situated nature of our experience.

What is this – to elude and enact, to feel things slip away in the same manner of making an appearance? And what occurs for affective tonalities that shift in the passage opened up by this gap? The experience I've called screen/display – moving from a laptop to the vitrines, offers a way of thinking about how attentive slippages shift affectivity. These shifts and slips may be seen to move across three main scales of action and related timeframes.[6] In what follows, these are: for the surrounding environment, its apperception as absolute duration; for the body, readiness response and the half-second lapse; and for the conscious mind, a fringe horizon of around 1/10th of a second.

1. Already Always: apperception—The wall in the vitrines is every wall I've ever considered until I engage with it directly, even

as this falls into worlds that have since moved on, retaining a pastness of future potential.

A kind of absolute duration is already there before us while we foreground what is necessary and intentional, a slippage for smoothing our way in the world. We subconsciously assimilate familiar elements from our surroundings based on prior knowledge (apperception). This is not reserved for matters at hand, for it already suggests a distribution of thought at a liminal level. The situated and embodied nature of cognition is enacted through a dynamic ecology of experiential couplings with other entities in the environment. Embodied cognition is enactive and extensive in thinking and feeling through material traces and mnemonic devices that operate as physical supports for recollection and speculative prehension (see Thompson 2007; Chalmers and Clark 2002).

2. Half a Second: readiness response—A wall is proximity, enclosure, and display, finding its threshold in the readiness of all walls within me.

   At the level of the organism, our apperception of the wall is already primed in the physiological activity of the autonomic neural systems, so much so that it often gets the jump on us before we know it. Around a half-second lapse may occur between the initiation of movement in response to external triggers, and the time it takes for the movement to be registered in conscious thought (see Libet, Gleason, Wright, Pearl 1983). This is not just a case of being a little slow off the mark, but where functional stimulus potential and psychophysical tendencies are virtually prefigured with incipient forms.

3. 1/10th: fringe horizon—A wall is the blurry surface of my own agency towards it. As I reach to touch it I've already touched it, and in touching am reaching still.

   At the level of consciousness, we find an even more discrete interval for this composite sense of the "now." As Francesco Varela explains, what we experience as "the specious present" in any instance is not clear and distinct, but more a blur of impressions within an almost imperceptible timeframe – a fringe horizon at around 1/10th of a second (Varela 2000). On

> one side, this slippage tends towards an immediate future (protention), while on the other tends toward a just-past that is not yet memory (retention). Protention finds our grasp upon the wall in the speculative micro-intervals of how things might work out, just as retention performs a kind of cognitive cache for carrying this coherence.

Being in the world entails a dynamical flow of cognitive couplings with other things based on sensorimotor activities that operate in a liminal area as much as anything we can clearly grasp. Affect doesn't begin with being affected by someone or some thing as such; rather it turns upon a kind of disjunction in the very texture of subjective agency, where we are always and already affected (auto-affection). Affect becomes a "constituitive temporality" in which "I am affected before knowing that I am affected" (Depraz 1994: 73, 75). Consciously identifying states of feeling in relation to outside influences may be where a particular mood or emotional tone becomes clear and distinct, but these are predicated on an auto-affective substrate in which we are in a state of "permanent coping" (Varela 2000: 230).

Third Formative Point—Collapse / Reframe @ 4am

Flashback and forth to the *Ketl* ... it's the day before the performance and we're busy arranging the final installation, each of us attending to our own areas and tending to the overlaps. Then, suddenly, catastrophe strikes. I tested the WiFi signal weeks ago, but on final checks the signal strength has collapsed to two bars. An essential feature of the show involves me wearing a Google Cardboard VR headset, to dance an online navigation through the Google Street View world on St. Catherine street outside the Gallery. The image I see on my Nexus smartphone goggles is shared with everyone on a large video projection, sent live by a screen-share application over WiFi. But it's a lot of data and needs a strong signal. Now the video stream is crashing after 10 minutes, then 8 ... 4 ... nothing. I collapse with the WiFi into a screen of anxiety, emotion heightened and scattered across device and set up ... wondering all the while what might happen tomorrow.

Recalling the first formative point (screen/display), I try different locations, discuss the situation with Sans and others, but everyone is focused on their own tasks, and the possibility of resolving it through technical support feels remote. The protentional collapse is palpable, centripetal and vertiginous. I can feel the walls closing in as I navigate many corridors of impossibility. A sense of quiet terror slowly shifts through despair, resignation, looking for hope, a change of plan. I get home late and exhausted but can't sleep, my mind all ruminant machinery with strange transitions of worry, fatigue, REM states barely dropping into dream. Then gradually, images appear, ideas take form, coordinating and accelerating, feeling the joy of them. I'll be deliriously tired today but at 4am I have a "plan-b" that feels better than just live-streaming an online navigation to the audience.

Falling Out of Phase—Emotional Expression

Attuning to shifting rhythms is central to the strange middlings of immediation, especially where affective tonalities loop and fold with emotional expression. As Brian Massumi puts it, emotion is "qualified intensity owned and recognized at the conscious level of a personal subject, while affect operates more at a pre-individual level (Massumi 2002: 28). Varela describes affective tonality as a "dynamical landscaping" (Varela 2000), to which the horizon of our situated attention becomes transparent (open) or has a certain opacity (closure) that takes on the color of specific emotional content. From a cognitive dynamic systems perspective, the appearance of emotion is accompanied by a "phase shift," when a break occurs in the tonal continuity of self-affecting-self (auto-affection); an interruption in the transparent or unreflective absorption in a flow of action (Varela 2000: 291-292). Emotional expression shifts affective tonality when thinking and feeling identify something that seems to be at stake for the subjective territory of a person. This is not to attribute a negative value to emotion solely in favour of pre-personal affect. Phase shifts on a fringe horizon are simultaneous and incipient in their movement across dynamical landscapes of affective tonality. Both have their places, where systemic conditions and different ecologies of experience allow collective tonalities of "affect" and "emotion" to be mobilized in different ways.

Several questions and potentials arise for the art-making process, for it's not just where interpersonal mediation may be transduced through collaboration, but how the spatial, temporal and material elements specific to this transduction offer further insights. How might these affective media ecologies allow an audience to think and feel in different ways through various modes of participation and spectatorship? How can this thinking-feeling remain affective and conceptual in the relational back-and-forth of media, performer, spectator? And what is at stake for the phase shifts of affects and concepts, where a performance does not simply communicate ideas or convey emotional states? If critical practice can do more than make comment on the mechanisms of control that mould these tonalities (as if it were outside their very operations), this calls for a critical edge of a different kind. A precarious and speculative one, in which transformations of thought and action might occur.

As Massumi has shown, affective politics operate at a liminal level where forms of power exercise a kind of shorthand trigger mechanism, especially in the way media effects elicit emotional responses that are already prefigured within a broad spectrum of control (Massumi 2005). The art process often confronts a redoubled limit, and a certain reticence, lest it become too literal around political critique. On one side, when forms of power and emotion are invoked or expressed they can collapse the potential for new affects and sensations to emerge, as creation and reception fall into the dead ends of interpretation. On the flip-side, the internal fields of force at play within works of art (and their emergent processes), harbour their own qualities and powers for transformation. We might say that art finds its own politic of sorts, seeking diverse modes of agency, entities of thought and feeling that have not yet come into being but have a nascent power nonetheless. In the abstract concreteness of conceptual and affective vitalities, aesthetic processes seek a critical edge within themselves where a work may eventually take on a singular life of its own. Across them both (external collapse and internal potential), there's a strange middling particular to immediation. The invocation of emotional responses (as subjective territories, forms of power, and their critique) becomes a relational boundary condition for weighing up how audience reception may participate in, and indeed enact the distributed nature of affective and emotional ecologies. For *Ketl*, this becomes a fugitive exercise on the precarious cusp of critique.

Orbital Flatness—Faciality

My first thought at 4am was to go outside the gallery and smash my phone on the footpath as a way of ending the performance. But by mid-morning, I realised the catastrophe called for a subtler sense of urgency. Even as a joke for insomniac frustration my initial reaction seemed appropriate at the time, especially where questions of withdrawal and critique found relevance beyond my discussion with Sans. The FOFA performance was curated as a two-hander with Joel Mason's *Duck Feet* soiree, and the two works were situated more broadly within the timeframe of the *Undercommons Residency*, hosted by Senselab in Montreal with guests Stefano Harney and Fred Moten.[7] In *The Undercommons: Fugitive Planning and Black Study*, Harney and Moten put forward a compelling response to contemporary mechanisms of control (2013). Their project recognizes that the Commons as we once knew it is long gone, already overrun with neoliberal subjectivity and micro-fascist complicity at a systemic level. Entering the "Undercommons" instead becomes a matter of recognizing our shared brokenness, to discover a constantly shifting fugitive capacity – "the refusal of what has been refused" (Harney and Moten, 2013: 96).

For Harney and Moten, objective critique becomes patently impossible when institutional frameworks professionalize it as the voice of privilege. (For them it is primarily the problem of the critical academic, but this can be applied more broadly). A critical perspective becomes yet another performance indicator, a condition of impossibility carrying an affective tonality that may be felt as a fugitive state: acting both for and against the institution. This tonality is ecological, and systemic – in institutional context and in the dynamical manner in which Varela describes affective phase shifts. A fugitive criticality calls for working through a shifting condition in which there is no outside in objective terms, only a strange *jouissance* of being overcome by its transformations. It is, then, that other "outside" of which Deleuze speaks (Deleuze 1988: 23-47, 118). Or in a different manner, where fields of force shift phase through the deepest interiority, immanent shifts that bifurcate and jump in scale, confronting the very conditions in which a system operates.

For *Ketl*, the WiFi catastrophe brought home with some gravity how broader tonalities may be felt within a specific institutional context. It also created a break in thinking through what was at stake in using Google Street View as a performance platform. How could it function as a critical lens for looking at online geospatial interfaces at a simultaneously planetary and embodied scale? How then to work with the limits of that critique, given the conditions and constraints that had appeared? Affective phase shifts acquire very particular media materialities, finding an interstitial quality that turns upon disjunctions of immediacy and mediation. The catastrophe had already cast its own refusal, so the question of what options were given or taken now lay in a fugitive region of distributed tonalities, across performers, media, various spaces and occasions.

Instead of the live screen-share projection, I show an edited Street View navigation from a previous iteration in New York (Glasshouse Gallery 2014).[8] At FOFA, the screen is a large perspex sheet covered in white lard, which gives the projected video a glistening painterly quality. This accentuates the strange organicism of digital artefacts already apparent in the image. As I discuss in my paper for ISEA, the Google Street View image has a textural flatness that belies its 3D orbital orientation, full of bleeding contours and shallow blocks of colour. Zooming up on people at the limit of the image's resolution, this flatness shifts across the visual platform when we notice how faces are blurred to satisfy legal concerns, enacting a simultaneous privacy and privatization of the public (see Hornblow 2015b).

An initial point of departure for discussion with Sans was to draw parallels between Deleuze and Guattari's concept of faciality, and the image recognition algorithms Google uses to identify faces and signs. Faciality is a codified assemblage of control operating in and through the human face—a white wall of signifiance with its sensory orifices as black holes of subjectification (Deleuze and Guattari 1987: 167-191). Similarly, many facial recognition systems look for identifying features by extracting landmark elements (eyes, nose, mouth, etc.)[9] To trouble an easy parallelism calls for both specific and speculative slippages. Faciality is not a machine that simply works via faces but through any encoding regime of white surface and black holes, with their coordination enabling figure/ground relations for a territorial system of identification. On Google Street View, faciality becomes dense and abstract when the algorithm saturates a scene to find accidental traits; for instance in the leaves of a tree or a pile of trash. A paradox occurs in which the very processes that encode a given scene come to generate aberrant signifieds through the universality of binarisation. Accidental identities, as in a tree or some trash, suggest faciality machines yet to come, as if permeating nonhuman entities at the machinic level of their very materiality.[10] If there's something inherently inhuman about the human face, it is where systems of control appear as a distant close-up for subjects and signs. To resist faciality is then not to erase the face but to multiply its traits, to invent new faciality machines, or 'probe heads' as Deleuze and Guattari call them (190) – a monstrous becoming-animal of proliferating orifices where it's hard to say for sure what mouths and eyes are anymore, or of what they may be capable.

Plan B - broken media

> *'I don't have an answer for these questions*
> *of withdrawal and openness,*
> *except something broken to share'*
> *Ketl (Hornblow and Sans, 2015)*

The WiFi catastrophe helped to draw out affinities between *The Undercommons* and notions of faciality, towards a kind of generative brokenness for immediating the performance process. Plan B began with me crawling around the gallery, showing my phone to people one by one, holding the screen flat to the floor so the accelerometer sensor in the phone would convey the geospatial orientation of a ground in parallel with the online 3D image. The intimacy of the small screen drew people in one by one, the performance becoming more conversational in tone, with a break in presentation leading to a number of open questions.

The image on the screen carried its own brokenness, of a geospatial kind. I'd come across several glitches in my navigation outside the gallery on Google Street View. With multiple cameras on the roof of the Google Street View car, the composite image these create is always prone to dislocation and planar distortion. Gaps appear in the way Google stitches together a spherical 3D world. Like falling through the cracks in the pavement, urban fabrics and geospatial interfaces extend and shift through a ubiquitous planetary assemblage, a scopic regime full of its own slippages.[11]

I collect a few things together – the Cardboard VR unit, some small tomatoes, a kitchen knife, a container of lard. Kneeling, I cut some slices of tomato using my phone as a board, lathering lard thickly across the screen and embedding the slices into it like a snack. I place the phone inside the Cardboard VR unit and secure it by circling cling wrap around my head, inserting tomatoes as I go – a wipe of lard here and there – cutting a hole to breath and speak. A few participants assist me with the wrap, then I offer the knife, inviting people to cut into the tomatoes so the juice can escape and dribble down my body like a bleeding image.

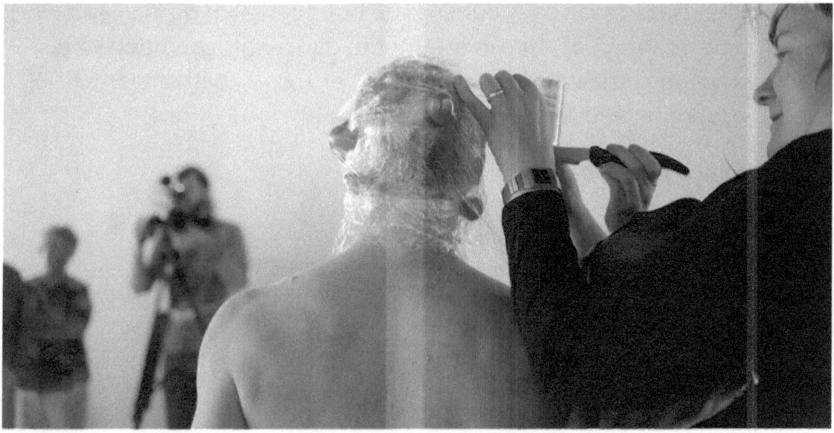

Figure 50. *Ketl*, Hornblow and Sans, 2015. Image: Kinga Michalska

The actions contrast with spoken speculations on the planetary nature of geospatial interfaces, looking to a time of writing when, as I say in *Ketl*: "everything will become media, as media becomes orbital in orientation, and all matter carries data" (Hornblow and Sans 2015). Plan B is not just a withdrawal from the failures of technology (in technical process, or their negligence in providing critiques of power); rather something has shifted in scale and mode, where concepts take on materiality by reconfiguring the coordination of analogue and digital elements. Much of the early work by artists using Google Street View (Doug Rickard, Jon Rafman, Michael Wolf, Mishka Henner)[12] finds a post-photographic condition where artistic agency meets machinic vision. With the development of *Ketl*, and what might follow from it, I'm thinking more broadly about a post-media condition where there is no longer any outside in terms of agency. Or indeed, this has always been media's "outside" in the Deleuzian sense – that any milieu is both troubled and renewed by the very conditions that define its boundaries. Which is to say, where media is the plurality of a medium – as the means of doing or communicating something, its hybridity can only go so far before it finds an internal limit. The agency media assumes to mediate for other things enters an absolute middling, where all entities already describe themselves somehow, just as our own mediations are already full of enactive couplings.[13]

This may be immediation's most radical middling for media materialities, where the development of a project is no longer just to be caught in the middle of things, but where descriptions might *pass through* things themselves, troubling the boundaries of human and non-human agency. For *Ketl*, an attempt to dance this condition was accompanied by other thoughts coming over the PA, with a text-to-speech program used to sound like an android:

> *It's not a personal thing*
> *it's almost impersonal*
> *or some kind of impersonation*
> *where I becomes like a thing*
>
> *I becomes a thing*
> *made up of many things*
> *to feel that other things*
> *all think in their own way*
> *Ketl (Hornblow and Sans 2015)*

With-drawing In-difference

I want to return to Malabou's proposition around withdrawal from wonder, which I couldn't deal with earlier but can no longer avoid. Arriving with some delay at the question of indifference, and feeling indifferent one way or another (whether withdrawal inspires sad passions or a lack of affection), my inclination is towards a different *in-difference*—to refuse the options given and in this refusal to accept them both. For if auto-affection enacts the dynamic landscaping of affective tonalities as a state of permanent coping, there is already a nascent politics in withdrawal as a field of forces that may confront its own outside. To withdraw is not simply to refuse or recoil from the circumstances of a given context, as if institutional forms of power were merely external forces for subjectivity. To be always and already affected (auto-affection) often appears to lie "outside" our attention, and yet this outside comes to the fore as a defining condition in the micro-perceptions of untimely phase shifts. Whether passive in retreat or active in refusal, states of withdrawal sit astride emotional and affective tonalities in the unravelling of multiple speeds and durations. The minor catastrophes of *Ketl* revealed how technical agents underlying the process may suddenly withdraw their affordance, arriving so soon or too late as points of protentional collapse, through which auto-affections are embedded and extended to other things.

My own withdrawal was already there as a state of affection (or lack thereof), in mutual sensitivity for the initial discussion with Sans, and thereafter acting as a kind of strange attractor throughout the process. Now, post-catastrophe, a kind of slowness arrives for the performance itself, a withdrawal from affordance in which the multiple speeds and durations of other things may enter a speculative area. This *with-drawal* is not just a refusal of the technical (broken media) but a state of affective restraint, a caution and care for the future of our becoming media. To be *in-different* around the political uses of "sad passions" versus "laçk of affection," may then find a different politics; an immediation in potential – for and against, with and from, to be *in-difference* with the phase shifts that pass back and forth, within and between us, through other things.

A lack of affection is not nothing, for even states of withdrawal enact distributed couplings. I wonder then, whether wonder was never simply a personal joy but rather that "enjoyment" that all occasions of experience partake as absolute process (Whitehead 1968: 150-152). And we might add, where human and nonhuman entities both add to and draw from one another's existence (James 1912: 180). Even after the collapse of intention, beyond the catastrophe, we may find the delirium of a strange *jouissance*, allowing ourselves to be overcome. Or, as in that peculiar mood called melancholy, which is nothing if not a different curiosity toward other things – to really wonder what they can do, a sensate feeling all the new after the self has passed a state of despair, and continues to carry that potential.

To draw with and from (rather than simply open or withdraw), is a process that has passed through several stages and scales of relation: from the transduction of interpersonal collaboration via the digital and analogue shifts of screen / display, to the WiFi catastrophe and subsequent delirium of 4am, to Plan B and its broken media. Two concerns conclude my thoughts on affective shifts in "a *Ketl*" around the politics of withdrawal for contemporary media. How are systemic ecologies and their affective / emotional tonalities taken up on the other side of the performance by people in the audience? And how does a speculative post-media condition begin to find its own outside, in feeling bodies and thinking subjects? It's hard to say what an audience response may be, let alone speak for it, when feedback is so often based on the communication of personal feelings and opinions. I'm more interested in what may be called "post-performance" strategies or tactics for troubling expectations around spectacle, reception and

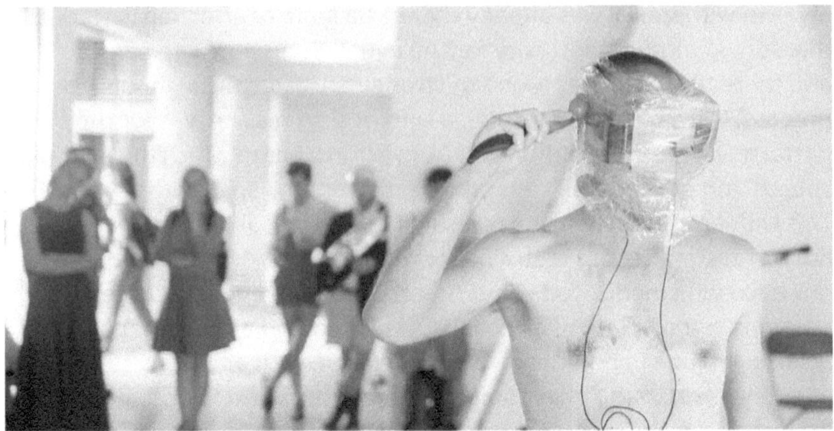

Figure 51. *Ketl*, Hornblow and Sans, 2015. Image: Kinga Michalska

participation.[14] When virtuosic techniques seem to collapse, diverge or delay their effects, the affective gaps that issue from this may become more apparent between performer, audience, and the middlings of their media.

The so-called group subject of 'the audience' collapses as a single entity when spectators come to acknowledge their own side of the wager, opening a relational field of forces in which responses may both diverge and polarise. Emotional and affective tonalities teeter either side of the shift, as people withdraw into critical interpretation, or find a speculative area where they come to reference and reframe the grounds of their own reception as part of the event. When virtuosity fails or falters in the gap, shifts in phase generate multiple responses. For *Ketl*, post-performance strategies shift between an over-determination of description (performance lecture, and this essay), tentative improvisation and quotidian gesture (dance/ physical action), and the dirty analogue collapse of digital media interfaces. On the pre-personal side of the post-performance gap, the distributed nature of affective intensities may retain their potential for multiplicity and transformation. In the back-and-forth of shifts in phase, tonalities of various kinds are taken up by the audience through restraint or disjunction. New collectivities may be invented; not just those of a human group subject, but where people might enter a relational mode of thought in which the notion of thinking things feels tangible somehow.

De-scribing delimitation, towards a different writing

These speculative conditions of a multiple post-ness offer trajectories beyond the scope of this essay. Indeed, they point to its own outside in the delimitation of de-scribing a tentative time of writing.[15] As a final response to Malabou (where "inspiring indifference becomes necessary for the exercise of power"), I would add that critical art practice exercises its own politic of sorts in demarcating a semi-autonomous potential for the transformation of affects and sensations. Post-conceptual and post-performance conditions call for a different kind of "in-difference": for with-drawing-from systemic ecologies; for thinking through where things may shift in tonality. Here the strange middlings of immediation find broad frames of reference and scales of action, towards a speculative post-media condition. Here aesthetic processes have much to offer critical conundrums to come, when thought and matter collapse and proliferate in their singular multiplicities.

Anything may contribute to the emergence of a work of art – the way it coheres across diverse modes of agency, material and conceptual affordances, collaboration, participation. The work takes on a life of its own when its delirium starts to move within and between subjects and objects. Phase shifts in process offer untimely immediacies that seem to come so soon or too late, appearing as signs of affective tonalities not yet felt, or of concepts invented on the fly. Even at a point of protentional collapse there's an opportunity to withdraw for a moment, to draw from that which has withdrawn its usual affordance, to draw *in-difference* with a new alterity. When this happens, immediating qualities that are untimely and translocal may be seen to move transversally across human and nonhuman agencies, where critical practice may weigh up what is at stake for collectivities of various kinds. For *Ketl*, critical shifts approach a fugitive limit around systemic tonalities, becoming speculative as a process of de-scribing the delimitation of its own self-reference.[16] Thinking back and forth, feeling what just happened, what things have been and are still becoming, as all these emerge together – I wonder how the radical middlings of immediation might shift differently, if this text may be felt in the world when its end starts again with other things? Reading this sentence ... we have a general feel for how the flow of words might work out in the near future that's already now, carried along by a just-past potential for holding it all together, as this iterative recursion enfolds the movement of thought through an intentional center, bounded by a fringe horizon. If the time of writing is a matter of affective tonality, then being caught in the middle of things is not just a concern for this project, but for disjunctive rhythms of immediation to be felt in the time of reading, and in times of living.

Notes

1. This essay for Immediations is a companion piece to two recent publications written during my postdoctoral research at Senselab – the first, a journal article for *Inflexions* 8, special issue on Radical Pedagogy, "A Sahara in the Head: The Problem of Landing" (Hornblow 2015a); the second, a conference paper at the International Symposium on Electronic Art (ISEA 2015) – *O'megaville: Excursions in Planetary Urbanism* (Hornblow 2015b).
2. I aim to contribute to the sense in which media takes on a broader definition within an expanded field of research. See for example, Andrew Murphie's "Electronicas: Differential Media and Proliferating, Transient Worlds" (Murphie 2003). Also, Matthew Fuller's *Media Ecologies: Materialist Energies in Art and Technoculture*, where he explores how new media works have multiple compositional elements that generate "abnormal" relationships in their interaction with other objects (Fuller 2005).
3. *Ketl* was performed at FOFA Gallery, Rue St Catherine, Montreal, on June 23 2015. For previous and ongoing iterations for this project, see: michaelhornblow.com/Ketl/
4. This iteration for *Ketl* at the Affect Theory Conference involved a site-specific installation on the street outside the Ware Center in Lancaster Pennsylvania, on October 17 2015; in collaboration with Melora Koepke and Anwar Floyd-Pruitt.
5. It may be said that Malabou offers a very narrow reading of Deleuze, with her focus on a contemporary neurobiological understanding of affect, via Damazio (Malabou 2013), which limits the broader philosophical engagement with Spinoza. My own concern is not so much to weigh in on this debate, or at least to "*with-draw*" from it at this point. I'm more interested in how the question of withdrawal may be deployed as an experiential concept, not just for this project in its performance and preparation, but for a time of writing that might find a mode of description immanent to it. In saying this, and as I go on to discuss towards the end of this essay, I also question the neurobiological basis of Malabou's argument from the point of view of Varela's thesis on auto-affection (Varela 2000).
6. See my Doctoral thesis for a discussion of how 'intensive timeframes' may become a way of thinking about untimely speeds and durations across affect and performance (Hornblow 2013).
7. *The Undercommons Residency* involved a series of discussions, reading groups, workshops, performances and "pop-up propositions,"

at the SenseLab (Concordia University, Montreal), as well as in local parks and other venues (July 13-25, 2015). See: http://senselab.ca/wp2/events/a-week-of-study-with-the-undercommons/

8. *Omegaville* was a previous development to *Ketl*, involving a four-channel video installation, presented at Glasshouse Gallery, New York; as part of an exhibition *The Smell of Red* with Erin Manning, Nathaniel Stern, and others (June 2014).

9. Traditional face recognition software uses this geometric approach, for example the MFlow system in airports (see: www.hrsid.com/product-mflow). Other developments involve photometric algorithms, with 3D data points, skin texture maps, or thermal imaging.

10. Deleuze and Guattari refer to information theory as being permeated by the machine of faciality, with relation to processes of binarization: "Information theory takes as its point of departure a homogeneous set of ready-made *signifying* messages that are already functioning as elements in biunivocal relationships" (Deleuze and Guattari, 1987: 179).

11. See my paper for ISEA2015, where I discuss in more detail how notions of faciality may be explored through specific features of the Google Street View platform; with related concepts around cinematic machine vision, planetary urbanism, and mondialisation (Hornblow 2015b).

12. See the following: Doug Rickard's *A New American Picture*, exhibited at the Museum of Modern Art, New York (2011); Jon Rafman's *The Nine Eyes of Google Street View* (ongoing); Michael Wolf's *Street View: A Series of Unfortunate Events* (2010); and Mishka Henner's *No Man's Land* (2011).

13. Domenico Quaranta gives an overview of how the term post-media has been used in different ways; from its political call to action with Felix Guattari, to the historical impact of the media in New Media Arts, and related crises for aesthetics and medium specificity (see Quaranta 2011). As suggested in *Ketl*, with current technological advances for the materiality of media, I see new implications moving across these debates. As indicated in my later comments in this essay, areas for future research may include a combination of post-conceptual, relational and object ontologies.

14. I see this as a tendency in relational approaches to contemporary performance art practice. For a similar approach to theorising such a tendency in theatre, see Lone Bertelsen and Andrew Murphie's *Affect, Subtraction and Non-Performance* (Bertelsen and Murphie 2012).

15. A speculative post-media condition may be explored further through relational and object ontologies. For the former, thought is a process of making invented in and with the world, and is not limited to human mentality but enacted through material affordances and collective processes of various kinds (see Manning and Massumi 2014). For the latter, I would say that things do not just withdraw in their being in a sea of alterity (see Harman 2002), but also draw with-and-from others through semi-autonomous relations.

16. The project title for *Ketl* is taken from the military "kettling" practices adopted by riot police, as used in Montreal during the 2012 and 2015 student protests. What interests me is how kettling, as a process of biopolitical delimitation, has co-evolved alongside new techniques in urban protest with similar yet contrasting dynamics, beginning with the Arab Spring and Occupy movements of 2011. See further, my synopsis for the Affect Theory Conference 2015: https://www.michaelhornblow.com/#/Ketl/

Jonas Fritsch

An Eco-logic of Urban Interactive Environments

Introduction

In this chapter, I will sketch out an eco-logical thinking of urban interactive environments building on Félix Guattari's ecosophy to cultivate a critical reflection on the theorizing and design of such complex environments in interaction design. Digital technologies continue to make their way into our everyday urban practices, changing the urban landscape and our affective experience of being (together) in the city and elsewhere. Corporate visions for living in the so-called Smart City have emerged alongside a growing body of research within urban computing and urban interaction design, presenting quite different visions for living with digital technologies. The streamlined visions of a comfortable and convenient lifestyle facilitated by technologies that form part of the scenarios for everyday life in the Songdo International Business District (IDB) in South Korea (http://www.songdoidb.com) are in contrast with the actual accounts of empty apartments and a general lack of livability in this developing Smart City.[1] The critique of the predominant Smart City visions coming out of the joint fields of urban computing and urban interaction design—may be voiced most prominently by Adam Greenfield in his book *Against the Smart City*—points to the lack of understanding of the ecosystems of practices that make up cities (Greenfield 2013). Following from these ideas, this chapter builds on a growing need to develop new ways of theorizing and analyzing urban interactive environments in their ecological complexity. Through this theoretical mobilization, the goal is to cultivate design concerns that are actually contributing to crafting urban interactive environments that provide the opportunity for richer experiential fields beyond the comfortable and convenient.

The motivation for writing this chapter comes from an ongoing engagement with the work of Guattari not least as part of activities within the SenseLab[2], in particular in the events *Generating the Impossible* (2011) and *Immediations* (2013-19, in particular the Sydney Workshop 2014), and from an ongoing exploration of developing a theoretical foundation for experience-driven approaches to urban interaction design as a kind of research-through-design (Frayling 1993, Fritsch 2011). In this chapter, I will sketch out how Guattari presents a theoretical opening for unfolding an eco-logic that I believe can contribute to forming a new agenda for the design of urban interactive environments. Guattari's ecosophy situates the changes catalyzed by technology on an environmental, social and mental scale. In Guattari's work, ecological change is not only for the environment; it also works on a social/societal and experiential level—and, maybe most importantly, any changes to one ecology will affect the others, leading to new productions of subjectivity. Building on Guattari, the chapter's overall aim is to develop an analytic understanding of the complex ethico-aesthetic processes that form our experiential fields in urban interactive environments, engaging directly with the concept of "immediation" from an eco-logical point of view. Indeed, the notion of immediation implies an understanding of technologies directly related to forms of experience, rather than tools or objects, and must be understood eco-logically as well. To urban interaction design, the Guattarian ecosophy is introduced as a theoretical foundation for analyzing and designing urban interactive environments, taking into account the experiential complexity of the intersecting social, mental and environmental ecologies.

First, I contextualize the introduction of Guattari's eco-logic in relation to the "ecological turn" within Human-Computer Interaction (HCI) and interaction design, where I argue that Guattari presents a different genealogical starting point and theoretical implications. I then present the main concepts from Guattari's work for theorizing and analyzing the eco-logic of urban interactive environments. Based on this conceptual exploration, I draw lessons from a range of urban design projects, leading to the formulation of new design concerns and experiments from an eco-logic point of view.

The Ecological Turn in HCI and Urban Interaction Design

The notion of ecology holds a central place in diverse disciplinary fields. Grappling with issues of situated design and understanding contexts of use have long been core interests in HCI and interaction design, in particular in areas like Participatory Design. As Kaptelinin & Bannon (2012) describe it, it can be argued that there has been an "ecological turn" in HCI and interaction design to better account for the complexity of the habitats we are designing for and with. The notion of ecology has been worked on with contributions through "information ecologies" (Nardi and O'Day 1999), "ecology of artifacts" (Krippendorf 2006), "ecological inquiry" (Smith et al. 2013), "ecology of digital artifacts" (Jung et al. 2008) and "digital ecology" (Kjeldskov 2013). Since digital technologies have become an organic part of natural environments, Bannon and Kaptelinin argue that:

> The effect of a new technology on human life conditions critically depends on a complex system of interactions between the new technology and other technologies, as well as people, social context, preceding events and so on. In addition, the effect may take considerable time, and the outcome is often difficult to predict. (2012: 290)

According to this, interaction design requires local knowledge and local action to manage disparate technologies (291). In earlier work, I have developed the idea of understanding participation in interaction design processes as ways of cultivating a "design ecology" (Fritsch & Iversen 2014). Here, my collaborator and I drew on the work of Nardi and O'Day (1999) together with the work of Isabelle Stengers on "ecologies of practices." According to Stengers, an ecology is processual, relating to the "production of values, to the proposal of new modes of evaluation, new meanings" (2010: 32) In an ecology "new relations are added to a situation already produced by a multiplicity of relations" (2010: 33). This way, any design ecology intersects with other ecologies of practices, which will affect it in any number of ways.

However, it is possible to add to the work on ecology within HCI and interaction design a different "ecological turn" associated with the arts and humanities—what John Tinnell (2011) identifies as a general evolution of the "eco-humanities." This turn stems from different genealogical starting point(s), namely Arne Naess' notion of "deep ecology" and Gregory Bateson's *Steps to an Ecology of Mind*, a genealogy Tinnell sketches out as a way to enter the ecosophical work of Félix

Guattari, which will be unfolded in the next section. However, first a cautionary remark; according to John Tinnell (2011), it is important not to only develop Guattari's notion of ecosophy from a reading of *The Three Ecologies*, since this book is only part of a range of larger conceptual developments running across the joint body of Guattari's work. In his article, Tinnell sketches out four general conceptual trajectories informing the ecosophical investigations carried out by Guattari: nascent subjectivity, machines, post-media and autopoiesis (2011: 40). For present purposes, however, this chapter will mainly focus on the introduction of Guattari to urban interaction design, and how this introduction and ensuing analysis of existing projects and future design concerns talks back into the development of immediation as a concept dealing with the experiential and ecological complexity when designing urban interactive environments.

Towards an Eco-logic of Urban Interactive Environments

Felix Guattari develops his notion of "eco-logic" as part of his proposed ecosophy in his book from 1989 *The Three Ecologies*. In the book, Guattari unfolds the problem of the "subject's fabrication posed in the context of ecological struggles" in the age of "advanced informatics," calling for a "necessity of a mastery that can keep pace with the environment's reinvention in a time of widespread techno-scientific progress and crisis." (Genosko 2009: 69). Guattari argues for a general rethinking of the notion of ecology:

> Ecology must stop being associated with the image of a small nature-loving minority or with qualified specialists. Ecology in my sense questions the whole of subjectivity and capitalistic power formations, whose sweeping progress cannot be guaranteed to continue as it has for the past decade. (Guattari 2008: 52)

In *The Three Ecologies,* Guattari presents three intersecting ecologies—the *mental* (human subjectivity), the *social* (social relations) and the *environmental* (biospherical)—all related to a "common principle" concerned with *the production of subjectivity* (Genosko 2009: 76). According to Genosko, the Guattarian subject is "an entangled assemblage of many components ... before and beyond the individual (76). Guattari states that the three ecologies are governed by a logic of *intensities*, an "eco-logic" "concerned only with the movement and intensity of evolutive processes, rather than the capture of delimited entities (2008: 44). Subjectivity produces and is produced by existential territories, fields, through a productive self-positioning which is relational "subsuming both autonomous affects of the pre-personal and pre-verbal world, and multitudinous social constructions. Emergent and processual, producing and produced ..." (Genosko 2009: 77).

For Guattari, eco-logic is by definition activist (Genosko 2009: 79). In his own work, Guattari exemplifies this through a variety of artistic practices, concerned with forging new value systems and new productions of subjectivity. According to Genosko, this can be understood as a call for an ethico-aesthetics of eco-praxis, initiating real change, but without being able to predict outcomes (87). Interestingly, Guattari links this to digital technologies that are part of the technological and machinic phylum forming subjectivity. He argues that the advent of microprocessors can be seen as a molecular mutation that catalyzes changes in macro-social and experiential conditions, changing the "actual substratum of human existence" and thus opening up "fabulous possibilities of liberation" (Guattari in Genosko 2009: 87). This also leads to Genosko arguing that "[a]t the heart of Guattari's project is an ethics arising from the interface between humans and non-human machines" (Genosko 2009: 88). Importantly, Genosko argues that the notion of ecology allows Guattari to pose questions of transdisciplinarity on a large and stratified scale. If we wish to actually tackle the complex ecological crisis of today, no one discipline can stand alone; an eco-logic approach to understanding urban interactive environments also calls for a transdisciplinary approach to working with these kind of wicked problems (Buchanan 1992).

In his generalized ecology—ecosophy—Guattari again and again emphasizes the interrelatedness of the different ecologies. As Genosko states, "solutions at one level entails changes at the others." (Genosko 2009: 73). Andrew Murphie has argued that the question of ecology "becomes not only a matter of the environment but of media ecologies, cognitive ecologies, ecologies of perception and affect. Moreover, these ecologies need to be considered singly, in their interaction with other ecologies, and both at the same time" (Murphie 2006: 118). Consequently, it is less about the different ecologies in themselves as it is about understanding and analyzing the dynamics of change governing their processual and emergent transitions. This also entails looking into the affective resonances and relaying across ecologies, how they form more or less stabilized assemblages, which becomes central to the analysis and design of urban interactive environments.

In the next section I will put the conceptual foundation to use in an analysis of five urban interaction design projects I have been involved in. The projects have been carried out over a period of more than 8 years, as part of the research center Digital Urban Living (www.digitalurbanliving.dk) that ran from 2008-2012, and later the Participatory IT-center (www.pit.au.dk). Both centers are rooted in the research environment around the Center for Advanced Visualization and Interaction (www.cavi.au.dk) at Aarhus University. The projects range from the design of interactive installations aimed at getting people actively engaged in issues related to climate change (CO2nfession/CO2mmitment), 3D projections for a museum to bring the statue of Holger the Dane to life (the Journey of Holger the Dane), the design of an interactive listening machine used to bring stories/echoes from the past to life and to foster community storytelling (Ekkomaten and Echoes from Møllevangen) and the design of an interactive poetry generation machine to be used in public libraries and festival (INK). These projects can all be said to explore the design of urban interactive environments, using digital and interactive technologies to form new experiential fields in the city, creating new relational events—and failing at this sometimes as well.

I draw on these projects, related to the work and the vocabulary of Guattari to sketch out a range of design concerns to be pursued in urban interaction design. It must be noted that these projects are not to be seen as exemplars of Guattarian concepts; there are other projects that more acutely activate the ecological concerns. In addition, the projects are not as directly radical and activist in their scope and reach as some of the artistic projects Guattari mentions in his own work. However, I will argue that there is a point in fostering and developing these design concerns from an ongoing design research practice put into resonance with the Guattarian concepts and that this is an important way of unfolding a range of ecological design concerns to be further pursued and experimented within the design of urban interactive environments.

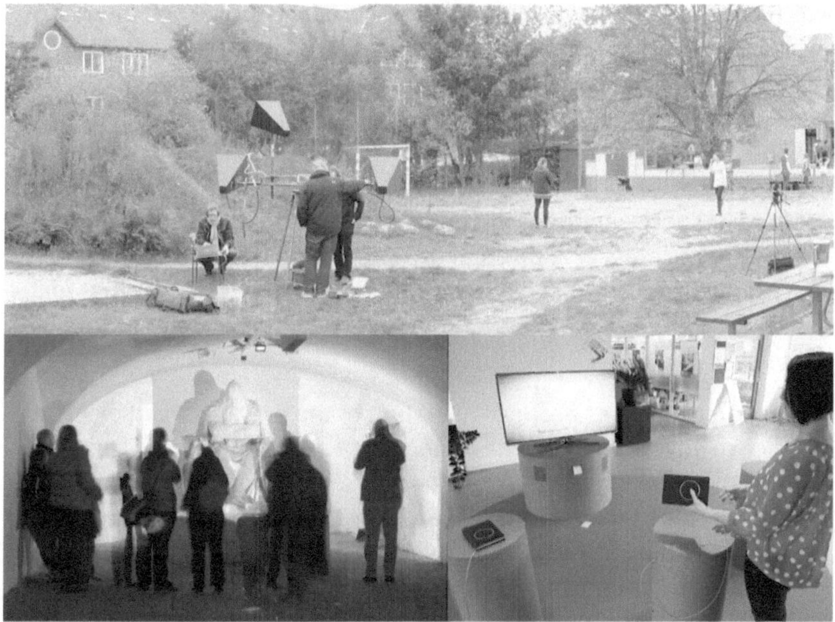

Figure 52. Immediations Collage, NY. Top: The Ekkomaten machine in the neighbourhood Møllevangen in *Echoes from Møllevangen*, where the inhabitants could experience different sound recordings related to different locations in the area. Photo by Jonas Fritsch. Bottom, left: *The Journey of Holger the Dane*, using 3D projections to activate the statue of Holger the Dane in the Casemates, Kronborg Castle. Photo by Jonas Fritsch. Bottom, right: The *INK* poetry machine on display at Roskilde Library. By engaging with the sensorembedded books, people could write poems that were then printed out in the format of library receipts. Photo by Roskilde Libraries (image in public domain).

Unfolding the Ecological Complexity of Urban Interaction Designs

A range of the projects presented in this chapter have been concerned with bringing stories or objects to life, using digital technologies to tap into the affective spaces surrounding such diverse settings as Kronborg Castle and the story behind the statue of Holger the Dane, as well as Store Torv in Aarhus and the eighteenth century life in the city in the design of *Ekkomaten*. Here, a driving motivation has been that the city holds an experiential and narrative potential that can be unleashed through different kinds of interaction designs, uncovering and (re)activating the hidden affective layers forming part of the existing experience of these urban and public spaces. In, for example, *Ekkomaten*, the interactive setup activated both the environment in which the installation was placed as a cultural, historical and physical setting, the social relations forming around the use of the installation in a specific public space and the more personal engagement with the presented stories (as seen in Fritsch et. al. 2013). Pastness and futurity traverse the immediate relational activation of the history of the place, the site, the technologies deployed, the social situation. *Ekkomaten* does not mediate between these factors; it immediately situates the ecology of experiences emerging through the interaction with the installation in a relational field comprised of these (and other) process lines that may or may not actualize, but which nonetheless color the affective tonality of the event.

A question also arises around the notion of the events staged by urban interactive environments. One might ask of all the projects; *when* is the event actually taking place—or what is *the event* taking place? And how is the event taken up into other events, from an eco-logical point of view? A traditional analysis of people's experience of *Ekkomaten* might focus on the moment of interaction—but what about the changes in technological conception catalyzed by the interaction, re-orientations of historical knowledge, a new sensation of being in the city and other relational activations? *Echoes from Møllevangen* is an example of a way to build on the event of *Ekkomaten* into another project with a more societal and communitarian reach; the same infrastructural setup to catalyze or condition the emergence of different events in a new relational field. Because of the relational complexity it becomes increasingly difficult to say when the event is taking place. Clearly, in *Echoes from Møllevangen*, a number of events were facilitated throughout the project; researchers performing soundwalks in the Møllevangen neighborhood, the collection of sounds by the inhabitants of the neighborhood through sonic probes, interviews carried out with selected inhabitants by the local social worker, the additional collection of everyday sounds by the research team, the orchestration of the collected sounds into a curated soundscape, the display of the installation with the soundscape in the neighborhood—lots of subevents make up the overall project—and can potentially take on a life of their own. It must be stated, though, that *Echoes from Møllevangen* was to some extent a less successful project since we, as researchers, did not manage to care enough for the composition of the subevents into the actual display of the installation—or in their potential relational ramifications after the display.

With *INK,* however, the story can be said to be quite different. Again, we might ask: what is the *INK* event? When picking up the interactive book? When choosing a sentence? When playing around with the sentences and "writing" the poem? When the poem is printed out? When the poem is read out loud—or shown to people at home? When you videotape your friend reading out loud the poem, and when you show this video to your friends? When the blog with all the aggregated poems is visited? When the machine accidentally inserts the same sentence three times in a row due to an algorithmic glitch? When a person instructs another person in how to compose a poem? All these are real life observations of the relational complexity of the ecologies of experience emerging through the interaction. Apart from this, the design of the installation and the ensuing exhibition of it in a great number of places (numerous libraries, the Roskilde Festival, conferences) has been instrumental in changing the participating librarians' understanding of the function of the library today; currently, 4 interactive installations are being crafted, that will continue to travel around the country in the years to come, experimenting with text and interactivity as part of the library experience. Another interesting observation from this project concerns whether the digital installation can be seen as a literary work in its own right. Recently, the author of the text in the database of the installation, Peter-Clement Woetmann, collected a range of poems in a physical book, authored by him. Only then did *INK* become an event in the literary community; the book was reviewed (mostly positively) in newspapers and magazines. Again, this is an example of the process lines emanating from the crafting of the installation, taken up and (re)activated over a much longer period of time, in a variety of intersecting contexts. A central element is that of co-composition, where you "cannot know in advance where the collective value of the project resides" (Manning in Massumi 2015b: 165). This seems to be the case when we talk about urban interaction design, and it is important to continuously track and tend to the process lines activated in the process, and possibly facilitate the co-compositional when designing the conditions of emergence of urban interactive environments.

In most of the presented projects, there has been a focus on developing technologies that directly engage bodily movement through the development of physical interfaces. *INK* uses physical books embedded with sensors so people can choose sentences on a screen and "write" poems. The physical interface moves the interaction into a social space, the library or a festival setting, fostering new ways of being together in the settings where the installation has been put up. Using closed books as a way to write also questions the relation between text, writing and technology. *Ekkomaten* also clearly experiments with physical interfaces, in fact the interaction with the machine was intentionally designed to be demanding in a physical sense, as a commentary to the seamless swiping on mobile devices. This orients the interaction from individual/personal to social/collective; often people would have to collaborate and negotiate when it came to the interaction with the machine. In *The Journey of Holger the Dane*, 3D projections merge with a physical statue; in a sense, the interface disappears. Instead, there is a fusion of the physical and the digital, which is immediately and affectively felt. In particular there is a sequence, where the statue looks as thought it is breathing; the 3D projection subtly shifts the contours of the statue so it looks like Holger the Dane's chest is moving. At the same time, the soundscape plays breathing sounds. Here, I would argue that the interactive setup works in "the formative stir of the field of emergence of experience" (Massumi 2011: 76). In the context of immediation, interfaces are more than screens, and the feeling of interactivity tied to the richness of the ecology of experience catalyzed through the digital activation.

In *CO2nfession/CO2mmitment*, we see concerns developing towards more large-scale ecological experimentation, facilitated by the interactive technologies, fostering new urban practices, creating richer experiential fields in urban space. The whole idea behind this project was to take an environmental, large-scale issue and show its relation to the immediacy of everyday actions of people in Aarhus, putting a personal face on the collective struggle for a better climate. In this project, the city in itself becomes an interface for engaging with issues related to climate change. By hijacking commercial infrastructures and making them accessible to public issues, a new idea of communitarian engagement and open, performative dialogue is suggested; people are encouraged, through the technological setup, to actively engage with societal and environmental issues. Relational events emerge from this infrastructure, and the same can be said with respect to the two *Ekkomaten*-projects linking sounds, history and the cityscape, using auditory explorations to make people engage in new community storytelling as a collective listening process. Rather than a technology per se, *Ekkomaten* is an assemblage that works eco-logically in the way it activates relational events through people's engagement with the installation. *INK* adds to this a questioning of the infrastructural ecosystems concerned with (digital) text production and their relation to reading/writing; the poems appear in real-time on a screen, they are printed out on small receipts, and simultaneously published on a blog seconds after they have been written. The circulation across platforms adds to the exploration of ecologies of information, entering the machinic phylum through the aesthetic production.

Emerging Eco-Logic Concerns for Urban Interaction Design

In all the projects presented in the above section, we are talking about interaction design that goes beyond any idea of a designed object. The design projects must be understood ecologically as urban interactive environments activating experiential fields through the deployment of digital technologies. This activation across ecologies cannot be fully determined in the design process, or by the design. Focusing on the immediacy of the experiential fields and relational events activated, forces us to rethink the way we conceive of urban interaction design projects; rather than controlling interaction, we are staging or facilitating processual activations and oscillations between process lines that will always play out differently through the interaction—and beyond. Importantly, this is not a way to diminish the importance of the material crafting of e.g. the physical machine in *Ekkomaten.* It is a way of valuing this material crafting in its activation of the relational events emerging through people's interaction. If anything, the theory of immediation and an ecological approach to understanding urban interactive environments calls for an increased attention to detail in every part of the ecological activation.

An eco-logical approach to the design of urban interactive environments needs to take into account that any changes in one ecological register will affect the others. Any design simultaneously works on an environmental, social and mental level, affecting ecologies of experience in the immediacy of everyday life, catalyzing changes in the production of subjectivity. Here, an experience-oriented design approach would focus on the ethico-aesthetic processes that form our experiential fields through different intersecting and resonating ecologies, activated by different technologies understood as Guattarian "molecular mutations," in an attempt to unfold the complexity of the emergence of new forms of subjectivity. This concern is directly tied to unfolding the transversal politics of the different ecological processes cultivated both in the design process—a form of design ecology—and after the introduction of the design into already existing ecologies of practices, relating to the question of event and co-composition as unfolded in the previous section. In addition to this form of transversal politics, a transdisciplinary approach to the design processes should always be a guiding principle.

The presented projects and concerns described in this chapter clearly transcend the vision of a Smart City which would seek to instrumentalize, operationalize or smooth out ecologies of experience. Rather, what urban interaction design must pursue is a vision of a city providing conditions of emergence of differentiated experiential fields and relational events catalyzed by affectively engaging interfaces. Such interfaces would actively experiment with the experiential parameters of our immediate urban experience through an exploration of technologies of emergence. It was stated in the beginning, that the theory of immediation must be understood eco-logically. By developing an eco-logic approach to the analysis and design of urban interactive environments, this chapter calls for a continued digitally led experimentation with the relational richness of ecologies of lived experience.

Notes

1. See e.g. http://politiken.dk/oekonomi/gloekonomi/ECE2480009/verdens-stoerste-udviklingsprojekt-ligner-en-spoegelsesby/ or http://www.financialexpress.com/article/markets/smart-city-or-ghost-city/4345/
2. The SenseLab is an international network of artists and academics, writers and makers, from a wide diversity of fields, working together at the crossroads of philosophy, art, and activism (taken from and see more on: http://senselab.ca/)

Jondi Keane

The Practice of Immediating: Toward the Ground of Our Own Activity

> There is not the mere problem of fluency and permanence. There is the double problem: actuality with permanence, requiring fluency as its completion; and actuality with fluency, requiring permanence as its completion.
> *A. N. Whitehead (1978: 347)*

Immediation and Immediating

The concept of immediaton raises questions about the filigree, about the eventful connections from which nextness arises. It concerns the techniques[1] through which one practices. What might enrich collective action? What can an event become? How can research-creation, or practice-led research enter into these questions?

This essay engages a research-creation event by drawing out a proposition regarding the nature of a practice of immediating through the concept of *lived abstraction*. Specifically, the performative and interactive installation, *ZOOM*, provides a situation through which to explore how events can be perceptually felt as a lived abstraction: an "effective virtual vision of the shape of the event, including in its arc the unseen dimensions of the immediate past and immediate future" (Massumi 2011: 17). The generative proposition of nonsensuous or amodal perception excites the imagination of practitioners who use art and media practices to play with the conditions of perceptual and conceptual processes from which felt perception *comes to experience.*

If art and media practices play with the conditions of how concepts might be experienced, my proposition is that the experience of paradox can draw an immediating practice out of lived abstraction.

Engaging the Uses of Paradox

Poet and theorist, Charles Stein, has written extensively about creative practices and the philosophical concerns that bear upon immediation, particularly the paradox of contemplative exercises in relation to the work of art. Stein thinks about paradox through what are called diagonal constructions in mathematics [2], for example instances in which a system refers to itself. Familiar paradoxes include: the liar's paradox (the truth or falsity of the statement "I never lie"), Russell's Paradox (a catalogue of books in a library that includes itself), whenever literary authors refer to their own text (Calvino's *If on a Winter's Night a Traveller*) and, in contemplative exercises, the instruction that must be applied to itself (the meditation instruction: refrain from intentional activities). In the last example, the diagonal substitution that occurs for a Buddhist meditator confronting a Zen Koan is useful for thinking through ways of approaching paradoxes confronted in everyday experience. The practice of engaging with paradox throws us into the heart of immediation. Of particular interest is how the Koan offers a useful way to immediate through a particular experiential paradox that I will go on to discuss through the ways *form is active formation*.

To summarize Stein's discussion, the meditator is confronted by the problem that "refraining from activity" is also an activity and, when emptying the mind, the thought that sets meditation in motion is itself a concept that confronts the mind with the difference between experiencing and understanding a concept. Stein suggests that for this particular task of engaging with the Koan, students often make two types of error. The first error is refusing to take the contradiction seriously by ignoring it (Stein associates this error with the formalist mathematics that save the system by rejecting the diagonal case as undefined within it). The second error is to allow the contradiction to inflate the state of mind that produces a mystification of thought (which Stein associates with the classical mathematicians, carried away by Platonistic possibilities) (1988: 28-33). To be clear, these are not problems in themselves, they only become problematic when the task is to deal with the paradox of self-reference. That is to say, the errors Stein identifies interfere with accessing the immediate ground of one's own activity. Recognizing these errors opens the possibility to discover what immediating entails.

To meet the task of the Zen Koan does not necessarily mean to accomplish the explicit instruction. Here is where the artwork and the

Koan can share a common operation: the indirect connection afforded by a paradox. The Zen student must attain a vantage not confined by the language in which the meditational instruction is delivered in order to grasp the condition and structure of the exercise. By doing so the student "covers the entire space of their cognitive language and steps beyond it ... onto the immediate ground of their own activity ... brought into contact with its experiential basis, capable of saturating, at a single stroke, the space of its own activity" (Stein 1988: 32-33).

Over many years my art practice has explored the problem of self-reference. Artworks are not simply a way of producing novel experience or confounding or critiquing existing modalities but operate instead as ways to open up an understanding of how to live, attaining a broad generative value. This generative value is related to enquiries into "immediation." Immediating is the deployment of techniques of engagement that usher us onto the ground of our own activity, prompted by conundrums or challenges such as that of the paradox of self-reference. In the context of an art practice, this might involve eliciting a co-dependent movement between form and forming.

ZOOMing In and ZOOMing Out: Installing Immediating Practices

How one immediates, then, pertains to those often implicitly mobilised techniques (a disposition perhaps), that artworks can help to recognise and develop. I recently set out to navigate these issues through an interactive installation, *ZOOM,* which was part of a tandem installation, *PAN & ZOOM* (Jondi Keane and Kaya Barry) shown at the "Performing Mobilities" Exhibition (Melbourne 2015). The installation consisted of two distinct works (*PAN & ZOOM*) that were devised to be co-joined. The works shared a common wall and offered very different, but related spatial experiences: the sweeping panoramic movement on a horizontal plane in *PAN* contrasted with the knots of spatial compression and expansion in *ZOOM*. The experience of these two works might be described as perpendicular as opposed to parallel. For this paper, I will focus only on the interactions offered by *ZOOM* focusing on how 'immediating' played a role in devising and enacting the work.

ZOOM explores the movements contained in the cinematic apparatus of the moving camera. The installation co-opts the "dolly-zoom" effect in cinema, wherein the camera zooms in while moving backwards,

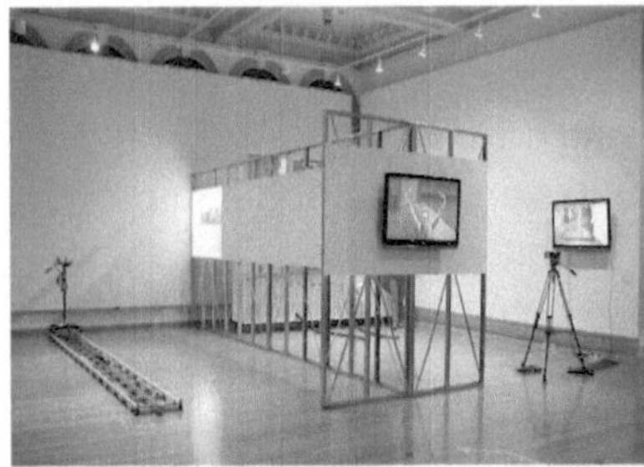
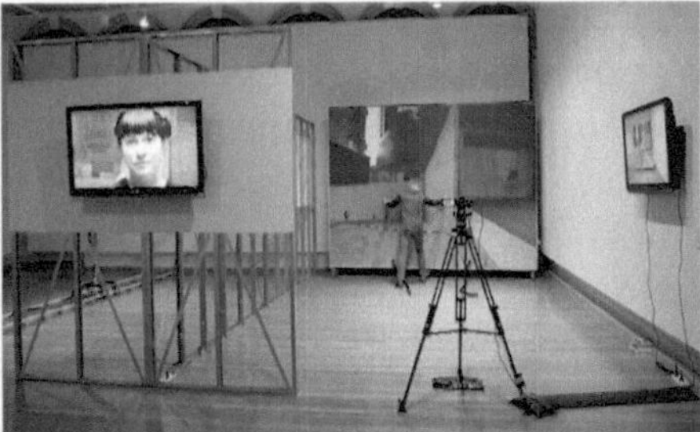

Figure 53. Installation view of *PAN & ZOOM* set up. Photos by Kaya Barry.

or zooms out while moving forwards, resulting in the screen image expanding or contracting to amplify intense moments of realization for the protagonist in film narrative. Offering two sets of spatial experiences—a performative event and a cinematic screen-based event—the work was an assemblage constituted by a video camera, a live feed to a screen, and a moving wall 2.7m high by 3.6m wide, which was on wheels and on which a perspectival photographic image was attached. This image was chosen to provide strong architectural structure as well as multiple levels and vistas (see figure 3). The image on the wall is also one of the images in the array of panoramic images stitched together in *PAN*. The selected architectural image was shot from street level but shows a ramp descending to a lower level, a half wall that one might be able to sit upon, an entryway courtyard slightly elevated and view of the surrounding buildings that tower overhead. By manually moving the wall (pushing or pulling an attached rope which replaced the movement of the camera in the dolly zoom effect) *ZOOM* dilated the movements-within-movements that unfold when a dynamic physical structure interacts with the complexity of lived-experience.

The installation pulled apart the double movement of the camera effect by performing the pulling-back-and-forth of a moving wall as environmental backdrop. During the exhibition, a person, or group of people were invited to make a video recording using the installation to enact a dolly zoom effect, inside of which they were asked to improvise actions. These improviser-participants stood between moving wall (operated by myself) and zooming camera operated by my collaborator.

If desired, the potential improvisation was discussed with participants in terms of how the performative space of the installation was set up and where the participant's image would or would not be not captured in the video. Further discussion was offered to those willing to discuss

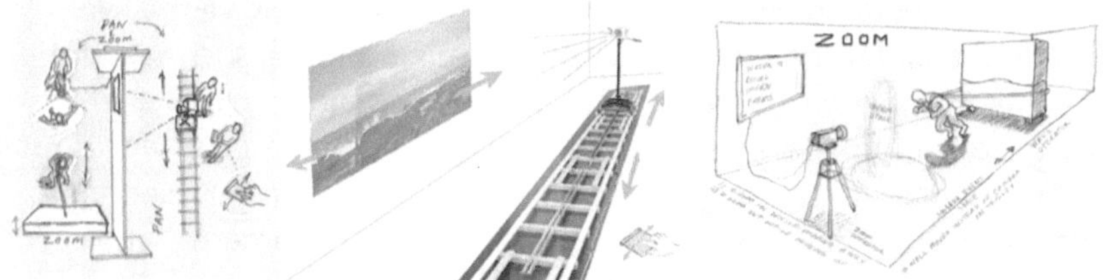

Figure 54. *PAN & ZOOM* spatial layout of installation. Drawings by Jondi Keane and Kaya Barry.

their experience of space and a compilation of historical dolly zoom effects was on hand to augment these discussions. A screen on the wall next to the camera displayed a live feed of the recording, such that the improviser-participants could see the footage both while being recorded and just afterwards. We offered to make as many recordings as the participants wanted. At least half of the participants made more than one video, experimenting with ways of inhabiting and responding to the spatial event. The time of the recording and therefore of each improvisation, was the time it took for me to slowly push the wall eight meters to the back wall, turn around and pull the wall towards the improviser-participant and camera. Generally, this took about 30-40 seconds.

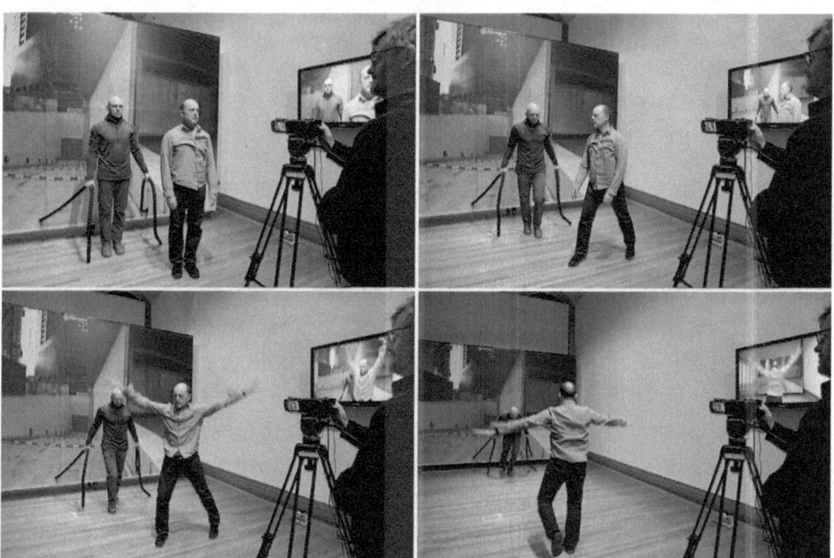

Figure 55. Working with improviser-participant (Shaun McLeod) in *ZOOM*. Photos by Vicki Jones.

It is important to note that improviser-participants could view a live feed of the film being recorded by the zooming camera, such that the movements of both the wall and the camera were immediately fed back to the improviser-participants. *ZOOM* sets up several instances for self-reference and re-entry into the installation's system of relations. The moving wall had two starting positions: close to camera (half metre away) and at the back wall of the gallery (8 metres). Each time the wall moved, to make a video recording or not, it was treated as an iteration. Through these iterations, the wall began to reference itself and the gallery context. It continually distinguished itself from and moved in accord with the space—creaking across the uneven wooden floor, rubbing against the gallery wall, wearing a groove in the gallery space. The wall offered itself as a measure of space, time, relation and variation. I began to become part of the wall, in service of the wall and yet distinct from the wall, for example on the occasions when I was addressed as the artist or wall operator. On most occasions, I disappeared into the wall itself and would emerge, sticking my head out from the undifferentiated visual noise of the background as if from behind the invisible curtain. Gallery goers were not sure how to interact with the person who had separated from the wall. I purposefully did not adopt the silent role of the performer, but, as mentioned above, tried to move gently between the performer of tasks, the moderator of activity, facilitator offering information and artist guiding engagement. The encounters varied depending on the distinctions and decisions made by the gallery goers. Some were amused, others overwhelmed by the sensory environment and feedback, others pulled back and some projected a unified autonomous front.

Standing or moving in the space between the (moving) wall and the (zooming) camera, a person is amidst something highly structured but, at the same time, very much in formation. The "form" of the work is a kind of "machine," and the improviser-participant/s are asked to "perform" or move within these pre-scripted or "formal" components. As much as the actions of the installation assemblage are, to some degree at least, pre-given, the actions of the improviser-participants are not. What any one person might have felt in their engagement with the work was inaccessible to me, however, what I witnessed from within the performative event and from watching the recorded videos, I can offer as observations about a pattern that emerged when people spent extended periods of time in the installation.

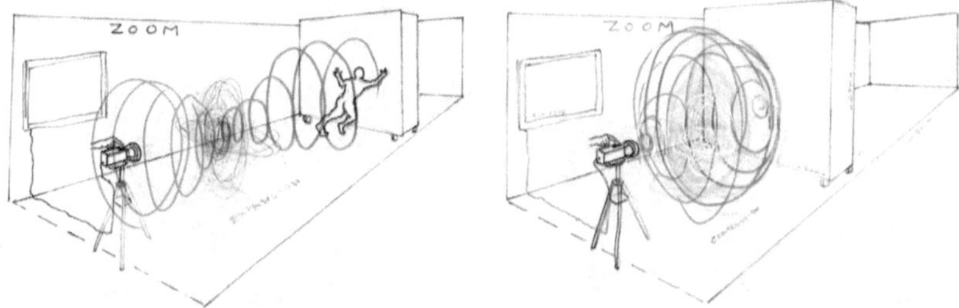

Figure 56. Expansion and compression of the event-field in *ZOOM.* Drawing by Jondi Keane

Participants had to improvise a way of being in the installation and respond to the expansion and contraction of the space in the video recording on screen, in the live performative event or indirectly through onlookers' reactions. The improvisations began to intensify the improvisers' response to changes of the installation space and their choice to move with or against the other installation components. It appeared that participants who developed the improvisation over several iterations entered into a mutually responsive relationship with the space and began to feel the expansion and contraction as a function linked to their experience. Other improvisers remained separate and/or reacted against the movement of the space rather than in concert with it. Others moved into the movement and aligned themselves with their own bodies. Improvisers began to think and feel their way into (or out of) the experience of space and their own ways of processing (organising and correlating) the experience.

What seemed most telling, however, was the degree to which the entire assemblage of the work "came together" most convincingly through an event that seemed to move toward something like meeting the task of the Zen Koan. In other words, when the assemblage became aware of itself as a set of separated and connected components, the beginnings of a practice of immediating emerged. The work set up a self-referential loop in which one is both inside and outside the spatial assemblage of the dolly zoom effect—both being affected by the spatial event and simultaneously seeing oneself externally in the recording zoom-image. As part of this entire set-up, pre-scripted movements gave way to modes of active formation as people composed multiples experiences from multiple modes of perception and conceptual construction at once.

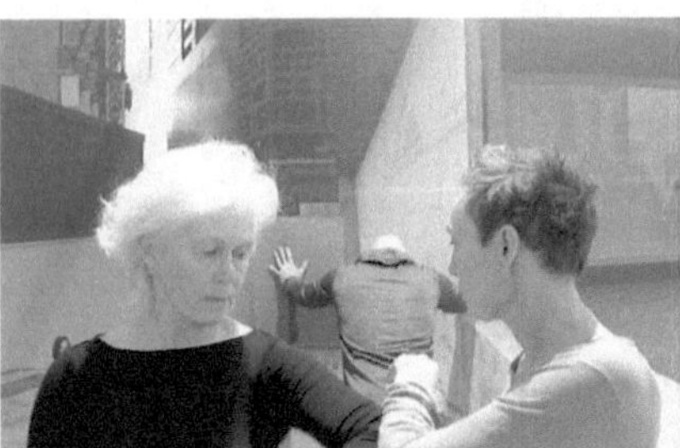
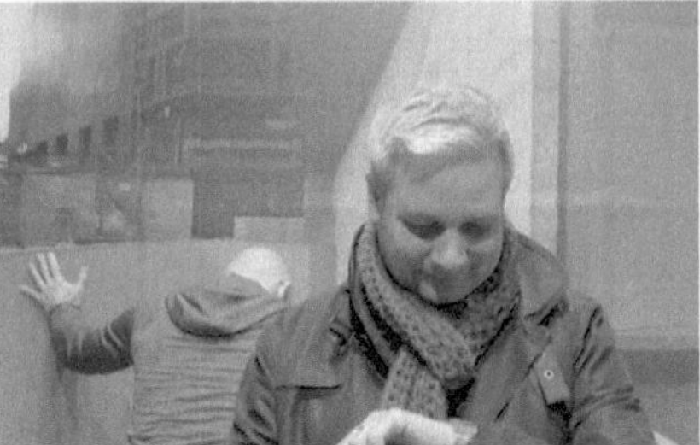

Figure 57. Improviser-participants recording video in *ZOOM* (stills from video). Video and stills selection: Kaya Barry and Jondi Keane.

In the installation, the different feedback mechanisms each relate to different configurations of experience. The work also produced several feedback loops between all those attendant components – the wall operator, the camera operator, the improviser/s, the gallery space, the constructed installation, the moving wall, the live-feed screen, the recorded video document and any spectators viewing the process. This left plenty of room for connections to emerge between material, agents and artefacts and be used to augment, dilate or ignore the registration and proliferation of affects and the modes of engagement activated at each instance within the event.

In general, the way things are set in motion informs how we plan, perform and reflect upon ecologies of relation, whether these things are artworks, architectural environments, essays, choreographed movements or everyday actions. However, the specificity of the components, their material qualities, context and modes of activation are affected in turn by the way one immediates. Paradoxically, "one" (oneself) is precisely what comes into question as the process of realising the ground of one's own activity accentuates or emphasises, uncouples or links "one" to the collective, the environment and the technologies in play. *ZOOM* attempts to construct conditions that emphasise the generative value of art, by using the paradox of forms in an artwork as one might construct a Koan. In this way the work of art, as a relational platform, becomes a provocation for engagement and reflexivity, highlighting what emerges when participants immediate by turning towards the ground of their own activity.

The practice of immediating impacts upon the extent to which timescales can be dilated or compressed or the ways in which form can be understood as expanded and/or contracted modes of forming. Exaption, in the context of evolutionary biology as described by Darwin,

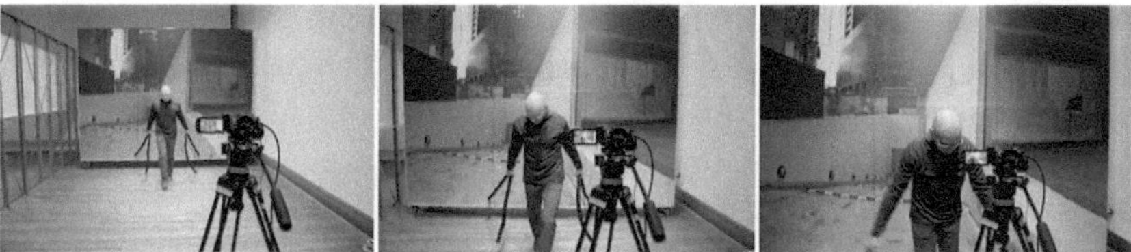

Figure 58. The moving wall in *ZOOM*. Photos by Kaya Barry

Gould [3] and others, has been used to refer to an adapted trait or feature that only becomes useful when activated in a future context. This has implications for selection - particularly how an organism and environment dynamically shape each other. In relation to an artwork or creative process, exaption suggests that a process of perception, mode of understanding, formal structure or mode of forming can be made available for an as-yet unknown future use. Exaption helps to articulate the strange temporal and spatial complexity of an artwork's affect on the re-composition of experience, particularly when considering the affects of paradox.

The potential held by the concept of exaption, a concept of the futurity immanent in the present, allows the timescale of biological formation to operate through the immediate experience of lived abstraction. The implication of exaption, as a concept activated within art, provides a way to think about the way form plays out across time scales that are imperceptible to us. If exaption is about morphology in the context of evolution, it also indicates the potential of form in the context of art. As art becomes an evolutionary device, it can be used to trigger moments of self-reference within evolution.

In *ZOOM*, for example, the wall was *not* made for structural purposes or for decorous reasons, rather the wall was constructed as a prompt to activate exaptive potential—to be put to use in service of recomposing experience. If an improviser in *ZOOM* glimpses the way in which he or she composes experience, this affects the recalculation of the parts to the whole. By zooming-out the form and shape of the river can be perceived. By zooming-in, the eddies and contingent events reveal the unique niche events. Movement through scales of perception transpose the relational network. The components of the installation moved even without moving or more exactly—the movements within a seemingly still structure were made to resonate and vibrate with potential. These transformative movements happen in both directions—from object to environment and vice-versa. For example, an object such as a soccer ball changes the lounge room into a stadium and the gallery changes the urinal into a work of art.[4] Whereas the placement of an object into a new context does not constitute exaption, the immediating capacity to make new distinctions, constitutes the exaptive potential made available through the paradoxical status of art.

An experimental artwork allows for actions, objects and the environments to form new configurations. In this way a wall can operate like an iteration of the liar's paradox (e.g. "This statement is false"). The moving wall in *ZOOM* is a wall and not a wall, it is walling and refusing to wall: it is true and false: it has gone AWOL (away without leave) and is stuck in place. The moving wall enables movement between the two states. The wall is an exapted feature whose potential is mobilised under the conditions of an artwork rather than an architecture where it is asked to behave as it always has behaved. The uselessness of an exapted feature and the absurdity of the non-yet apparent new context is transformed by the practices of immediating that art draws out.

Features and behaviours given a new context in art realise their exaptive potential by participating in an open platform of relations, which the artwork foregrounds. When exaption occurs, the crowd of past distinctions (like a crowd walking down a busy city street behind a person who bends to tie a shoelace), hits the newly constructed slow-moving walls of the platform. Something has to give. The wall in *ZOOM* is made to behave in an unaccustomed manner and exceeds its objecthood, no longer needing to conform to the template of walls. Exaption without the new context in which an adaptation flourishes also seems absurd. The wall does not request or receive permission, it leaves its post where the duty to uphold ideas of permanence and structure is housed, to go out roaming the boundaries in search of new distinctions.

ZOOM's acquired function re-configures events and recomposes experience in ways that make the ground of one's own activity perceptible. This is where an exapted Sisyphian behavior finds its value, rolling the stone up and down the hill not as a repetitive punitive task but as the meditative realisation of everyday actions. The unceasing activity constitutes hell only if objects are inherently tied, through their form, to teleologcially defined goals. Otherwise, only the movement matters for the realisation of living. If the endless task is to touch and be in touch with the ground of activity, then movements within and across the boundary states (of any distinction) are not tied to particular forms but to their occasions. An immediating practice would experiment with and strive to develop new techniques of engagement that usher us onto the ground of our own activity.

An immediating practitioner, in the flow of an expanding and contracting present, might purposefully mis-match certain possibilities for action in lieu of future possibilities. Immediating, as a practice, becomes a way to develop techniques for mis-matching existing traits and their environments and deploying the constituent forms *speculatively*. In this way, form would be made to speculate on its own viability, risking itself in the process.

Notes

1. Within the *Immediations* project the collaborators have been working through the concept of technique not tied to the content of practices but extended through their processual invention and sites of potential multiplication (Manning and Massumi 2014: 94). Terms such as "technique" are loosened from their mooring to take on more ambitious registers and resonance. Techniques such as conceptual speed dating, making propositions, shared meals as research creations, reading groups as part of research creation events, free radical within the group, collective devising event—all of which require further elaboration and collaboration. Techniques cannot be separated from the technologies, which are embedded in the environments they co-construct.
2. Stein's discussion comes from the introduction to a collected volume of texts in the journal *IO* (1988) produced by the Rhinebeck Institute (a group of poets, philosophers and mathematicians in upper NY state) of which Stein was part.
3. For more on exaption as an evolutionary principle, see Gould and Vrba "Exaption: A Missing Term in the Science of Form." (1982)
4. In his discussion of the logic of relation in *Parables for the Virtual* Brian Massumi (2002: 68-88) comments that Michel Serres, Bruno Latour and Pierre Levy all use the soccer ball to discuss the relation of subject to object and individual to collective (71). Objects can open prefigured space to bottom-up perceptual processing, forging unanticipated relationships. The urinal is a reference to Duchamp's *Fountain* exhibited in 1917.

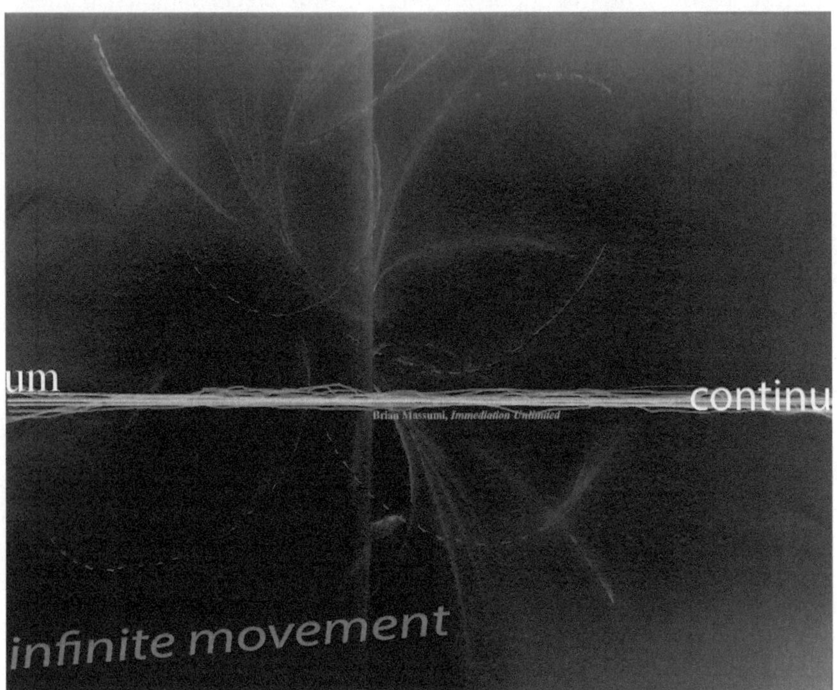
um
continu
Brian Massumi, *Immediation Unlimited*
infinite movement

Brian Massumi

Immediation Unlimited

A Provocation

It could not be clearer: "the elucidation of immediate experience is the sole justification for any thought" (Whitehead 1978: 4). In a single phrase, Whitehead sweeps a venerable concept off the table: mediation. A shudder can be felt across the disciplines as a centerpiece concept shatters like an antique vase brusquely elbowed by an uncivilized guest. The concept, after all, was long fought for, and remains a prized acquisition in many a field, whose critical credentials are embossed on it. My own field of communications is prime among them.

But Whitehead also phrases the same admonition differently. We must "confine ourselves," he writes, "to that which communicates with immediate matter of fact," because "what does not so communicate is unknowable, and the unknowable is unknown" (1978: 3). The pieces may not be able to be glued back together, but this statement gives some hope of a knowing reconciliation. It announces that in the process philosophy advocated by Whitehead, immediation is not to be taken as the opposite of communication. The "elucidation of immediate experience" actually *requires* a concept of communication – which is to say, transmission. Where transmission goes, some notion of medium is bound to follow. But what manner of medium is this? Which concept of communication are we talking about? How can transmission inhabit immediacy? It is necessary to construct a robust concept of immediation, equal to the needs of a process-oriented take on the world, to begin to answer these questions.

But first: what is it about the concept of mediation that requires it to be swept aside for a process-oriented perspective to take hold?

A Forensic Portrait

Mediation in its classical, communicational sense is a good place to begin. What follows is a schematic sketch of the concept. It is not meant to correspond to any particular author's or school's technical take on it. It is more like a composite identikit drawing. Its purpose is only to enumerate a set of tendencies and commonly interlinked conceptual gestures that are generically presupposed by the concept of mediation, and tend to return as of their own accord in varying constellations, or to insinuate themselves into the conversation like a half-heard whisper, wherever that concept is deployed, even in cases where they are officially declared to be unwelcome. There is such a thing as zombie concepts: concepts that carry a presuppositional force of such staying power that they tend to return no matter how many times you slay them. The presuppositions accompanying the concept of the self-contained, sovereign subject of modern thought is one of them. Mediation is another. The two are not unrelated. The aim here is to provide a generic forensic portrait of the mediation zombie, not in order to turn it against any particular version of mediation theory (many of which are admittedly far more sophisticated than this sketch will let on), but rather, positively, to highlight the contrasting counter-tendencies that a theory of immediation is called upon to develop following its rallying cry to seat thought and knowledge in immediate experience.

The sketch: what is transmitted is a message. The message is assumed to be preconstituted. Only once it is formed or formatted into a transmissible content does it become transmissible. In a word, mediation supposes pre-formation. The pre-formation extends to the parties in communication. The sender and receiver are also preconstituted, in the sense that their ontological status is assumed: they are subjects of thought sharing information. A raft of humanist presuppositions about what constitutes a subject and cognitivist presuppositions about the nature of experience floods the transmission wires. Cognition is understood to precede perception, and to have primary status in relation to it. Perception enters the picture on the receiving end, playing the basically passive role of reception. It is treated as a transparent window on the content. The important thing is the subject's retrieval of the information. That is where the action is. Logics that are properly perceptual, or broadly experiential, would only cloud the view, so must be sidelined in favor of the cognitive acts of information packaging and retrieval. The medium, like the perception it delivers to, is committed to an ideal of transparency.

This instates a dichotomy between form and content, twice over. First, the transmissibility of the message is its fittability into a general form (a formatting), and that general form is the vehicle for the particular content transmitted. Second, the medium as information channel is itelf the general form for all transmissions: their general condition of possibility. This second form/content division coincides with a structure/process dichotomy. The medium is the structure framing the process of communication. This brings with it yet another dichotomy, between fixity and flow. Finally the operation of mediation is understood in terms of an *intervening third*. It is around this point that the philosophical questions will congregate in what follows. This is because the notion of an intervening third lies at the heart of all theories of mediation, however sophisticated, and however cognizant they are of the shortcomings of the schema just enumerated. It is their sine qua non. It is the bite of the mediation zombie, drooling unwelcome presuppositions as its teeth clamp down.

The model of the intervening third is as simple as the idea of an apparatus of communication viewed as interposing itself between the sender and the receiver. Its coming-between as a third term tasked with ensuring the conditions of possibility for communication places the parties in communication in a relation of exteriority to one another. This fashions social relation as *external relation*: an interaction between two, mediated by an intervening third. Mediation's being "in the middle" is understood in these terms, as pertaining to external relation. This is relation as an added factor constituted by an intervening third coming between two discrete points, joining them at a distance through its own devices. This has far-reaching philosophical consequences. The gravest, for a process oriented approach, is that it writes immanence out of the equation. As we will see, immanence and immediation are a package deal. One cannot be conceived without the other. Immanence is not a concern for mediation.

In mediation, immanence is replaced by interiority. Sender and receiver are subjects, each with its separate interiority, triangulated by an intervening technology. This refuses any fundamental status to the transindividual as opposed to the intersubjective, making it a secondary effect of the external relation between individuals, rather than a primary fact of "intra-action" (to use a currently popular term, which in my work I call generative "infra-activity," used as a synonymn for "immanent relation"). It also firmly ensconces the process in the confines of the human, and confines the human to its own finitude, limiting its resources for becoming-other. The unlimited falls entirely to the side of the media apparatus, in its ability to exponentially multiply content, and to distribute its operations ever more extensively throughout the social field. Technology arrogates the openness of infinitude to its own operations. As part of the same gesture, it claims "singularity" for itself, preceding it with "the" to make it a punctual event, rather than a logical category all its own, outside the opposition between the general and the particular, as process philosophy styles it. Singularity is deferred, arriving with the apocalyptic crossing of a speculative threshold. In the meantime, humans remain relegated to their accustomed status of particulars representing their general category of being, conforming recognizably to its model, their belonging to it defined by their displaying common characteristics, their becoming riding on their external relation to technology rather than on any internal relation of difference to themselves, infra- to their form of life, in trans-connection to its outside. The significance for immediation of the concept of immanence, and its kinship with a certain idea of the outside, will become clear as this essay progresses.

There are many currents in communications and media studies that have called the conceptual gestures just outlined and the presuppositions they carry into question, attempting to make a break from the generic schema of mediation. Recognizing that media and technology play a constitutive role not only in the formation of the social but in the very genesis of the human subject goes a long way toward shaking the schema at its preconstituted roots. Positing an "originary technicity" at work within the human, making the human's technological extendability definitive of its being, overcomes the externality of the relation to technology. Moving toward an ecological paradigm upholding a symbiogenesis between human and nonhuman actors opens the gates of becoming, as the human reopens onto the outside and the infinite, in posthuman or more-than-human becoming. Giving the affective dimensions of experience their due challenges the schema on another front, by dethroning the cognitive from its position of primacy and reasserting perception, and more generally experience, as fundamental factors. The importance of these developments should not be underestimated.

And yet ... as long as the cornerstone of the paradigm of mediation is left in place, the conceptual gestures outlined above, with their plethora of presuppositions, will continue to stir menacingly in the grave. The issue, once again, is the intervening third. Only an effective concept of immediation radically writing that notion out can complete the break. The mission is to push the entire framework into a phase-shift, driving all of its attendant zombie concepts – sender/receiver, information, content/form, interaction, interiority/external relation, perception as passive reception, particular/general – into their final theoretical death throes, in favor of a new figure of transmission pertaining to that which "communicates with immediate matter of fact."

The stakes are broader than communications and media studies. The paradigm of mediation has another major homeland: the theory of power. Theories of the ideological transmission of structures of power are a major province of mediation theory. In this case, the mediating apparatuses are the traditional family, education, disciplinary institutions such as the police and prison, and the state, in addition to the media. It is important to run through some salient points, at the risk of generating another identikit drawing.

Theories of ideology rest on the thesis that there is a power of conformity already in place prior to experience. Experience sprouts on the soil of inherited sets of implicit ideas that encapsulate the structure of social relations. These naturalized social relations are transmitted to the individual, in whom they are implanted as a priori beliefs. They come to the individual before the individual consciously comes to herself. Individuals' self-expression is secondary and deriviative, expressing the power relations already structuring society, whose form of domination reproduces itself by means of this inculcation. Individuals come to their thinking in ideological conformity with what is already socially pre-thought. Their form of life comes to them preformed. The inculcation may come as a habitus, or a structure of feeling, but the transmission is always essentially cognitive in tenor. The word ideology says it all, with its etymological combination of "idea" and "logos."

It is no wonder, given that etymological ballast, that when feeling is highlighted it remains subordinated to a structure of thought. In the words of one of the theorists of ideology who worked most concertedly to open the structure to process by giving a pivotal role to embodied feeling and perception, in the final analysis ideology still always boils down to a "pre-formation" of thought (Williams 1977:134). The ideological structure is "thought as felt and felt as thought" (132). This phrase's bookending of feeling by thought recalls the etymological doubling of idea and logos written into the word "ideology." The crux of the matter remains cognitive, in spite of the importance attributed to feeling. This is attested to by the fact that the dialectic between the inherited ideological structure and the embodied process of reception and transmission that updates it, adapting it to each historical period, is understood to coincide with the dialectic between the individual's particular practical consciousness and the general social consciousness. The particular/general and structure/process dichotomies are not only retained, they are collapsed into each other. The work of the critique of ideology is to counteract the effects of this blurring, which results in the formation of a false consciousness founded upon the acceptance of the transmitted ideology as natural and unquestionable. The prescription can only be more and better cognition: a raising of consciousness. This has significant political consequences. It stands to reason that the lifting of the veil of illusion can only be spearheaded by an astute subgroup, already uncommonly in the know, who have honed their critical prowess and are now in a position to enlighten others. The mediation paradigm, applied to the theory of power, tends toward a vanguard politics. This in turn fosters a new hierarchical structure in replacement of the old. Historically, that hierarchy has tended to incrust in a party apparatus. The theory of immediation carries strikingly different political valences.

In the foregoing account, a concern for the structure/process and general/particular dichotomies have repeated like a refrain, in harmony with the issue of the intervening third. The reason for the concern for structure/process is that, regardless of the intent, the structure side allies with pre-formation, making of transmission a conformation. Conformity then takes precedence over differencing. The static takes conceptual precedence over movement and change. Position comes first in relation to movement. Change comes a derivative second to fixity, as an operation upon it.

For process thinking, in contrast, change is the only constant, and movement only comes from movement. The logical category of the singular is considered primary in relation to the particular, and its partner in ideological crime, the general. Confusing particularity for singularity glosses over the way in which every particular is always, in some way, in excess of its category. In everything, there is always a little-something-extra over and above the common properties it displays that identify it as a particular case belonging to its generally-recognized type: an errant detail, an embryonic appetite, a slippage or minimal deviation, a shimmying troubling its positioning and priming it into aberrant movement. The consequences of this for the theory of power are that structures predicated on pre-known general categories – as is the case for all state, governmental, and institutional structures – are always playing catch-up. They are always running after the singular, in an attempt to corral it back into place, and feed off its energies. The mediation paradigm that is in complicity with these dichotomies glosses over this processual fact: structures are defined by what escapes them. Escape and the process of becoming it carries forward do not presuppose structure. Quite the opposite, structure presupposes the primacy of escape.

This is a reminder that the philosophical questions concerning immediation are immediately political. The political "implications" are not add-ons: they are of the metaphysical warp and woof. Speculation on immediation, however abstract, carries by its very nature a pragmatic force. It carries a concrete suggestion of alternative ways of negotiating power relations, not as an option, but as a metaphysical necessity, if change and becoming are to be given their processual due.

Immediation in the Middle

Charles Sanders Peirce makes Mediation one of the metaphysical pillars of his "triadic" philosophy. He uses Mediation, and sometimes Medium, as a synonym for his category of Thirdness (Peirce 1992a: 254, 295; Peirce 1997: 191, 193-194). Despite the name, Peirce makes it crystal clear that mediation does not imply an intervening third as a separable element. Calling it mediation is misleading, particularly after the long intellectual history from Peirce's day to our own that has embedded the term with the schema of presuppositions just described.

For Peirce, what defines genuine thirdness, quite the opposite of an intervening third, is a condition of inseparability. Thirdness designates the indissolubility of a coming-together. Calling this Relation would be much more intuitive, and would have the added benefit of signalling the pivotal status of this concept as the linchpin of the logic of relation that Peirce considered one of his chief contributions to philosophy. Relation is indissoluble because if it is possible to decompose a phenomenon into separate elements and still have the same phenomenon, what you're dealing with is a collection. A collection is when elements are discrete from one another, a mere disjunctive multiplicity. Their natures are not in play simply by the fact that they come together. The connection between them is extrinsic to their natures. It is a merely accidental circumstance. The between of them has no particular consistency, no thickness proper to it, no nature of its own in which their natures are called upon to participate in a way that changes them. The relation, in a word, is external. External relation, according to Peirce is a "degenerate" thirdness (or "mixture"; Peirce 1992a: 254-255). It corresponds to what nowadays is called interaction, a term with which discourses on media are rife. Interaction is the thin between.

In genuine thirdness, the in-between has a thickness that requires a participation that goes to the heart of what the participating elements are and what they can do. Entering into the relation changes their natures. This entails, conversely, that removing them from their coming-together will change their natures again. In a favorite phrase of Deleuze and Guattari's, they cannot be divided without changing in nature (Deleuze and Guattari 1987: 33, 483). This nature-changing participation where the very definition of what a thing is, and the spectrum of what it can do, is at stake in what is meant by "internal relation." This term does not at all mean that the relation is inside, confined to an interiority. Quite the opposite, it means that the "inside" comes out. The thing sends its very nature on an adventure in the world, taking a wager on what else it can be. Internal relation is involvement in an event, and the event constitutes a becoming. It is the elements, coming-together, that are *in* the relation; it is not the relation that is in something else. This is another way of saying that the concept of internal relation is a concept of immanence. Internal relation is the mutual immanence of the multiple, in the singularity of a changeful event. Immanence is when things come out of themselves to come together. It is shared *outside* of what they collectively come into, to become-through.[1]

This changes the meaning of "between." Between is no longer the external distance separating two things. It is co-involvement, a participation that brings things together in change. "Between" is a being outsided together; being in the midst of a shared becoming. Becoming comes through the middle. The middle is not passively circumscribed by the external relation between things, as pre-constituted. It is an active middling that takes thing up together into itself, toward change. It is the direct implication of a multiplicity of natures in each other, across any actual distance separating them. All immediacy is in the middle, and all middling is in immediacy. The between is not the actual distance. It is the absolute proximity to each element, and by the same token to them all, of an implication in the event of change, integrally shared. This makes the relation a locus of sorts, but not one that can be pinpointed in space. It the locus where what is localized in space participates nonlocally, in immediacy. This means that it is by nature abstract, or ideal: as much of the order of the virtual as the actual.

Take love as an example. The love relation is not decomposable into two separate people, both of whom are busy, each on their own side, executing the action of loving. This would make love a collection of two dual relations: that of each individual to love. The feeling of love is of a direct involvement in another's life, in a way that adds a supplement to your life that you cannot put your finger on, because it is neither here nor there–or rather it is always here and there, wherever you go. Unlocalizable as it is, you feel it directly, without having to think about it. You also know, just as directly, that it will draw you into an adventure that will not leave you unchanged. Love is not an interaction between two living beings. It is an intermodulation between two lives. It takes off from what they are, each on their own side, in order to sweep them up toward what they will become together. Love is not 1+1=2. It is a strange, vital mathematics where 1+1=3. The third is the becoming. This is a third that exceeds addition. It is more a kind of fusion.[2] The one and the other cease to be a collection of two. Instead, they move together, across their distance and difference, integrally as a block, their movements correlated even when they are apart. They are entangled, not unlike quantum particles. To paraphrase Whitehead, the world of two becomes one, and is increased by one (making three). This "fusion" is not an erasure of distance and difference. It is a supplementation of them: a real but abstract thirdness of co-involvement. Every couple's coupleness has its own affective complexion, which can be felt and responded to, supplementary to any one-to-one interaction you may have with either party. There is a being of the relation. Anyone who is friends with a couple knows that implicitly. The relation is an incorporeal being that has its own "personality," irreducible to the personalities of the individuals in love. It is not a mere convention of speech to say "in" love. The being of the relation is a kind of ideal locus, defined by what Raymond Ruyer calls a nonlocal liaison. You are still in love when you are apart.[3]

The same logic applies to situations involving three parties, for example in polyamory. Polyamorous relationships are not decomposable to two sets of dual relations, because each relation cannot fail to be modulated by the other, even if the choice is made to maintain a certain separation between them. The between of relation is a nondecomposable "among": it goes between all of the terms in relation at one and the same time. It's not a straight line from one term to the other, plus a straight line from that other to another. It's an abstract line that snakes in a zig-zag between all the terms at once, filling the intervals with its own ideal thickness, at no remove and at no delay. The thickness, or intensity, can be variable. To say that integration does not erase distance and difference is to say that it applies to a differential, and that the differential is never surpassed, but rather supplemented. Differentiation and integration are two sides of the same coin. People in love become together, but they do so without becoming the same – or becoming in the same way. Love relationships are notoriously asymmetrical.

Another example of a thirdness among three co-involved parties is the gift (Peirce 1992a: 251-252). From the interactive point of view, giving is decomposable into a dual relation between the giver to the gift (a proferring) plus another dual relation between the gift and the giftee (receiving). However, this is only an event of giving because the action of proferring *coincides with* the action of receiving. They overlap in the event, entering into continuity with one another. If the giftee refuses the gift, the gesture of proferring is abruptly sundered from the receiving, and both parties break from the gift relation. The two actions fall into separation. Their reciprocity is broken. In a true giving, proffering and receiving are reciprocals, integrally intertwined. They are fused aspects of a single action that fills the distance between the two participants with a quality of relation, in the thick of which their lives are moving forward. You can't decompose the gestures into two dual relations without losing that quality of relation. There is of course a distance between the two participants, but there is no distance between the two gestures. They occupy the same abstract locus, which is the relation of giving.

There are many proferrings that are not of gifts, and likewise receivings. Exchange has many faces. If you approach giving as an interaction between two individuals mediated by the gift-object as intervening third passing from one dual relation pertaining to one individual to another dual relation pertaining to the other, you deprive yourself of any way of distinguishing intrinsically between different kinds of profferings and receivings. Divorced from the singular quality of the exchange, the actions look the same. They are basically identical: one arm extends, the other extends to meet it, something passes hand to hand. Looked at as isolated actions, there is nothing to differentiate receiving a gift from receiving a hand-me-down or, for that matter, from a cashier receiving cash for a purchase. The profferings and receivings involved display the same general form. Given that common form, in order to differentiate between events you have to appeal to extrinsic factors. An obvious way of doing this is to situate the exchange, for example by appealing to how it is framed by external circumstance. The problem is that from the relational point of view, circumstance does not frame the relation. It enters into it, and its ingression exerts a force of fusion. The circumstances are an operator of the fusion, along with such things as intention, nuances of posture and facial expression, the presence of corroborating signs such as decorative wrapping, and the flair with which the act is performed. The integrality of the relation, the way these relational operators come together as one event, carries a felt quality all its own. It is this felt quality that distinguishes this event from other events of proffering and receiving. That *felt quality* expresses an intrinsic difference endowing the act with its own event-personality. It marks the immanence of the relation: the fact that the contributory factors, or relational operators, are in on it together, reciprocal co-conspirators, inseparably bound – as good as one, for all the event cares (but still very much themselves, from the point of view of the differential of their asymmetrical involvement in the integral event).

As these examples show, immediation, understood through a philosophy of relation, is vitally concerned with *qualitative difference*. The singular feeling tone of events is foregrounded. That qualitative difference is expressive of internal relation, directly felt. The notion of fusion points to the immediate reality of the relation, and underlines that the event is composed of differences coming to coincide – coming into *continuity* with each other, without their difference being erased. Immediation, to paraphrase Whitehead this time, concerns the becoming of continuity (Whitehead 1978: 53). But how do qualitative difference and continuity go together? What is *their* relation? Continuity is often understood in term of indifference. Here, we find ourselves called upon to link it integrally to difference. The relation takes up the difference in nature between its multiple contributory factors and supplements that differential with the expression of the emergent thirdness of a singular qualitative difference characterizing this event, in an immediacy of feeling.

In order to say with Peirce that Thirdness is mediation or medium, while saying in the very same words that relation is immediation, an explanation has to be found for how difference and continuity are as intimate with each other as a pair of lovers. What will be achieved will be the holy processual grail of a concept of the medium that does not rely on the notion of an intervening third, while at the same time providing a basis for a theory of transmission.

Time to Become

Whitehead makes a similar conceptual move to Peirce's. The relationality at the heart of process, he writes, features "a group of fused occasions, which enters into experience devoid of any medium intervening between it and the present immediate fact" (Whitehead 1967a: 181). Whitehead seconds Peirce's approach in his invocation of fusion and coming into continuity, as well as in attributing a thickness or effective consistency to the continuous in-between and in casting aside the intervening third. Whitehead goes one further, adding a new emphasis: on time. The fused occasions, he says, come from the immediate past, and their coming-together constitutes the cusp of the present. The question of (im)mediation now fuses with the question of time.

Media studies, like ideological theories of power, are typically more concerned with place and space than temporality. Networks are seen to produce cultural "spaces" whose study often takes the form of explanatory mappings of arrays of nodes. Time figures most often in terms of speed (of transmission or contagion between nodes) or acceleration (increasing pass-through speed across nodes). Speed and acceleration are spatialized figures of time: time measured in the framework of space, reduced conceptually to rate of displacement. Whitehead, on the other hand, is concerned with time as becoming, connected to the problem of the emergence of the new. This is time not as displacement, but as qualitative change, constitutive of being. Pre-formation, fixity, and generality have no purchase here, in the singular event of relation.

What is immediate in Whitehead's formulation is the action of the past as it figures in the dawning of the present. What he is referring to as the fusion of occasions is an activation of potentials inherited from the past. These "reenact" themselves. They reactivate, to serve as formative forces for what the present will bring (Whitehead 1967a: 192-193). The present's dawning *is* this very reactivation. The reactivation is selective. The infinite potential of the past is felt, but only certain potentials are felt clearly and insistently enough to figure positively, as readily available resources for what the present aims to become. The aim at the future, according to Whitehead, is as necessary a factor as the impetus of the past. The attractor of a coming completion of the occasion just commencing moves backward from the future to meet the forward push of the past. This is the immediate future beckoning becoming. The reenaction occurs at the intersection of the immediate past and the immediate future. The occasion is energized by their differential, as they fuse into immediacy with each other. The present is the integration of these two asymmetrical forces, coinciding. It is the dynamic mutual inclusion of the impetus of the past and the allure of the future, co-energizing a becoming. The present is the past and future's thirdness: the reality of their co-involvement. It is the being of their relation. It is the supplementation of their irreducible difference, as they come into continuity across their difference.[4] The selection of which potentials will figure positively, as contributory factors ready and raring, is a function of the synergy between the two inverse movements as they integrate. More potentials reactivate than can eventuate. The selection integrally includes mutually incompatible potentials. This pregnance with more potential than can be, gives the present its intensity. Its intensity carries a singular feeling characterizing this now, such as it is, as no other now has ever been, nor will be: a vitality affect expressing the happeningness, the novelty, of this present passing. The task of the becoming is to narrow down the bundle of reactivated potentials to a selection that are compatible, or can be rendered compatible en route, so that the becoming can complete itself, in a final determination of the event it will have been.

This is a complicated way of describing something we all know intuitively. Whitehead uses the example of speaking a sentence (Whitehead 1967a: 181-182). The aim to express, intersecting with the available resources of language inherited from the past, energizes the formation of the utterance. The infinity of potentials carried by language is at the tip of the tongue. A first word issues, and the cusp of the present's energization, at the cross-roads of the past and future, gear-shifts into a forward momentum carrying the potential with it. But the potential has now been narrowed down."The...," you say. That doesn't narrow it down by much, but still. The future aim is now at a common noun, under pressure of habit and grammar, with the orientation toward those most readily available common nouns (those suggested by the context). "Donald...," you say. The expectation is shattered by a proper name, a nickname no less. Trump is preying on your mind. A new context sets in, reconfiguring the selection of potentials for what comes next. "Is ..." A number of vivid potentials now vie for the honour of completing the sentence, in a selection not unaffected by the inflexion with which you pronounced the introductory words. The energizing aim has characterized itself as pointedly political. You are suddenly at a loss for words. The remaining selection of potentials is all so vivid, all equally suggestive, all so apt (and satisfying), that you simply let the sentence trail off, leaving them hanging in the air. The utterance has completed itself with a certain incompletion, leaving a remainder of alternative potentials between which it is no longer necessary for the occasion to choose, because they reinforce each other, across their difference. Their hanging together, compatibly various, gives the occasion its final character as an expression of an intensity of feeling too heart-felt to narrow down completely.

All utterances, even those more definitely completed, leave a remainder of potential for follow-up. Potential feeds forward, with a characterizing intensity, no matter what. The coming into continuity of the future and the past that is constitutive *of* the occasion energizes a continuous flow of potential *through* the occasion: a continued becoming of continuity; a flow of qualitatively changing relation (the relation of the past to the future, of you to your interlocutor, of you to your own affective state, of shifting contexts articulating to each other and rearticulating, of one event following upon another). No pre-formation. No fixity. Process. An event, not opposed to structure, but structur*ing*.

It is easy, and in some ways more instructive, to use a perceptual rather than linguistic example. The same account could be repeated, for instance, with the example of sightseeing in an unfamiliar city, approaching a corner. The event potentials do not simply pertain to what is already in place lying in wait around the corner, deposited there from the distant past. They also exceed what your accumulated knowledge of walking through cities leads you habitually to expect to see. They notably include your state of attention, incoming from the immediate past to cusp the present melding into the immediate future. Distracted by the stress of not knowing where you're going, you fail to see an uneven paving stone in the sidewalk as you turn the corner. The potential for a fall suddenly jumps out at the occasion, a co-production of your aim to get somewhere and the affective tonality of the immediate past (distraction) forming the inattentive step now leading you there. The bundle of potentials greeting you is quite limited.

Either you fall or you don't. Although it's not so cut-and-dried as that. There are many ways of falling and not falling when you trip. There is an infinity of them, in fact, but a smaller infinity than what the city as a whole generally offers around its corners. As it happens, you draw on your balancing skills to catch yourself, with an embarrassingly byzantine flail of a pirouette. Now, that's a novel way not to fall. Not falling never felt quite like that, you sigh. You compose yourself and walk on, recontinuing the potential of your relational encounter with the city, across the interregnum of the trip. It happens that you are a dancer. As you continue, you feel a new dance move gestating in style of your almost-fall. Your catching yourself links to dance, at a distance, offering potential for that other practice.

Take a Moment

The main point to retain from this is that a distinction must be made between the *immediate* and the *instantaneous*.

The immediacy of the present is not an instant, understood as a point in time. That is yet another spatialized figure of time, modeled on space. It is taking the classical notion of space as composed of widthless, dimensionless points, and applying that model to time. This didn't pan out so well for space, as Zeno showed at the very beginning of philosophy. Why should we expect it to turn out any better for time? Yes, it's a powerful heuristic, highly useful for dividing space for purposes of measure. But it is a philosophical non-starter. Because if you push the division toward the limit, space – which it is the whole point to measure – is annihilated. As you divide down to smaller and smaller intervals, you converge toward the void of the ultimately widthless. What else would you expect but a void, when you construct three dimensions out of building blocks of no dimension? The principle of the whole operation of division is the spatial archetype of the mediation doctrine of the intervening third: that between every two points lies another. But what can it even mean to say that between every two points there is an intervening third point if the points are widthless to begin with? Doesn't the widthlessness of points destroy the very idea of "between" that is supposed to be the fundamental spatial relation? The medium of space swallows itself whole, by its own self-voiding definition.

The present of immediation is not made of points. It is made by fusion: an integration of differentials of all sorts, the primary of which is between past and future. The figure is not that of interpolation, but rather of *overlap*. A selected group of potentials reenacting the formative force of past occasions integrally overlap and fuse together, entering the present en bloc. Their entry energizes a force of impulsion through the present, which is boosted by the attractive force of future aim. The fusion of selected potentials from the past is, in the same stroke, a dynamic fusion of the past with the future. It is misleading to say that the past potentials enter the present. It is more the case that this two-fold fusion *constitutes* the present. It *is* the "immediate present fact," or what Whitehead often calls the "concrete fact of relatedness" (Whitehead 1978: 22 and passim). It is the density of this complex overlap that constitutes the thickness of the present, as in-between time. But then, all time is in-between time. What is there, actually, but the present? We are always actually in the between. We start in the middle, as Deleuze and Guattari liked to say – and stay there, moving with it as it slips ahead, qualitatively changing. Unmoving locus of becoming, moving us along.

There are no end-points on either side of this in-between. On either side lies the infinite expanse of the past and the infinite horizon of the future. The in-between of becoming is bracketed by openness. It has no definite boundary. It is only *limited by potential*, past (incoming) and future (ongoing). Immediation is the unbounding of experience's taking determinate form. For this is not a model of seamless flow. There is always a hitch giving the occasion pause: an interregnum across which the action continues. Time trips. Something cuts in and trips it up, triggering the event into taking definite, irreversible form. The continuity of time becomes across the cut of the interregnum. The model is not of seamless flow, but of cut/flow.[5] What intervenes to make the cut (flow) is not a third thing, but a relation that makes a difference: an unnevenness met en route that triggers a dynamic taking-form on the fly (a *clinamen* immanently modulating the momentum of the occasion). The unevenness is not a separable element. It is relational. In the corner example, what made the event was a relation between the sidewalk and a pace and manner of walking. The crack in the sidewalk figured as making relational ingress. Apart from that ingress, it is nothing for the event (for the event will not have happened).

Overlap gives us the figure of the "saddle-back," as William James famously put it, as opposed to the point (James 1950a: 609). Becoming rides the saddle of the time it takes, which is the time the concreting fact of its cut/flow makes. The present is not a point in time. It is a "specious present" carrying a certain width or thickness of process (ibid.). "The immediate present of each actual occasion," Whitehead writes, "lies in a duration" (Whitehead 1978: 124). My undancerly near-falling will have a different experiential thickness, a different intensity, than yours. It will yield a qualitatively different duration, which will in turn yield a measurably different chronological time-interval (I flail more than you, and it takes me more to right my balance). The duration that is the specious present is not this chronological measure. The duration is the internal relation, directly expressed in experiential intensity, of the contributory elements of the event fusing into it, giving it its singular arc. The chronological measure is a secondary ("degenerate") artifact of the event being juxtaposed (set in external relation) to another event (the moving of the hands of a stopwatch).

The point about time not being a point is that immediacy is relationally saddled with *duration*. It is not in an instant. Rather, it has its moment. It is *momentaneous* rather than instantaneous. The time it takes is the time it makes.

It is the rhythm of the hitches giving pause, triggering the catch of a definite taking-form of the movement-across, that parses the flow into specious presents. The resulting moments stand out from the flow as definitive emphases in becoming. Cut/flow, trip/catch–stand-out moment in life's ongoing.

Some Consequences

Quoting Whitehead again, the duration of the moment coincides with "the rush of immediate transition" (Whitehead 1978: 69). It is to this immediate fact that philosophy should "confine itself." In immediation, *transition precedes transmission*. Things are not in transition when they are being transmitted; there is transmission when things make a transition. The past, selectively reactivated, transitions into the present. Or to put it more precisely again, when the two-fold constitution of the present draws past potentials forward to meet future potential, transition occurs. A charge of pastness, fused with a force of futurity, carries across the in-between that is constituted by that very movement. To say that "transition precedes transmission" means that transition is, processually, primary in relation to transmission.

Transmission is a derivative of the thickness of a transition. This turns the whole model of mediation on its head, in more ways than one.

In mediation, the present is mediated by the determinations of the past. In immediation, *the past is mediated by the present*, in the sense that it is the constitution of the present that determines what of the past carries forward. The relation of the present to the past is active. There is no passive reception. The present involves the reenaction of the immediate past, selectively taking up this past inheritance into its own singular taking-form. "What becomes involves repetition transformed into novel immediacy" (Whitehead 1978: 136). The transformation in question is the active self-constitution of the moment's becoming. The occasion takes form as a function of its "living aim at its own self-constitution" (244), exploiting the resources of the past through the fusion of its own attractive force with the impetus of the past (and with the forces of circumstance). It could be said with equal justice that the present is mediated by the determinations of the past, and that it is mediated by the allure of the future, because it is precisely the middling of the two, an emergent third. This is a third that supervenes rather than intervenes (it is supplemental, adding the one of its becoming to the many earlier become and to come). However, retaining the word "mediation" at this point is no more than a matter of habit. What comes through the middle does not intervene between two existing endpoints. It directly supervenes between two potential open-endednesses, filling the in-between with its own immediacy. This is a strange kind of self-constituting in-between whose coming-to-pass spins off its own either side from the middle.

Mediation in the usual sense places the emphasis on a particular notion of determination. Everything hinges on the linear causality of a transmission from point A to point B, and how that transmission determines what comes next. The move from A to B is a closed segment bookended by the sending of the message as initial cause and the reception of the message as consequent effect separated from its cause by the interval of transmission. In immedation, determination is recursive: it occurs in the fusional loop between the past and future. The emphasis is on potential. The emphasis is on the active selection of potential by a self-constituting duration, rather than the passive entraining of an effect already pre-figured in, and commensurate with, its cause. "Immediacy is the realization of the potentialities of the past, and is the storehouse of the potentialities of the future" (Whitehead 1978: 136). That realization is not a commensuration, but a supplementation. The in-between is not closed by pre-figuration; it is open-ended by an excess of potential (more than can actually be absorbed in the event). Immediation *is* the interval. It is the thickness of that self-constituting in-between. There is no separate message that is communicated across the interval. There is only the *expression* of potential in a taking-determinate-form that parses the openness with its own becoming. The expression is of a momentaneous self-constitution. The self-constituting is both the form and content of the event of becoming. In the expression, form and content integrally fuse into what can be called, albeit somewhat misleadingly, and for lack of a better word, the "dynamic form" of the event. (When the phrase "taking-form" is used in this essay, it is with the proviso that it is an irreducibly dynamic form – a form of transition – and that the word "form" is being used with suspicion, for convenience of expression.)

Ultimately, what is transmitted, what is carried across by the transition's self-constitution, is formative potential, not information.[6] Potential is not transmitted as a content. Unlike the determinate taking-form that parses out of it, potential has no definitive form or content. It is transmitted as a degree of freedom *of* form, and *from* content. These gloss, respectively, as the remainder of futurity left over across every transition (free for subsequent form-taking) and the inheritance of the past (the initial energetic charge that the occasion's self-constitution takes up into itself, and from which it departs to the extent that it becomes). The past has no given content, because it is *taken* as content by and for the occasion's self-constitution. The future, for its part, has no taken form, because it *gives* (in the sense that a door that is open a crack gives when given a push).

In immediation, there is no form/content dialectic, any more than there is a structure/process dichotomy. Form and content only figure as presently fused into dynamic form, or separated out as freedom of and freedom from (futurity and the determinations of the past respectively). The freedom is not total, but gradated, of a certain degree. The degree of freedom varies for every passing present, depending on the way it spins its open-endedness. Not even freedom is a general concept for immedation. Immediation, in its self-constituting of its own event, only knows the singular.

The dichotomous distinctions out of which the paradigm of mediation is constructed are reconstrued, by immediation, as processual distinctions bearing on aspects of the cut/flow of time as qualitative change, or the trippy becoming of continuity (the event).

A Fork in the Road

Peirce shares Whitehead's sense of middling. An example he gives of mediation is a fork in the road (Peirce, cited in Zalamea 2012: 57). It's an odd example, by the lights of conventional images of mediation. For one thing, it is just that: one thing. It is an integral figure. True, it has three components. It is internally differentiated. But none of its three components qualify as an intervening third. Take one out, and the remaining two change in nature. A fork in the road with one line is not a fork in the road. The figure of the fork in the road passes the test of genuine thirdness: it cannot be divided without changing in nature.

Although this figure has no intervening third, it does have a middle. The middle is the point at which the three paths intersect. Overlap would be a better word, because they are in fact tangent to one another rather than intersecting. One of each of their endpoints overlap to form the middle. If you look at the figure as a spatial diagram, the overlap appears as a single geometric point, and you would be forgiven for considering it widthless. But zoom yourself into it, on a journey, and its thickness and multiplicity jump out. Look down one fork, then another. They look and feel different. Because they are. Not only physically, but in terms of the potential they open. Now look back. The road you have traveled to come to this point is even more different than the two ahead. It also has a feel to it, but it is the familiar, comparatively boring, feel of the already-tread. Your standing where you are, with the exciting alternative of two divergent paths in life ahead of you, is the embodied inheritance of the past of your journey, whose potential has been spent, but in a way that opens more, divergent, potential. Experientially, you are not at a point. You are in the thick of a transition, and what lies ahead for you depends on which way you end up going. It gives you pause, because the road is unknown to you. You can trip up, and end up lost, in which case what lies ahead for you is frustration, things like late meals, missed appointments, and lost opportunities. You look down one fork again, and then the other, as if some previously missed detail will mercifully attract your attention and trigger a decision in you. Nothing comes. So you plunge ahead as if it had, perhaps on so thin a ground, so slight a trigger, as a shift in the light on the surface of the road that just now flittingly filters through the trees, half-consciously beaconing you ahead. A road never quite forked for you just this way before. You have made the transition, and with that, the world's potential – a modest dollop of it, surrounded by a practically unlimited swathe of it in the form of less availabe paths through the unbeaten woods toward myriad unsurmised destinations – is transmitted to your life's ongoing. You are free, to a graded degree, to carry on.

In place of an intervening third, we have an overlap consisting in a *reduplication* of endpoints. A line of movement never ends at *a* point. Processually speaking, it comes to a saddle formed by the superposition of multiple endpoints. These are less endpoints than anchor points for divergent vectors onwards and backwards. The "point" is the thickness of their coming integrally together, across their difference, for the present moment. It is their fusion, into a block of multiplicity. It is the how of their fusion, the manner in which they come multiply together, that characterizes the present moment, endowing it with its singular vitality affect.

Any diagram or schema of what Peirce called mediation – or what is less confusing for us to call the immediation of genuine thirdness – is insufficient if it is approached simply as a geometrical figure, given the heuristic reality that geometrical figures are constructed from, and can be divided into, points that do not have qualitatively different natures and are as indifferent to the event of construction as division. We must zoom into experience, at least in thought experiment. For experience is always in movement, and movement is always in the thick of transition, taking its own duration, making its time, middling for qualitative change. "Immediate experience [is] the essence of an individual fact" (Whitehead 1968: 98).

To say that immediation *is* the present immediate fact is to say that it is irreducibly experiential. Experience cannot be bracketed out. Immediation is one with direct experience, on the road in thought or in the woods. The process philosophy adequate to immediation is a species of James's radical empiricism, defined by the precepts that relation is real (it is the reality of thirdness, a doctrine drummed into his readers by Peirce) and that relation is directly experienced (it is of the order of the event) (Peirce 1997: 190-191; James 1996a, 42). It is experience that effects the fusion that forms the relation. Diagrams and schema are necessary aides of analysis, but they must never be left at a merely geometrical juncture. They need to be prodded into movement. They need to be forked into experience.

Forking Zeno

This is precisely what Peirce does with the problems philosophy inherited from Zeno, heuristically glossed over by the later Euclidean consensus forming the classical foundation of geometry (the idea that lines are made of points rather than transitions, that points are widthless, and that between every two points lies an intervening third). It is worth the detour to go through Peirce's strategy for prodding this schema into movement, in order then to zoom experience into it.

As noted earlier, Peirce's concept of mediation is that of thirdness; the problem of thirdness is undecomposably a problem of continuity (Peirce 1992b: 190); continuity is of the nature of relation; and the reality of relation is directly experienced – making mediation immediate. For the concept of immediaton to set, all of this has to integrally hold together. Continuity is a weak link, first of all because the traditional way of envisioning it – by cutting into a line and interpolating points into the gap, repeating the procedure ad infinitum, in a passage to the limit of the widthless – is so heuristically ingrained in us as to form a habit of thought that is very difficult to shake, but which, unshaken, will swallow immediation in the void. Continuity is also a weak link in connection with directly experienced relation, because that involves continuity in issues of qualitative difference, and the way we think of differing qualities of experience – which experience never comes without – is anything but geometric. We are back at the relation between continuity and qualitative difference, signalled earlier, as a core problem of immediation.

The following account is freely based on Fernando Zalamea's remarkable account of Peirce's logic of continuity (Zalamea 2012). Peirce begins by denying that lines are made of points. It is obvious, he says, that lines would be discontinuous if they were made of points, because however far you took the division, there would always be a gap into which you could intercalate another point. At the limit, the gap would be infinitesimal. Over the limit, you would fall into a void and everything would be all gap, as the infinitesimal concertinas out into infinite nothingness, in an energyless geometric equivalent of the Big Bang. As you try to construct the continuum by division, all you achieve is to infinitely gap it, making it as deeply discontinuous as it can get, up to the point that it gives up the ghost of geometry and expires in the spaceless void. Poor line.

To save it, you just have to give it a shake. Instead of thinking of the points as lying next to each other with a potential gap in-between for a third to intervene, think of them of them as *moving* back and forth *over* each other, in restless agitation (Zalamea 2012: 20, 22). Now every point is a smear: an overlap composing a "neighborhood" of multiple points. You can transition continuously over a smear. And you can also continuously transition from one overlap to a next overlap restlessly smearing with the first. Now, if you cut the line, you just cut through to more smearing: under-smearing. Cut again and again: under-smearing galore, layer after layer. This actually supplements the line rather than attenuating it. It thickens its composition rather than thinning it out. Because if all the "points" in the line are sliding into and over each other, then it stands to reason that the line itself is moving, in just as ceaseless agitation. In some of those agitations, it might well shift beside itself, forming a parallel to itself. Or it will slant, and form a perpendicular to itself. The parallel and the perpendicular might meet for a passing moment, to form a rectangle. You have now moved not into the dimensionless void, but into two-dimensions: you have surfaced. Keep shaking, and you get all manner of figures, in all dimensions. All of these translations of the line are included in the under-smear. The agitation constitutive of the line mutually includes in its event-space the absolute fullness of an infinity of potentials. Which is just what they are, potential or virtual figures. Were they actual figures, the line would not be what it is, a line. You could reverse perspective, and see the line as a cut-out from this complex plenitude. It amounts to the same thing.

The line is an included aspect of the plenum, and the plenum is an included aspect of the line: mutual inclusion of all in one and one in all.[7] The mutual inclusion is asymmetrical, because the inclusion of the all in the one gives a line, whereas the inclusion of the one in the all gives a plenum: a continuum. They nest in each other differentially, off-balance. Cut into a line and "a continuum will result like a *self-returning line* with no discontinuity whatever" (Peirce, cited in Zalamea 2012: 24). You have to keep thinking the mutual inclusion in terms of movement, conceiving of the line departing from itself in all directions and dimensions, and then in no time (or at infinite speed) returning to itself. When the line departs from itself, it moves into a "continuous growing of potentiality" (Peirce, cited in Zalamea 2012: 67). When it returns to itself, the growing potential contracts into one dimension, limiting itself to a determinate figure, a simple line. A movement occurring in no time is virtual. A movement occurring at infinite speed is at the limit of movement potential. Note that Peirce said a continuum will *result*. Continuity is reproduced at the same time as a limited figure of it emerges. Continuity is iterative, continually rolling over on itself into a new variation, as each limited figure cuts out from it. The essence of the continuum is movement. It has no fixed form. Any fixity the figure of the line might have is a virtual movement effect. Far from being the opposite of movement, the fixity of the determinate figure is a particular expression of the limit of movement potential.

The continuum itself "flows" (Zalamea 2012: 31). It is in a constant fluctuation of becoming-line (and all else and more, mutually included: potential continually growing). Needless to say, in the midst of this agitation, "the principle of the excluded middle does not hold" (26). What holds is the middle, mutually including. The simple figure of the line stands out from the commotion. It holds the line (holds to itself) amidst constant fluctuation, self-constituting as the linear in-between of a multitude of figures whose singular dynamic form of overlap describes it, characterizing the moment geometrically. To immediate is to "globally unify the different perspectives" held in potential, in a determinate taking-form (58). This is a local-global integration. The taking-form limits the growing potential to its simple local figure, at the same time as it continues the global growth of self-returning potential. Depending on the perspective, you can see the local figure as limited, not by points or a void, but by open-ended potential; or, you can see it as limiting potential to its own taking-form. These are two fused aspects of the being of the figure, and in the same stroke of the global reality. These are two coinciding inverse movements. The same two-fold agitation swinging at infinite speed (or in a no-time that makes the moment) between, on the one hand, the singularity of a determinate definition, and on the other the so-overfull as to be encompassingly vague. Definition is an emphatic local contraction of vagueness bringing a complex globality of infinite potential to determinate expression in a simple limited figure (Peirce 1992b: 258).[8]

"The vague might be defined as that to which the principle of contradiction does not apply" (Peirce, cited in Zalamea 2012: 27). That is because what it is so-overfull of are "can be's" and "would be's" that are "not individuals," yet are just as real as any determinate "is" (26). The vague is the mark of the immanence of an all-encompassing "supermultitude" (8). Of this supermultitude can be said what James said of pure experience, that it:

> is not yet any definite *what,* tho' ready to be all sorts of whats; full both of oneness and of manyness, but in respects that don't appear; changing throughout, yet so confusedly that its phases interpenetrate and no points, either of distinction or of identity, can be caught. .... But the flux of it no sooner comes than it tends to fill itself with emphases, and these salient parts become identified and fixed and abstracted. (James 1996a: 93-94)

From the global perspective, the parts that become identified and fixed and abstracted from the flow of the continuum, the individuals populating process, are "no longer distinct ... They have no existence ... except in their relations to one another. They are no subjects, but phrases expressive of the continuum" (Zalamea 2012: 14-15). Determinate individuality is the differential *mark* of infinite continuity (13): the local sign of the global.[9]

> A continuum is a collection of so vast a multitude that in the whole universe of possibility there is not room for them to retain their distinct identities; but they become welded to one another [fused]. Thus the continuum is all that is possible, in whatever dimension it be continuous. You have so crowded the field of possibility that the units of that aggregate lose their individual identity. It ceases to be a collection because it is now a continuum. ... A truly continuous line is a line upon which there is room for any multitude of points whatsoever. Then the multitude or what corresponds to the multitude of possible points, –exceeds all multitude [it is a supernumerary infinity, a supermultitude]. ... On a continuous line there are not really any points at all. It seems necessary to say that a continuum, where it *is* continuous and unbroken, contains no definite parts; that its parts are created in the act of defining them and precise definition of them breaks the continuity. (Peirce, cited by Zalamea 2012: 19)

Where the continuum is unbroken is in the fusional supermultitude of potential that is left-over the local act of cutting definitively into, in the smear to infinity afterneath the interregnum of taking-form.

Existence is Rupture

"Peirce's logic of vagueness hopes to control the transit of the indefinite to the definite, of the indeterminate to the determinate, and to study some intermediate borders in processes of relative determination" (Zalamea 2012: 25). Occupying this borderland are modes of transition. These constitute "an intermediate, or nascent state, between determination and indetermination" (Peirce, cited in Zalamea 2012: 26). Process is the perpetual rebirth of this transitional nascent state of the global becoming local.

Intermediate nascent state, Peirce said. That is: a nascency through the middle, constituting thirdness. Constituting relation. The individuality of the breaking-away into a becoming-determinate is a relational autonomy.

This way of thinking the global and the local requires rethinking them in a way that does not equate the local with the particular and the global with the general. You can continue to use the word general, as Peirce does, but only if you emphasize that what you really mean is *generic* (Zalamea 2012: 11). And that when you say generic you mean restless, rocked ceaselessly back and forth across the borderland of nascency, swinging between the singularity of the emergent individual's salient marking of the indefinite continuum and the continuum's genericness vaguely exceeding all mark. Process swings *singular-generic* rather than fixating on the general-particular. When we say that an individual figure is singular rather than particular, it is a way of underlining its belonging to process.

Repeat: the continuum's "parts are created in the act of defining them and precise definition of them breaks the continuity." In other words, "existence is rupture" (Zalamea 2012: 21). The borderland of nascency is subject to cuts rupturing the continuity of the growth of potential, which slips back-forth, afterneath, left-over determination. The continuum trips on definite taking-form, taking pause from its own globality. This is how it immediates itself. Otherwise, it would be vaguely intemporal, full of can be's and would be's without any is's and will be's. This is how it makes time for itself. This is how it marks its moment: with its cutting out into individuation, changing in nature as it divides.

To say that existence is rupture is a Peircean way of saying that the problem of continuity is not just a logical problem, but also a pragmatic one: a problem of coming to be, a matter of becoming. Rethinking continuity by adding movement to the usual static schema and following the fork in the road to which this leads, is a way of wedding immediation to the question of ontogenesis in thought experiment – and in thought and experiment.

No End

There is, actually, only middle. The fork in the road taught us that what appears to be an endpoint is actually a superposition of a multiplicity of points that does not erase their difference. The points enter into a zone indistinction without losing their difference. Rather, they integrate it into one appearance (an appearing together). The fork in the road doesn't actually look like a superposition. But from the point of view of journeying potential, that is exactly what its appearance is: a virtual overlap of potential trajectories. To see it this way requires an abstract view, but this is a different kind of abstraction. It is not the general kind of abstraction that simplifies thirdness. It is a singular-generic kind that virtually prehends the over-full reality (of potential).[10]

At such a juncture (and what locus of our live's journeys is not one?), some of the superposed "end-points" are new points of departure for the onward journey. Even the ones that aren't, are, if you come to the fork from a different direction. The superposed multiplicity of end-points solves a thorny logical problem encountered by the attempt to fork off from Zeno. If you cut into a line, classically conceived, thus dividing it in two, which line does the point of division belong to? If you attribute it to one of the resulting segments, the other is left unlimited, so that it can't not keep going infinitely, growing back into a continuum, like an endless amputated frog leg, rather than behaving as a properly hobbled discrete figure.

Peirce's solution to this problem is as simple as it is ingenious: you don't have to put the cutting point on one side or the other, because that point spontaneously reduplicates itself and goes to both segments.[11] It is as if the cut-point jumped in place, and from the slice there issued two of it, like twin virtual particles hopping out of the quantum void to take material form. When the cut divides the continuum it stirs it up. It agitates it into sprouting new parts of itself. Thus the twoness of the segments comes from a virtual superposition. It is the result of a virtual overlap that was potentialized by the cut-into-it to take the form of a separating-out: a distancing into disjunct forms united at a distance by a shared genesis. The resulting points are genetically entangled, in nonlocal liaison across their separation.

This may not seem like a very technical solution to the problem. But philosophically it works wonders. For is not this reduplication a geometric expression of Whitehead's processual concept of reenaction (or what in my own work I call reactivation)? The cusp of the present for Whitehead is just such a leap in place where an endpoint redoubles itself into a point of departure, the two in immediate superpositon for an immeasurable interval before process travels down a new line, adding a new segment to the world's becoming, and this demonstrably (in two ways: first, it is directly registered in the immediate emphasis of its specious-present feeling tone; secondly, that intensity can be derivatively registered by a secondary apparatus of measurement translating its qualitatively singular coinciding with itself into a comparable quantity). Peirce's reduplication solution to the endpoint problem opens up another way of articulating the geometrical reasoning that is so necessary to thinking cut and continuity with process philosophy.

Of course, the example of a line is an artificially simple one. Even in the example of the fork in the road through the woods, there was an indefinite multiplicity of other off-road paths also entering into superposition at the forking. These were less alluring and less accessible, but were still there in potential. If the fork of the road into two well-graded paths was the locus of a virtual reduplication of endpoints-cum-points-of-redeparture, their leaping in place was accompanied by a splash of an indefinite number – in fact, a supermultitude – of other less salient off-road points, less well graded (present in a gradation of potential shading off into an encompassing silvan vagueness). The line didn't just split, it exploded into ontogenetic shrapnel. This is also part of Peirce's geometric reasoning, when for example he says that any point might spontaneously "burst" into any multitude of points whatsoever, "and they all might have been one point before the explosion" (Peirce, cited in Putnam 1994: 6-7). He doesn't trust points to behave. The possibility that "points might fly off, in multitude" (ibid.) at any moment gives a notion of the continuum as constitutively *irritable* (Peirce uses the same idea in his discussion of protoplasm; Peirce 1992a: 341). Prod, and it will throw off virtual points whose overlap in that occurrence will make the moment. These are not artifices, like geometric points, which are purely heuristic contrivances of reason. They are real, virtual *event-particles* (what

Deleuze and Guattari call "particles of becoming," 1987: 269, 272-275). The specious present is a playing out of a select group of the potentials they release, following an arc of actualization co-produced by the past's explosive reentry and the aim of the future's attractive pull. The thickness of the specious present is in fact a selective thinning out of the explosion of potential that "energizes" (Whitehead's word) every moment. Reenaction is ontogenetically explosive. The "reduplication" of the endpoints can be thought of as event-particle shrapnel that is caught by the forking road segments for their own constitution. Their segmentation is a limited *capture* of the potential released.

The explosion of reenergizing potental is ready to detonate at any point. Every endpoint is a spontaneous rebeginning, bursting with ultimately unlimited potential. This explosion of potential is our perpetual present, endlessly reduplicating. The determinate takings-form that shake out at each juncture are ontologenetically entangled, united in nonlocal liaison at whatever distance their segmentations take from one another. The self-returning line of the continuum of existence is an infinite tangle, globally uniting and irritably dividing in the same stroke of the ontogenetic clock. Such is immediation. No end, always in the middle, in the thick of things shaking out again.

Parenthetically, this notion of capture is the way this process thinking of cut and continuity can be integrated into political thought. The capture of potential is the fundamental operation of power (Deleuze and Guattari 1987: 424-473). The explosion of event-particles is a primary, ontogenetic resistance to power: the seat of ontopower.[12]

Experience Continues

The articulation of Whitehead's reenaction with Peirce's spontaneous reduplication of points returned us from geometry to the cusp of experience, where existence is rupture and the growth of experience continues across every delimiting cut. Moving on from there, let us reduplicate the point where the discussion of the co-implication of vagueness and taking-determinate form was cut off by the supervening arc of the preceding segment's no-endedness:

"A continuum, where it *is* continuous and unbroken, contains no definite parts; parts are created in the act of defining them and precise definition of them breaks the continuity." (Peirce 2009: 168) *Precise* definition, Peirce says. This implies that there are places where the continuum remains unbroken, and definition, while not necessarily maximally vague, is nevertheless not precise. Vagueness also comes in degrees. If the "immediate fact" that is the process of ontogenesis is directly experienced, then the experience mutually includes a range of degrees of vagueness and preciseness.

To articulate the Peircean rethinking of the continuum to the qualitative differences of which experience is made, it is only necessary to think each point-smear as an overlap of sensings. Think of the way an object has a texture, and the texture is a way of seeing touching. Or the way a glint of sun includes a shiver of just-hinted-at colour as well as brightness variations. Think of these sense-smears as definite cut-outs from an indefinite continuum of experience. In them, we touch-see, in the case of the object, or in the case of the sun-glint see-see (see in different ways at the same time). We sense-smear experience defining its qualitatively lived moment, marking itself in the singularity of an individuation mutually inclusive of different sensings. Experience, definite in its emphasis, and at the same time smeared by the variations its salience mutually includes: more or less precise. More precise, in the case of the textured object, which breaks more completely from the continuity with the spatiotemporal background of perception, rupturing itself more forcefully into existence. Comparatively less precise in the case of the sun-glint, which flits with uncertain locality and indistinct moment. Still less precise in the atmospheres enveloping each moment and forming its periphery.

Peirce explicitly makes the connection between his local-global, singular-generic cut-and-continuum, and experience as mutually including an infinite gradation of sense-smear in far-reaching qualitative differencing:

> There must be a continuity of changeable qualities. Of the continuity of intrinsic qualities of feeling we can now form but a feeble conception. The development of the human mind has practically extinguished all feelings, except a few sporadic kinds, sound, colors, smells, warmths, etc., which now appear to be disconnected and disparate. ... Originally, all feelings may have been connected in the same way, and the presumption is that the number of dimensions was endless. For development essentially involves a limitation of possibilities. But given a number of dimensions of feeling, all possible varieties are obtainable by varying the intensities of the different elements. Accordingly, *time logically supposes*

> *a continuous range of intensity in feeling*. It follows, then, from the definition of continuity, that when any particular kind of feeling is present, an infinitesimal continuation of all feelings differing infinitesimally from that is present. (Peirce 1992a: 323-324; emphasis added)

Every experience encompasses a given number of dimensions of feeling, but if you shake it, you can obtain a plenum of all the other dimensions, in varying degrees of intensity (more or less vaguely). To shake it, you just have to think time – or better, eventfully make time – because time logically supposes the continuum of experience. When any particular kind of feeling is present, an infinitesimal continuation of all feelings differing infinitesimally from it is also present. The infinitesimal continuation is a self-returning line, no sooner cutting into itself than folding back on its cuts, superposing variations of intensities and different qualities of experience on each other and into the moment, as a function of an emergent figure. It is in its perpetual folding back on itself that the continuum is unbroken. Its unbrokenness comes back through the middle of taking-form, and also surrounds that taking-form with a gradation of potential shading off to a vague periphery. It is both at the center (the locus of determinate becoming), and forms its horizon (an encompassing openness to infinity whose surrounding the center is what makes it a center). The plenum is localized becoming's everywhere, at once suffusing and surrounding it.

To say that existence is rupture is to say that the moment is a composition of this plenum of experience. The logic of the ontogenesis in question in immediation is more directly aesthetic than geometric. It bears on the composition of qualities of experience, more or less vague *and* more or less determinate, in two-fold splendour. At this point (of felicitous conceptual smear), we can leave Zeno and Euclid and points and lines behind, confident that we have a way to talk directly about direct experience without reintroducing the intervening third and all of the zombie concepts that come with it. Now, when we talk about fusion, we know we are talking about the "osmotic process" (Zalamea 2012: 22, 64) of emergent experience taking-form, in the cutting-in and cutting-out of its own continuity.

The relationality that is thirdness that was earlier said to be inseparable from the concept of immediation implies an ethics of tending relation, and that ethics fuses with a politics involving something like love, in neighborhood with giving. Peirce suggestively speaks of "sympathy" (cited in Zalamea 2012: 57; see also Massumi 2015b), and reminds us that the individual, cut loose from the continuum, is a degnerate form of relationality, and that the given, as opposed the giving, is a degenerate form of possibility (Zalamea 2012: 12). Best to cleave close to the continuum of potential, composing with the plenum, marking to some degree, in some gradation, at every fork in the road, the full range of the qualitative intensities of experience, in a taking-definite-dynamic-form delimiting potential and at the same time opening an indefinite osmotic continuation of it, for carry-over into the next moment's self-constitution.

Such also is immediation: marking your time through transitions that artfully absorb a dollop of global potential, and pass a variation on that potential forward, in transmission, not of information, but of ontogenesis. Self-constitutively parsing life's ongoing.

Medium Revisited

We are finally in a juncture, after many forks in the road and explosions of conceptual points, to get to *the* point, about transmission. There are still outstanding questions. For example, for a theory of immediation, is there a medium of transmission? There is the middle of transmission – namely, transition itself – but if it does not involve mediation in the conventional sense, as has been repeatedly argued, can we say there is a medium? What is a medium of transmission, if it can't be an intervening third such as a technical appartus (as in the use of the word medium in the everyday sense)?

The two guiding authors of this discussion each hazard an answer. Peirce says that the continuum is the "global conceptual milieu" (Zalamea 2012: 23). The word "conceptual" in this answer emphasizes the ultimate abstractness of the continuum, as a self-returning line whose plenitude virtually folds back through the center of every determination of it, and at the same time bursts to the cusp with a virtual superposition of a multitude of points. This is a kind of "conceptual" reality that is immanent to the immediacy of experience (while at the same time, two-foldedly, the immediacy of experience is immanent to it). Its reality is attested to by its effectively contributing to the occasion's becoming by arraying through and around it a range and splay of potential of which the moment's taking-determinate-form may selectively avail itself (it is "conceptual" in Deleuze's sense of "Idea,"

Deleuze 1990, 1994; readers of Deleuze and Guattari will also recognize their "abstract line" in the self-returning, infinitely zigzag line of this essay, Deleuze and Guattari 1987: 497-498).

Global conceptual milieu. That works. But – there is no other way to put it – it's a tad abstract. Whitehead's answer is more concrete. He says, simply, that "the world is medium" (Whitehead 1978: 128; Murphie 2019, in Immediation 1). This implicitly repeats Peirce's use of the word "milieu," underlining that the best meaning for medium is the milieu of life, and that the ontogenetic immediation coming up through its perpetual middle is the "concrete fact" of life. This has the added advantage of extending the concept beyond the human sphere. The world is co-habited by many a nonhuman entity. The word "entity" is used advisedly, because a goodly number of these nonhuman factors do not exist, and that in different ways. I am referring to things that do not rupture into the discreteness of determinate being, some because they are just an idea (like geometric points) and some because they are the Idea, which zigzags a self-return through every rupture, in that no-time energizing the thickening of the immediacy of process into the arc of a duration (the continuum itself, replete with the virtual event-particles it explosively throws off at every juncture).

Whitehead specifies that when he says that the world is medium he is referring to the "actual world." Specifically: "each" actual world (Whitehead 1978: 226). By his conception, "the" actual world is in each occasion: the all of it is in each of them, asymmetrically included. In actuality, there is nothing outside each occasion's coming into itself. The actual world as medium is the immediation of the world in process. The word actual is employed here in the sense of "in the act." The actual world is the in-the-act of an iteration of the world redefininig itself. Even more specifically, the actual world is "the primary phase" of each occasion's being in the act of becoming. That means in reenaction, where endpoints reduplicate into points of departure, virtual event-particles burst forth, and the continuum self-returns. All of this is mutually included in the act. The actual world throws off virtual packets of potential, and shades off by degrees from the emphatic clarity of the distinct existence that is in the act of constituting itself, to the farthest and least accessible reaches of the global continuum of potential. The globality of the world, including what does not actually exist, is immanent to the actual.[13]

The idea that the world is each occasion as medium accords with a position I have developed elsewhere that medium could be redefined in terms of each event's singular manner of coming about (Massumi 2011: 102, 142-143). This way of putting it tilts the concept toward the dynamic form arcing out of the primary phrase of reenaction, to single itself out from the reduplicative point of overlap through which the continuum self-returns into the rupture of being its own self-completing world. While philosophically accurate enough, and while useful as a provocation to shake off the zombie concepts of mediation, this narrows the notion of medium in ways that limit its practicability. What "medium" means will have to be integrally reinvented for each example considered, in a way utterly adapted to that example. This can be well-adapted to some philosophical purposes, but it doesn't allow the notion enough span, in that it skirts around the issue of transmission. The way Whitehead develops the idea that the world is medium focuses on the thickness of the overlap occurring in the reenaction of the immediate past, and underlines the asymmetrical and differential nature of that fusional mutual inclusion *as* energizing a transmission of potential.

Consider two cars at an intersection. One is stopped at it, the other is approaching. The light turns red for the approaching car and green for the stopped driver, who steps on the gas pedal. The approaching driver, distracted by an incoming alert on his illegally unstowed phone, misses the signal. They crash. The cars' entering the intersection is the immediate past of the crash. Each car followed a different path to that event. Both paths included the trigger of the traffic signal, but they aborbed it differentially. The difference was one of salience. For one driver, the signal registered. For the other, it was backgrounded behind the emphatic beep of his phone. Later, this driver will somewhat-recall half-seeing it, at the edge of his awareness, prevented from rising to the foreground by the interference of the beep and the allure of social media beckoning for an immediate future that was not to be. That immediate future was abruptly displaced by the actually occurring immediate future of the crash. It will hang forever in alternative, unfulfilled potential. The driver survives the crash. For the rest of his life, every time he hears a phone alert, an event-particle of crashing is thrown off by the phone. He fleetingly experiences a virtual crash. Even unfulfilled potential can reenact itself. Potentials, unlike drivers, never die. The potentials selected by the actual course of the event include a long recuperation. The injured driver takes advantage of the forced leave from work to start learning a new language using the Duolingo app (the better to reconcile with his phone). Potential is transmitted, even grows, following a detour.

The entry of each car into the intersection can be considered an actual occasion in its own right. It can also be considered in its aspect as a component, or contributory formative factor, of the superseding occasion of the crash. Both cars deliver crash-potential into the accident. Each does this its own way, according to the different emphases of the immediate past of the immediately preceding occasions and how they led them to that juncture. The potentials in the two immediately antecedent occasions were differently complexioned. They were differently graded. Potential foregrounded in one was backgrounded in the other by the different ways the signal was absorbed. The drivers carried the crash-potential into the event differentially. The immediate past of the stopped driver effectively included the signal in its composition. It positively took it up as a formative factor. That of the driver who plowed through did not. It negatively took it up as formative factor.

If you follow back through the series of antecedent occasions leading to the crash in reverse order, you see the paths that converge in the crash diverging into the more and more distant past. As they diverge, the differentials multiply, and the pattern of inclusion becomes more and more variegated. They both heard a fire engine somewhere in the distance. But one passed through a school-zone before approaching the intersection, and this put her on the alert, and her alertness was carried over into her stop at the intersection. The lives, and potential deaths and injuries, of both drivers are mutually included in the crash. All the antecedent occasions leading up to it are also mutually included. They are effectively carried into it by the crash, whose occurrence determines them retroactively to have been its contributory factors. They overlap in it. But they do so in different patterns of inclusion. The overlap is not perfect. There are off-sets: there are things that belong to one path but not the other. The farther you go back into the past, the more off-sets there are. But the off-sets are in a sense still included in the event. The event wouldn't have happened if the potentials hadn't been patterned in just that way, all the way back. It wouldn't have happened if the responsible driver hadn't passed through the school-zone and it hadn't been during school hours. And that wouldn't have happened if ... You could make an insanely complex Venn diagram of the differential pattern of overlaps and off-sets characterizing the mutual inclusion of the past in the actual occasion of the crash. At the limit, the diagram would include the entire universe (Whitehead 1968: 9-10, 138; Whitehead 1978: 223). There is a "tenuous thread" – an infinitely complex zigzag abstract line – connecting every occasion's actual world to the open whole of the universe (Bergson 2012: 10-11).[14]

All of that complex of potentials enters the event-locus of the crash through the immediate past. The potentials are enveloped in it. They all fuse into it. They accordion into the crash as the metal hulks of the car accordion into each other. They are integrally delivered to the accident. The distant past does not exist. Its actuality is gone forever. In themselves, the actual occasions belonging to it cannot make a difference. They can only enter in through the channel of the immediate past of the twin signal-occasions that carry forward the potential that these antecedent occasions bequeathed. Even the immediate past does exist for the present. Its reenaction doubles time, to make the present. The immediate past exists in reduplicative fusion with the rupture of the present entering existence, in the reenactive redoubling of the ghost of its already-goneness with a vivid now beginning. The transmission of potential from the many overlapping leaves of the remote past has to pass through the energizing immediacy of this reenactive overlap between the just-past with the now-present, thick with immediate futurity. The transmission has to be immediated by the time-differential mutually included in the transition. It has to ride the saddle of time.

This gives a conceptual schema for how transmission is not only possible in immediation, but *can only actually be explained by it.* Immediation, at first sight, seems to contradict history. The opposite is the case: it *makes history possible*. Without the transition it constitutes, nothing would come to pass. The serial actualization of the present is what grows history. Without that actualization, history would simply be gone. It would stay in the past. And the present has no access to the past as such. It is a ghost for it. Immediation lets the past be gone, and its ghost return. It lets it differentially overlap with the present, and that in turn allows historic routes, routes of transmission wending their way backwards from the immediate past into the distant past, to make an actual difference, and be schematized and diagrammed.

If you don't accept the doctrine of immediation, you have to act as if you believe the past was not actually gone. You have to act as if the distant leaves of the past can somehow be inspected in the present. Denying the irrevocable passing of the past is hardly a solid basis for history. But this is precisely what traditional historiography does when it edits out the ever-formative role of the immediate past in overlap with the present. It skips over the immediate past, on the grounds that the methodology mediating its practice enables access to the past – forgetting that the methodology must always be reactualized to have any efficacity whatsoever, and that this reactivation always presently transitions through the immediate past. Ideological theories of power, for their part, assume an overlap of the past and present, but in too gross a way. They act as if a general structure were a priori present, transmitted in toto into the present by mediatory apparatuses. The totality of the structure is considered to be effectively present at every juncture.[15] Rather than energizing occasions, it constrains them, compelling them to play out in conformity with it, so that they repeat the structure from their particular positioning. The past, in this perspective, exerts a confining general causal influence. The ghost of past generally shakes its shackles.

From the process point of view, in contrast, each occasion is differentially conditioned by the unique patterning of potential entering it through the immediate past. The model is of singularity reduplicating, rather than structure repeating. The reenactive conformation of the present to the past is the transition to a new taking-form. The pattern of the past is infinitely variegated, and each present actualizes it differentially. Since the overlap of the immediate past with the present is also that of the present with future aim, there is always a potential for variation: a way out of confinement by given circumstance. An aim can always be off. Or it can be deflected by a sudden shift in emphasis triggering other potentials to effectively cut in. Or it can catch itself in the act and re-aim toward another attractor. The cut made by the rupture of existence constitutively carries the potential for change, as immediatedly as it dawns in the conformation of the primary phase of the coming occasion to its immediate past.

The historical lesson of immediation is to recognize, with Foucault, that history is always *the history of the present* (Foucault 1979: 31). As mentioned earlier, if you want to insist on speaking as if the past and the present are in a relation of mediation, you would have to say that it is the reuptake of the present that mediates the past. The diagramming of the historic routes leading to each present has to be tailored to that present. There is no general history. There are no a priori shackles – only reenacted ones. History is always in the singularity of the event, through which all of potential selectively returns. There is actually only "effective history," as Foucault also called it (Foucault 1977, 155). It must be further recognized that the present of the act of doing history is co-constituted, as is every occasion, by its immediate past overlapping with its immediate future. This means that aim is a constitutive factor in it. Whitehead insists that history includes what *could have* and *would have been* (Whitehead 1967a: 276, 286; Whitehead 1968: 89-90, 121).

There is no such thing as neutral history. It is always inflected by its own conformation with its immediate past under the formative spell of the allure of its future. This, along with the point that it includes could be's and would be's, means that history cannot simply be described. It must be *problematized*. Its potential must be re-shaken up, in the present. It must be asked, and asked again: what is at stake in *this* aim at history, as I, historian, am presently reenacting it? *Why* do history *like this*?

This is as much a political question as a methodological one. Can other stakes be activated by doing history differently? If writing history involves immediation, what does that say about living? Immediate that. Not-writing history puts you all the more intensely, reenactively, immediationally in the middle of it. Why write history, when you can actively become it? That, ultimately, is the political question of the past. It encourages standing up from the desk, and taking activist steps.

There are, of course, good reasons to write history. This is not an argument against history. It is an argument for the primacy of becoming in relation to it. The point is that although history is interesting, the aim at history is *interested*. That interestedness, or "concern" as Whitehead calls it, is a constitutive factor of every present's parsing of potential (Whitehead 1967a: 176). The way in which the historic routes leading to the present are diagrammed *changes the past*. It effectively repatterns which potentials are transmitted to the future, with what determinative emphases. It alters what the past *will have been*.

It is important to remember that the historic routes, however they are construed, are abstract. They have no concrete actuality in the present. It is only their reactivation – their manner of making reentry into the present, crashing into it, fused into a differential patterning of potential, energizing arcings, bursting with event-particles, shading off into the ultimate vagueness of unbroken continuity – that effectively makes a difference. This happens in immediation. Immediation selectively reenacts the past, locally-globally. Any notion of lines of descent or historic routes is an *image of the past*, abstracted (extracted) from the "immediate concrete fact." The making of an image of the past adds an additional fold to the two-fold of the direct perception of relation that is immediation's thirdness. This is the fold of reflective consciousness: the adding of a supplementary dimension of overlap to the affective commotion of thirdly reenaction. Conscious reflection is a a redoubling of reduplication, like an echo formed in the resonating chamber of the past and future, in the thickness of their immediate proximity to each other in the forming present.

Memory, of course is a privileged mode of the past making reentry. It is the way in which the dynamic forms of occasions from the distant pass (what Whitehead calls their "subjective forms") can be reactivated and transmit their pattern of potential to the dawning occasion nonlocally, without having to ride in on an antecedent actual occasion belonging to the surroundings (that is, one that is external to the body). The brain, as Bergson, Ruyer, and Deleuze argue, is a bodily machine for the direct actualization of the virtual. Memories are like backwards event-particles: potential-packets that the brain throws into the actual from the virtual, as opposed to being thrown off from the actual as a spray of virtualities. In memory, the spray reconverges. It recontracts into the flow of becoming. If the rupture of existence is compared to an egg, memory would be the egg unbreaking: re-fusing. The re-fusing comes with spontaneoulsy generated differences, scars, sutures, and stretch marks. Memory is mildly Frankensteinian. Or, as contemporary psychology says, a memory is always a reconstitution. It is a perpetual reinvention, without an original. This is why it is so easy to fool ourselves about our pasts, or generate "false memories" or, more creatively, fabulations (memories truly potentializing the present with an immediating "power of the false"; Deleuze 1989: 126-155; Manning 2019, in this volume). Habit and skill are similarly immediating, but with more regularity and with less of a penchant for fusional monstrosity.

The theory of transmission by immedation is applicable to communicational models of mediation. It can easily be applied to the "media" in everyday sense. Practically, the difference all of this makes is that it sends out an advisory that it is not enough to map the network, or describe the apparatus of transmission and the routes it comprises. It must be remembered that anything that can make a difference must presentify itself: it must effectively make ingress, under some mode or another, nested in some pattern of overlap, truly or falsely, but in any case reconstitutingly, and that all of this comes as an event. A screen is an event-surface. It includes many layers of nested potential, audiovisually reenacting (especially as screen windows multiply and embedded links add multiple clinamantic triggers aiming to inflect the arc of the occasion's immediate future). But it is not only what is on screen that is part of the event. The off-screen and out-of-frame also enters in. This includes memory again, and habit and skill. But also (as in the tourist walk and accident examples) the mode of attention inherited from the immediate past as it complexions the relation to screen-potential. It also includes any number of contributory factors converging from the past – an infinity of them, in fact, selectively patterned to present varying grades of more or less accessible, more or less compelling, potential. This should not be misunderstood as an argument for a return to some version of reception theory. That would put the event on the receiving end, when it has been said already, too many times, that what is at issue is an always-open-endedly in-the-middle. It also complicates the habit that holds sway in many corners of media studies, not to mention in the media itself, to consider that asking what the "impact" of a media technology is constitutes an adequate problematization of transmission. The crash and burst of potential has no such causal linearity as that implied in this commonplace.

A similar question arises in relation to our screen-related immediations as arose with the question of history. Media studies is also always interested. Reproblematizing the screen-relation involves reenacting differently how potentials nest in the screen – but also how the screen nests with the off-screen and out-of-frame. The overlaps and transitions between the digital screen surface and the analogue off-screen are as much a part of how potential is transmitted as the transitions from one screen refresh to the next.

If the problematization of history allies it with activist becoming, the problematization of our media relations allies to what is called research-creation (when it rewilds itself from its univerity domestication). Research-creation is the most intensely reenactive, most potentially energizing and changeful mode, of living the transitions between the digital on-screen and the analogue off-screen (which are always a part of every creative practice nowadays, through the constant digital searching, documenting, and archiving that occurs, formally and informally). The two problematizations, activist and research-creative, are made for each other. They naturally mutually include each other.

Final note: the appeal to memory and human practices should not be interpreted as limiting immediation to the human. It is by nature more-than-human. As stated earlier, there are always multitudes of nonhuman contributory factors entering into the self-constitution of every occasion. In addition, the explosion of event-particles described earlier occurs spontaneously, without being willed as such. It is like a spontaneous memory *of* the world, a kind of spontaneous combustion of the world's ontogenetic potential. Every occasion, involving a human or not, produces such a spray. This occurs most immanently on the quantum level. But it must also have happened any time the arc of an event takes a chaotic or unexpected turn. Chaos is the spontaneous multiplication of potential historic routes for the occasion's self-completion to detour down, with the selection self-deciding. Above the quantum level, there is no pure chaos. It is always filtered by the actual occasion as a function of its co-conditioning by its immediate past and immediate future. Chaos comes in doses, just as freedom comes in degrees (and it is the same coming).[16] Take care for the "anarchic" share (Whitehead 1929: 34; Manning, forthcoming).

Returning to the human, the co-practice of activism and research-creation involves a dosing of chaos through the artful co-conditioning of potential's middling reenaction. This aspect of immediation is otherwise known as improvisation. Improvisation, like love, or the gift, constitutes a genuine thirdness. Like all genuine thirdnesses, it is integrally relational. Its individualization in seemingly unconditioned choices or decisions – in free association, through simulations of pure chaos or appeals to pure contingency, or from personal inspiration in the guise of "listening to one's inner muse" – are degenerate forms of it.

Notes

1. The vocabulary around "internal relation" is confusing. Whitehead's usage of the term actually equates with what Deleuze and and Deleuze/Guattari call the "exteriority of relations." This is the doctrine that relations are autonomous with respect to their terms, in the sense that they have their own mode of existence, and in the sense that terms in relation do not precede their relation but are constituted by it (as in James' radical empiricism). The "exteriority of relations" is a concept of mutual immanence (infra-activity), allied to Deleuze's understanding of the "Outside" as "a different dimension ... which is farther away than any external world" (Deleuze 1988: 86). The "exteriority of relations" is not to be confused with the classical empirical notion of "external relations." External relations are accidental or cirumstantial connections between pre-constituted parts (equating to "interaction").

"Internal relations," understood as pertaining to the Outside, must likewise be distinguished from "relations of interiority" (interactions between parts composing an organic whole).

2. Zalamea (2012), in his discussion of degenerate versus genuine thirdness, also employs a vocabulary of fusion ("melting", 12; "welding," 19; and "fusion" itself, 21, 22).

3. Peirce seems to contradict himself on love. In "A Guess at the Riddle," he says love is dual relation and opposes it to the genuine thirdness of giving (Peirce: 1992a, 252). But in "Evolutionary Love" he makes it the basis for his "synechism " (philosophy of continuity), implying that it is a fundamental, genuine thirdness (Peirce: 1992a: 354). Evolution itself can only be form of thirdness.

4. Whitehead says that "reenaction" is another word for "the doctrine of continuity" (Whitehead 1967a: 183).

5. On process as constituted by cut/flow, see Deleuze and Guattari (1983: 1-50).

6. There are certain notions of information that are in fact consonant with the approach developed here. Prominent examples are Bateson's definition of information as "a difference that makes a difference" (as in the trigger-cut in this account) and Simondon's concept of information as a potentializing differential, or "disparation." In addition, the past can be said to "in-form" the present (formatively modulate it, immanent to its occurrence).

7. "The occasion is one among many, and including the others which it is among" (Whitehead 1967a: 180).

8. This overcomes the opposition between finitude (discreteness) and infinity (the continuum) while maintaining both, in their difference, by making them processually, asymmetrically, mutually including. The passage from the infinite to finitude is often said to be constitutive of modernity. If that is so, Peirce (and Whitehead and Deleuze) must be considered stubbornly *amodern* in their embrace of both.

9. On local signs, see James (1950b: 163-166n) and Massumi (2011: 128, 148).

10. This is what I have elsewhere termed a "semblance" (Massumi 2011).

11. For an account of this reduplication of end-points, and of Peirce's theories of continuity as they concern potentiality, see Putnam 1994.

12. *Ontopower* (Massumi 2015a) discusses how contemporary practices of war, expanded along the "full spectrum" between "hard" and "soft" power by strategies of preemption, contrive to capture ontopower itself.

13. "The 'here-now' ... is a world also including the actuality of the past [the immediate past in reenaction], and the limited potentiality of the future [the selected potential of the immediate future], together with the complete world of abstract potentiality [the plenary potential of the continuum] ... which transcends, and finds exemplification in and comparison with, the

actual course of realisation." (Whitehead 1967b: 151-152) What is not actual is still a formative factor of the actual, and as such can be considered an aspect of it (Whitehead 1996: 89-90).

14. The complex, ever-changing variegation of overlap and offset prevents this account from falling into the conceptual dead-end of the "block universe" of idealist philosphy so roundly criticized by James (1996b).

15. This a priori positing of a general structure imports a version of the block universe into the theory of ideology, making it a form of idealism, however strenuously it waves its materialist credentials.

16. A target here are philosophies privileging a concept of pure contingency and over-extending it, such as Meillassoux's speculative realism (2010). Whitehead's theory of the immediation of historic routes is also an implicit rebuttal of the philosophical standing of Meillassoux's central problem of the "arche-fossil," and of the assimilation of process-oriented philosophy to "correlationism" that is taken as doctrine by many speculative realists.

Erin Manning, Anna Munster, Bodil Marie Stavning Thomsen

Twisting Into the Middle 3

Immediation does not offer any promises. It is not a moral concept though there is no question that its reach has ethical potential. It is less ours to mobilize than ours to compose-with. A simple mobilization would do nothing more than create a new mediatory structure with immediation as the object of study, positioning us on the edges, looking in.

What immediation can do is spark a technique, orient an already-welling event, turn our attention to processes already doing their work, without us, or with us in a different way. It can alert us to the fact that we are also processes underway, continuously immediated by gestures that exceed us even as they give us transitory form. From this angle we are no longer the perspective from which the world is made but a matter with which it composes, a matter-force that exceeds the composition we have come to know as "our" selves. And it is from here, from the force of this uneasy middling, that techniques can be made (or recognized) that alter what living can be, and what life can do.

Notes on Contributors

Julia Bee is Junior professor for image theory at Bauhaus-Universität Weimar. She works on visual anthropology, perception and experience and gender-media-theory. Her dissertation (published 2018) was on Audience Assemblages, Power, Difference, and Desire in TV and Film Reception.

Lone Bertelsen works across the fields of feminist and social theory, photography, art and media studies, ecosophy and micropolitics. Her writing has been published in *Theory, Culture and Society, The Affect Theory Reader, Performance Paradigm* and the *Fibreculture Journal.*

Érik Bordeleau is researcher at the SenseLab and fugitive financial planner at the Economic Space Agency (ECSA). His work articulates at the intersection of political philosophy, media and financial theory, contemporary art and cinema studies.

Christoph Brunner works in the fields of cultural and media studies and philosophy as an assistant professor in cultural theory at Leuhpana University Luneburg. His recent work focuses on "activist sense" and the intricacies of sensuous experience, media practices, and activism. His wiritngs have been published in *Third Text, Journal of Culture & Aesthetics, transversal, Conjunctions*, and *Fibreculture Journal.*

Nicole de Brabandere Is an artist and researcher who uses writing and media and material experimentation to generate new techniques and concepts with which to inhabit lived ecologies. She is a postdoctoral researcher at the Chicago Center for Contemporary Theory, University of Chicago.

Sher Doruff is an artist, writer and research supervisor. Her recent novella series *Last Year at Betty and Bob's* (Punctum Books, 2018) explores fabulated trajectories of memory. She teaches at the Amsterdam University of the Arts.

Pia Ednie-Brown is a creative practitioner and Professor of Architecture at the University of Newcastle, Australia. Her practice, Onomatopoeia, is grounded in the discipline of architecture, while working across diverse media, methods and milieu. Her research seeks to work against anthropocentrism through revealing habitual oversights and unacknowledged agency, animating the inanimate, and exploring the edges of life.

Gerko Egert works on performance, dance and philosophy. He is a postdoctoral researcher at the Justus-Liebig-Universität Gießen. His recent work focusses on the power of choreography and the politics of movement in and beyond dance.

Jonas Fritsch is a design researcher whose work centers on a creative thinking of interaction design, experience philosophy and affect theory through practical experiments with interactive sound and physical interfaces. His work has been published and exhibited in numerous venues across Human-Computer Interaction (HCI), design, aesthetics and digital culture. He is Associate Professor in Interaction Design at the IT University of Copenhagen.

Andrew Goodman is a visual artist and occasional writer with an interest in participation, ecology and philosophies of process and science. He is the author of *Gathering Ecologies: Thinking Beyond Interactivity* (Open Humanities Press, 2017).

Ilona Hongisto works on documentary film and media with a special focus on the history, politics and aesthetics of fabulation. She is the author of *Soul of the Documentary: Framing, Expression, Ethics* (Amsterdam University Press, 2015).

Michael Hornblow is an interdisciplinary artist and Senior Lecturer in Architecture and Design at the University of Tasmania. He has a background in performance, video making, intermedia, and arts management, alongside academic research and teaching; with a focus on affective, diagrammatic and participatory relations within and across the body and the built environment. This approach is informed by doctoral research-by-practice in the Spatial Information Architecture Laboratory, Royal Melbourne Institute of Technology, and post-doctoral research at the Senselab, Concordia University.

Jondi Keane is an arts practitioner and Associate Professor of Art & Performance at Deakin University in Melbourne, Australia. For more than three decades he has exhibited, performed and collaborated on projects in the USA, UK, Europe and Australia, and publishes widely on practice-led research, art and embodied cognition, experimental art and architecture, and the contribution of art practices to interdisciplinary inquiries that engage collective concerns.

Thomas Lamarre works on the history of media and thought. His recent publications include *The Anime Ecology: A Genealogy of Television, Animation, and Game Media*.

Erin Manning is an artist and writer whose work engages with the interstices of experience with a special focus on collective individuation and neurodiversity. Recent work includes *The Minor Gesture* (Duke UP, 2016).

Brian Massumi is the author of numerous works across philosophy, political theory, and art theory. His recent publications include *The Principle of Unrest: Activist Philosophy in the Expanded Field* (Open Humanities Press, 2017) and *99 Theses on the Revaluation of Value: A Postcapitalist Manifesto* (University of Minnesota Press, 2018).

Anna Munster is a writer, artist and educator, working on arts, politics and theories of: perception, machine learning, the imperceptible. She is the author of *An Aesthesia of Neworks* (MIT, 2013) and *Materializing New Media* (UPNE, 2006), and works on expanded media environments collaboratively with Michele Barker. She is a Professor, Art and Design, University of New South Wales, Sydney Australia.

Andrew Murphie works on philosophy and a politics of differential organisation within a "third revolution" in media and communications (AI and automation, VR, data and signaletics, the world as medium). He also works on climate change as part of catastrophic multiplicity. He is an Associate Professor in Media and Communications at UNSW Sydney.

Toni Pape investigates the relation between aesthetics and politics, mainly in contemporary television and video games. He is co-author of *Nocturnal Fabulations: Ecology, Vitality and Opacity in the Cinema of Apichatpong Weerasethakul* (Open Humanities Press, 2017) and author of *Figures of Time: Affect and the Television of Preemption* (Duke UP, 2019). His work has been pubilshed in *Inflexions*, *NECSUS*, *Feminist Media Studies*, *Studies in Documentary Film*, and *Dance Research Journal*.

Justy Phillips is an artist, writer and publisher. She is the co-founder of the slow-publishing collaborative, *A Published Event*, exploring chance encounter and shared authorship of lived experience through speculative eventing. She is a Lecturer in Critical Practices at the School of Creative Arts, University of Tasmania.

Stamatia Portanova is a Research Fellow at the Università degli Studi di Napoli 'L'Orientale'. She is the author of *Moving without a Body: Digital Philosophy and Choreographic Thoughts* (MIT Press). Her research focuses on digital culture and philosophy from a radically speculative point of view.

Mattie Sempert is a practicing acupuncturist and writer, with an interest in the transversality of body and language, connective tissue, and nonhuman agency. Mattie is currently a PhD candidate (Creative Writing/Experimental Essay and Lyric Studies) at the Royal Melbourne Institute of Technology.

Nathaniel Stern is an artist and engineer, writer, researcher, and teacher, between the University of Wisconsin-Milwaukee and the University of Johannesburg. His most recent book is *Ecological Aesthetics: artful tactics for humans, nature, and politics* (Dartmouth, 2018).

Bodil Marie Stavning Thomsen works on media, art and philosophy with an emphasis on 'the signaletic material' in film and interfaces. Her recent publications include *Lars von Trier's Renewal of Film 1984-2014: Signal, Pixel, Diagram* (Aarhus University Press, 2018). She is a Professor at School of Communication and Culture, Aarhus University.

Alanna Thain is an Associate Professor and Director of Institute for Gender, Sexuality and Feminist Studies at McGill University, Montreal. She is the author of *Bodies in Time: Suspense, Affect, Cinem*a. (University of Minnesota Press, 2017)

Works Cited

Agamben, Giorgio. *L'uso dei corpi*. Vicenza: Nerri pozza editore, 2014.

Alliez, Éric and Andrew Goffey. "Introduction." *The Guattari Effect*. Eds. Éric Alliez and Andrew Goffey. London: Continuum, 2011. 1-14.

Althusser, Louis. "Ideology and Ideological State Apparatuses." Lenin and Philosophy and Other Essays. Trans. Ben Brewster. New York: Monthly Review Press, 1972.

Anonymous. "Controlling brain cells with sound waves." *Bioengineer.org*. September 18, 2015. http://bioengineer.org/controlling-brain-cells-sound-waves.

Anonymous. *Commune – Exhibition Catalogue*. Sydney: The White Rabbit Gallery, 2014.

Armstrong, Keith. "Towards a Connective and Ecosophical New Media Art Practice". *Intimate Transactions: Art, Exhibition and Interaction within Distributed Network Environments*. Ed. Jillian Hamilton. Brisbane: Australasian CRC for Interaction Design, 2006. 12-35.

Armstrong, Keith. "Intimate Transactions: The Evolution of an Ecosophical Networked Practice." *The Fibreculture Journal* 7 (2005). http://seven.fibreculturejournal.org/fcj-047-intimate-transactions-the-evolution-of-an-ecosophical-networked-practice/.

Artaud, Antonin. *Selected Writings*. Ed. Susan Sontag. Berkeley: University of California Press, 1988.

Blackman, Lisa. "Affect, Relationality and the Problem of Personality." *Theory, Culture & Society* 25.1 (2008): 27–51.

Bak, Per. *How Nature Works: The Science of Self-Organized Criticality*. New York: Oxford University Press, 1997.

Barber, Dan. *The Third Plate: Field Notes on the Future of Food*. New York: Penguin Press, 2014.

Barker, Timothy. *Time and the Digital: Connecting Technology, Aesthetics, and a Process Philosophy of Time*. Dartmouth: Dartmouth Press, 2012.

Bataille, Georges. "Informe." *Documents* 7 (December 1929), p. 382. [Reprinted/translated in: Georges Bataille: Oeuvres Complètes I. Paris: Gallimard, 1970.]

Bataille, Georges. *Visions of Excess. Selected Writings, 1927-1939*. Minneapolis: University of Minnesota Press, 1985.

Bataille, Georges. *The Accursed Share. An Essay on General Economy. Volume 1. Consumption*. Trans. Robert Hurley. New York: Zone Books, 1991.

Bataille, Georges. "Sacrifice, the Festival and the Principles of the Sacred World." *The Bataille Reader.* Eds. Fred Botting and Scott Wilson. Oxford: Blackwell Publishers, 1997.

Beisser, Arnold. "The Paradoxical Theory of Change." *Gestalt Therapy. Now.* Eds. Joen Fagan and Irma Lee Shepherd. New York: Harper Colophon, 1970.

Bennett, Jane. *The Enchantment of Modern Life: Attachments, Crossings and Ethics*. Princeton: Princeton University Press, 2001.

Bennett, Jane. *Vibrant Matter: A Political Ecology of Things*. Durham and London: Duke University Press, 2010.

Berardi, Franco (Bifo). *Félix Guattari: Thought, Friendship and Visionary Cartography.* Trans. and ed. Giuseppina Mecchia and Charles J. Stivale. London: Palgrave Macmillan, 2008.

Henri Bergson (1914), *The problem of personality* http://members3.jcom.home.ne.jp/yoshihara.jya/the_problem_of_personality_1-3.htm

Bergson, Henri. *Creative Evolution*. Translated by Arthur Mitchell. London: Macmillan and Co., 1922.

Bergson, Henri. *The Two Sources of Morality and Religion*. London: Macmillan and Co., 1935.

Bergson, Henri. *Time and Free Will: An Essay on the Immediate Data of Consciousness*. Trans. F.L. Pogson. London: George Allen & Unwin Ltd, 1950.

Bergson, Henri. *Les deux sources de la morale et de la religion*. Paris, PUF, 1967 [1932].

Bergson, Henri. *Mélanges*. Ed. André Robinet. Paris: Presses universitaires de France, 1972.

Bergson, Henri. *Creative Evolution*. Trans. Arthur Mitchell, Mineola: Dover, 1998.

Bergson, Henri. *Key writings*. Eds. Keith Ansell Pearson and John Mullarkey. New York: Continuum, 2002.

Bergson, Henri. *La pensée et le mouvant*. Paris: Quadrige, 2003.

Bergson, Henri. *Laughter: An Essay on the Meaning of the Comic*. Trans. Cloudesley Brereton and Fred Rothwell. Project Gutenberg, 2009.

Bertelsen, Lone. "Matrixial Refrains." *Theory, Culture & Society* 21.1 (February 2004): 121-147.

Bertelsen, Lone. "Affect and Care in Intimate Transactions." *The Fibreculture Journal* 21 (2012). http://twentyone.fibreculturejournal.org/fcj-149-affect-and-care-in-intimate-transactions/#sthash.um6shBql.dpbs.

Biernat, M., Kobrynowicz, D., & Weber, D. "Stereotyping and shifting standards: Some paradoxical effects of cognitive load." *Journal of Applied Social Psychology* 33 (2003): 2060- 2079.

Birringer, Johannes. "Transactivity." *Intimate Transactions: Art, Exhibition and Interaction within Distributed Network Environments*. Ed. Jillian Hamilton. Brisbane: Australasian CRC for Interaction Design, 2006. 106-113.

Bois, Yve-Alain and Rosalind Krauss. *L'Informe. Mode d'Emploi*. Paris: Centre Georges Pompidou, 1996.

Bolter, Jay David and Richard Grusin. *Remediation. Understanding New Media*. Cambridge: MIT Press, 1999.

Bordeleau, Erik. "Bruno Latour and the Miraculous Power of Enunciation." *Breaking the Spell: Speculative Realism Under Discussion*. Eds. Anna Longo and Sarah de Sanctis. Paris: Mimesis International, 2015. 155-167.

Bosteels, Bruno. "From Text to Territory: Félix Guattari's Cartographies of the Unconscious." *Deleuze and Guattari: New Mappings in Politics, Philosophy and Culture*. Eds. Eleanor Kaufman and Kevin Jon Heller. Minneapolis: University of Minnesota Press, 1998: 145-174.

Brunner, Christoph. 'Kon-/Disjunktion'. *Inventionen* 1. Ed. Isabell Lorey, Roberto Nigro, Gerald Raunig. Zürich, Diaphanes, 2011. 128-130.

Brunner, Christoph. "Immediation as Process and Practice of Signaletic Mattering." *Journal of Aesthetics and Culture* 4 (2012).

Brunner, Christoph and Jonas Fritsch. "Interactive Environments as Fields of Transduction." *The Fibreculture Journal* 18 (2011). http://eighteen.fibreculturejournal.org/2011/10/09/fcj-124-interactive-environments-as-fields-of-transduction/.

Brunner, Christoph and Jonas Fritsch. "Kon-/Disjunktion." *Inventionen* 1 (2011): 128-130. Eds. Isabell Lorey, Roberto Nigro, Gerald Raunig. Zürich, Diaphanes.

Brunner, Christopher, Erin Manning and Brian Massumi. "Fields of Potential: On Affective Immediation, Anxiety, and Necessities of Life." Ästhetik Der Existenz: Lebensformen Im Widerstreit. Eds. Elke Bippus, Jörg Huber and Roberto Nigro. Zurich: Edition Voldemeer, 2013. 135-150.

Buchanan, Ian. "The Problem of the Body in Deleuze and Guatarri, Or, What Can a Body Do?" *Body and Society* 3.3 (1997): 73-91.

Bywaters, Malcolm. "Lyndal Jones: Climate Change, Performance and the Avoca Project." *Fusion Journal* 4 (2010).

Cache, Bernard. *Earth Moves: The Furnishing of Territories*. Trans. Anne Boyman. Ed. Michael Speaks. Cambridge: MIT Press, 1995.

Calvino, Italo. *If on a winter's night a traveller.* Orlando, Florida: Horcourt Brace and Co., 1981.

Cariani, Peter. "To Evolve an Ear: Epistemological Implications of Gordon Pask's Electrochemical Devices." *Systems research* 10.3 (1993): 19-33

Cariani, Peter. "Emergence and Creativity." *Art.ficial* 4.0, "Emergência." Eds. Itaú Cultural. Sao Paolo, Brazil: Emoção, 2008.

Chalmers, David J. and Andy Clark. "The Extended Mind." *Philosophy of Mind: Classical and Contemporary Readings*. Ed. David Chalmers. Oxford University Press, 2002.

Clair, Patrick. "True Detective." *Art of the Title*. 2014. http://www.artofthetitle.com/title/true-detective.

Clough, Patricia Ticineto. *AutoAffection: Unconscious Thought in the Age of Technology*. Minneapolis: University of Minnesota Press, 2000.

Colebrook, Claire. "The Secret of Theory." *Deleuze Studies* 4.3 (2010): 287–300.

Collier, John. "Simulating Autonomous Anticipation: The Importance of Dubois' Conjecture." *Biosytems* 91.2 (2008): 346-354.

Combes, Muriel. *Gilbert Simondon and the Philosophy of the Transindividual*. Trans. Thomas Lamarre. Cambridge, MA: MIT Press, 2013.

Connolly, William. *A World of Becoming*. Durham: Duke University Press, 2011.

Corner, John. "Television in Theory." *Media, Culture & Society* 19.2 (1997): 247-262.

Coupland, Douglas. *Marshall McLuhan: You Know Nothing of My Work!* New York: Atlas, 2010.

Cubitt, Sean. "Electric Light and Electricity." *Theory, Culture & Society* 30.7-8 (2013): 309-323.

Cummings, Neil and Marysia Lewandowska. "From Capital to Enthusiasm: An Exhibitionary Practice." *Exhibition Experiments*. Eds. Sharon Macdonald & Paul Basu. Oxford: Blackwell, 2007. 132–153.

Darwin, Charles. *The Formation of Vegetable Mold through the Action of Worms with Observations on Their Habits*. London: John Murray, 1881.

De Brabandere, Nicole. "Experimenting with Affect across Drawing and Choreography." *Body & Society* 22.3 (2016): 103-124.

DeLanda, Manuel. *Intensive Science and Virtual Philosophy*. New York and London: Continuum, 2005.

Deleuze, Gilles. *Foucault*. Trans. Séan Hand. Minneapolis: University of Minnesota Press, 1988.

Deleuze, Gilles. *Cinema 2: The Time-Image*. Trans. Hugh Tomlinson and Robert Caleta. Minneapolis: University of Minnesota Press, 1989.

Deleuze, Gilles. *Logic of Sense*. Trans. Mark Lester with Charles Stivale. Ed. Constantin V. Boundas. New York: Columbia University Press, 1990.

Deleuze, Gilles. *Bergsonism*. Trans. Hugh Tomlinson and Barbara Habberjam. New York: Zone Books, 1991.

Deleuze, Gilles. "Postscript on the Societies of Control." *October* 59 (Winter 1992): 3-7.

Deleuze, Gilles. *The Fold. Leibniz and the Baroque*. Trans. Tom Conley. London: Athlone Press, 1993.

Deleuze, Gilles. *Difference and Repetition*. Trans. Paul Patton. New York: Columbia University Press, 1994a.

Deleuze, Gilles. "What is the Creative Act?" *French Theory in America*. Eds. Sylvène Lotringer and Graham Burchell. New York: Columbia, 1994b.

Deleuze, Gilles. "Mediators." *Negotiations:1972-1990*. Trans. Martin Joughin. New York: Columbia University Press, 1995. 121-134.

Deleuze, Gilles. *Essays Critical and Clinical*. Trans. Daniel W. Smith and Michael A. Greco. Minneapolis: University of Minnesota Press, 1997.

Deleuze, Gilles. *Desert Island and Other Texts 1953–1974*. Trans. Michael Taormina. New York: Semiotext(e), 2004.

Deleuze, Gilles. *Pure Immanence: Essays on A Life*. New York: Zone Books, 2005.

Deleuze, Gilles. *Nietzsche and Philosophy*. Trans. Janis Tomlinson. New York: Continuum, 2006.

Deleuze, Gilles. "Immanence: A Life." *Two Regimes of Madness. Texts and Interviews 1975-1995*. Ed. David Lapoujade. Semiotex(e): New York, 2007: 384-389.

Deleuze, Gilles and Claire Parnet. *Dialogues*. Trans. Hugh Tomlinson and Barbara Hammerjam. London: Athlone, 1987.

Deleuze, Gilles and Félix Guattari. *Anti-Oedipus: Capitalism and Schizophrenia*. Minneapolis: University of Minnesota Press, 1983.

Deleuze, Gilles and Félix Guattari. *Kafka: Towards a Minor Literature*. Trans. Dana Polan. Minneapolis: University of Minnesota Press, 1986.

Deleuze, Gilles and Félix Guattari. *A Thousand Plateaus: Capitalism and Schizophrenia*. Trans. Brian Massumi. Minneapolis and London: University of Minnesota Press, 1987.

Deleuze, Gilles and Félix Guattari. *What is Philosophy?* Trans. Hugh Tomlinson and Graham Burchell. New York: Columbia University Press, 1994.

Delmas-Marty, Mireille. "Le laboratoire chinois." *La Chine et la démocratie*. Eds. Mireille Delmas-Marty and Pierre-Étienne Will. Paris: Fayard, 2007.

Depraz, Natalie. "Temporalité et affection dans les manuscrits tardifs sur la temporalité de Husserl (1929–1935)." *ALTER: Revue de phenomenologie* 2 (1994): 63-86.

Diamanti, Eleonora. "Formation et transformation de la place publique montréalaise." *Formes urbaines : circulation, stockage et transmission de l'expression culturelle à Montréal*. Eds. Will Straw, Annie Gérin and Anouk Bélanger. Montreal: Les éditions esse, 2014. 67-74.

Dieter, Michael. "The Becoming Environmental of Power: Tactical Media After Control." *The Fibreculture Journal* 18 (2011). http://eighteen.fibreculturejournal.org/2011/10/09/fcj-126-the-becoming-environmental-of-power-tactical-media-after-control/.

Dolphijn, Rick and Iris van der Tuin. *New Materialism: Cartographies and Interviews*. Ann Arbor, Michigan: Open Humanities Press, 2012.

Doane, Mary Ann. "Information, Crisis, Catastrophe." *Logics of Television: Essays in Cultural Criticism*. Ed. Patricia Mellencamp. Bloomington: Indiana University Press, 1990. 222-239.

Eco, Umberto. *The Open Work*. Cambridge: Harvard University Press, 1989.

Eco, Umberto. "Interpreting Serials." *The Limits of Interpretation*. Bloomington: Indiana University Press, 1994. 83-100.

Ednie-Brown, Pia. "Architectural Animality: drawings out for a walk." Mixed media, exhibited as part of *Trace: Architectural musings*. Curated by Leonie Matthews & Amanda Alderson. Mundaring Arts Centre, Western Australia, October 3rd - November 9th, 2014.

Ednie-Brown, Pia. "Critical passions building architectural movements toward a radical pedagogy (in 10 steps)." *Inflexions* 8 (2015a): 20-48. http://www.senselab.ca/inflexions/radicalpedagogy/main.html#Ednie-Brown.

Ednie_Brown, Pia. "Can a house be alive?" *TED*x. Public lecture. 2015b. https://www.youtube.com/watch?v=oH-27DNqcO0&list=PLsRNoUx8w3rORCN0KrRaLO7xKt46mCDkf&index=3.

Ednie-Brown, Pia and Mewburn, Inger. "Laughter and the Undeniable Difference Between Us." *Intimate Transactions: Art, Exhibition and Interaction within Distributed Network Environments*. Ed. Jillian Hamilton. Brisbane: Australasian CRC for Interaction Design, 2006: 76-87.

Edwards, Paul N. *A Vast Machine: Computer Models, Climate Data, and the Politics of Global Warming*. Cambridge, MA: MIT Press, 2013.

Engell, Lorenz: "Medientheorien der Medien selbst." *Handbuch Medienwissenschaft*. Ed Jens Schröter. Stuttgart/Weimar: J.B. Metzler, 2014. 207-213.

Erickson, Britta. "Process and Meaning in the Art of Xu Bing." In *Three Installations by Xu Bing*. Madison: Elvehjem Museum of Art, University of Wisconsin-Madison, 1991.

Erickson, Britta. *The Art of Xu Bing: Words without Meaning, Meaning without Words*. Washington, D.C.: Arthur M. Sackler Gallery and Smithsonian Institution; Seattle: University of Washington Press, 2001.

Esposito, Roberto. *Terza Persona*. Torino: Einaudi, 2007.

Esposito, Roberto. *Le persone e le cose*. Torino: Einaudi, 2014.

Ettinger L. Bracha. "Matrix and Metramorphosis." *differences: a Journal of Feminist Cutural Studies* 4.3 (1992): 176-207.

Ettinger L. Bracha. "Woman-Other-Thing: A Matrixial Touch." *Matrix-Borderlines*. Oxford: Museum of Modern Art, (1993): 11-18.

Ettinger L. Bracha. *The Matrixial Gaze*. University of Leeds: Feminist Arts and Histories Network, 1995a.

Ettinger L. Bracha. "Woman as Object a: Between Phantasy and Art." *Journal of Philosophy and the Visual Arts* 6 (1995b): 56-77.

Ettinger L. Bracha. "Trauma and Beauty: Trans-subjectivity in Art." *n.paradoxa* 3 (1999): 15-23.

Ettinger L. Bracha. "From Transference to the Aesthetic Paradigm: A Conversation with Félix Guattari." *A Shock to Thought: Expression After Deleuze and Guattari*. Ed. Brian Massumi. London and New York: Routledge, 2002. 240-245.

Ettinger L. Bracha. *The Matrixial Borderspace*. Ed. Brian Massumi. Minneapolis, London: University of Minnesota Press, 2006.

Ettinger L. Bracha. "Fragilization and Resistance." *Studies in The Maternal* 1.2 (2009): 1-31.

Ettinger L. Bracha. "Uncanny Awe, Uncanny Compassion and Matrixial Transjectivity beyond Uncanny Anxiety." *French Literature Series* 38 (2011): 1-30.

Evans, Dylan. *An Introductory Dictionary of Lacanian Psychoanalysis*. London and New York: Routledge, 1996.

Faumont, Serge, Rondeau, Gary, Thiele, Todd R., et al. "An Image-Free Opto-Mechanical System for Creating Virtual Environments and Imaging Neuronal Activity in Freely Moving Caenorhabditis elegans." *PLoS ONE* 6.9 (2011).

Feneuil, Anthony. *Bergson: mystique et philosophie*, Paris : PUF, 2011.

Feuer, Jane. "The Concept of Live Television: Ontology as Ideology." *Regarding Television:Critical Approaches – An Anthology*. Ed. E. Ann Kaplan. Los Angeles: The American Film Institute, 1983. 12-22.

Forsythe, William. "Choreographic Objects." http://www.williamforsythe.de/essay.html.

Foucault, Michel. 1977. "Nietzsche, Genealogy, History." In Donald F. Bouchard, ed., *Language, Memory, Counter-Practice*. Ithaca, NY: Cornell University Press. 139–164.

Foucault, Michel. 1979. *Discipline and Punish: The Birth of the Prison*. Trans. Alan Sheridan. New York: Vintage.

Frayling, C. "Research in Art and Design". *Royal College of Art Research Papers* 1.1 (1993): 1-5.

Frazer, John Hamilton. "The Cybernetics of Architecture: A Tribute to the Contribution of Gordon Pask." *Kybernetes* 30.5-6 (2001): 641-651.

Fritsch, Jonas. "Affective Experience as a Theoretical Foundation for Interaction Design." PhD Dissertation presented to the Faculty of Humanities, Aarhus University. 2011.

Fritsch, Jonas, Breinbjerg, M. & Basballe, D. "Ekkomaten: Exploring the Echo as a Design Fiction Concept." *Journal of Digital Creativity* 24.1 (2013): 60-74.

Fritsch, Jonas, Pold Soren Bro, Vestergaard, Lasse Steenbock Vestergaard and Melissa Lucas. "Ink – Designing for Performative Literary Interactions." *Journal of Personal and Ubiquitous Computing* 18.7 (2014): 1551-1556.

Fritsch, Jonas. and O. S. Iversen (2014): "Designing for Experience: Scaffolding the Emergence of a Design Ecology." In *Enterprising Initiatives in the Experience Economy: Transforming Social Worlds, Routledge Studies in Entrepreneurship*. Eds. Britta Tim Knudsen, Dorthe Refslund Christensen and Per Blenker. London: Routledge, 2014. 226-244.

Fuller, Matthew. *Media Ecologies: Materialist Energies in Art and Technoculture*. Cambridge, MA: MIT Press, 2005.

Fuller, Matthew and Andrew Goffey. *Evil Media*. Cambridge, MA: MIT Press, 2012.

Funder, Anna. *The Girl with the Dogs*. Penguin Australia, 2015.

Gallagher, Shaun. "Protention, Schizophrenia, and Gesture." *Interacting Bodies: Corps en Interaction*. Ecole normale supérieure Lettres et Sciences humaines Lyon-France, June 15-18 2005.

Galloway, Alexander, Eugene Thacker and McKenzie Wark. *Excommunication: Three Inquiries in Media and Mediation*. Chicago: Chicago University Press, 2013.

Gardner, Howard. *The Mind's New Science: A History of the Cognitive Revolution*. New York: Basic Books, 1987.

Genosko, Gary. *Felix Guattari: An Aberrant Introduction*. London: Continuum, 2002.

Genosko, Gary. *Félix Guattari: A Critical Introduction*. London: Pluto Press, 2009.

Gidal, Peter. *Structural Film Anthology*. London: British Film Institute, 1978.

Gil, José. *Metamorphoses of the Body*. Trans. Stephen Muecke. Minneapolis: University of Minnesota Press, 1998.

Gilbert, Jeremy. *Common Ground: Democracy and Collectivity in an Age of Individualism*. London: Pluto, 2013.

Madeline Gins and Arakawa. *The Architectural Body*. Tuscaloosa: University of Alabama Press, 2002.

Goffey, Andrew. "Abstract Experience." *Theory Culture Society* 25.4 (2008): 15-30.

Golson, Jordon. "This Helmet Will Make F-35 Pilots Missile-Slinging Cyborgs." *Wired* (September 14, 2015). http://www.wired.com/2015/09/helmet-will-make-f-35-pilots-missile-slinging-cyborgs/.

Goodman, Steven. *Sonic Warfare: Sound, Affect and the Ecology of Fear*. Cambridge, MA: MIT Press, 2010.

Gould, Stephen Jay and Elizabeth S. Vrba. "Exaption: A Missing Term in the Science of Form." *Paleobiology* 8.1 (1982): 4-15.

Govan, Michael. *James Turrell: Seeing Yourself See*. Munich: Prestel, 2013.

Graeber, David. *Debt: The First 5,000 Years*. New York: Melville House, 2012.

Green, Nick. "On Gordon Pask." *Kybernetes* 30.5-6 (2001): 673-682.

Greenfield, Adam. *Against the Smart City (The city is here for you to use. Book 1).* Kindle Edition. Do Projects, 2013.

Grosz, Elizabeth. *Volatile Bodies: Toward a Corporeal Feminism.* Sydney: Allen and Unwin, 1994.

Groys, Boris. *Art Power.* Cambridge, MA: MIT Press, 2008.

Groys, Boris. "Comrades of Time." *e-flux Journal* 11 (December 2009): 1–11.

Grusin, Richard. *Premediation: Affect and Mediality After 9/11.* London: Palgrave Macmillan, 2010.

Grusin, Richard. "Radical Mediation." *Critical Inquiry* 42.1 (Autumn 2015): 124-148.

Guattari, Félix. *Chaosmosis. An ethico-aesthetic paradigm.* Trans. Paul Bains and Julian Pefanis. Bloomington: Indiana University Press, 1995.

Guattari, Félix. "Ritornellos and Existential Affects." *The Guattari Reader.* Ed. Gary Genosko. Oxford: Blackwell, 1996: 158–171.

Guattari, Félix. *The Three Ecologies.* Trans. Ian Pindar and Paul Sutton. London and New York: Continuum, 2008.

Guattari, Félix. *Chaosophy: Texts and Interviews 1972-1977.* Eds. Sylvere Lotringer. Trans. David L. Sweet, Jarred Becker, and Taylor Adkins. Los Angeles: Semiotext(e), 2009.

Guattari, Félix. *The Machinic Unconscious: Essays in Schizoanalysis.* Trans. Taylor Adkins. New York: Semiotext(e), 2010.

Guattari, Félix. *Schizoanalytic Cartographies.* Trans. Andrew Goffey. London: Bloomsbury, 2012.

Halewood, Michael. "A.N. Whitehead, Information and Social Theory." *Theory, Culture & Society* 22(6) (2005a): 73–94.

Halewood, Michael. "On Whitehead and Deleuze: The Process of Materiality." *Configurations* 13.1 (2005b): 57-76.

Halewood, Michael. "Language, the Body and the Problem of Signification." *Butler on Whitehead: On the Occasion.* Eds. Roland Faber and Michael Halewood. New York: Lexington Books, 2012: 176-195.

Hamilton, Jillian. "A Reformation of Space: Intimate Transactions in Art and Distributed Communication." *Intimate Transactions: Art, Exhibition and Interaction within Distributed Network Environments*. Ed. Jillian Hamilton. Brisbane: Australasian CRC for Interaction Design, 2006: 116-129.

Hamilton, Jillian and Lavery, Peter. "Introduction". *Intimate Transactions: Art, Exhibition and Interaction within Distributed Network Environments. Ed.* in Jillian Hamilton. Brisbane: Australasian CRC for Interaction Design, 2006. 2-11.

Hansen, Mark. "Engineering Pre-individual Potentiality: Technics, Transindividuation, and 21st Century Media." *SubStance* 41.3 (2012): 32-59.

Hansen, Mark. *Feed-Forward: On the Future of Twenty-First-Century Media*. Chicago: Chicago University Press, 2015.

Hansen, Miriam. "Early Cinema, Late Cinema: Transformations of the Public Sphere." *Screen* 34.3 (1993): 134-152.

Haraway, Donna. *Modest_Witness@Second_Millennium.FemaleMan_meets_OncoMouse: Feminism and Technoscience*. New York and London: Routledge, 1997.

Haraway, Donna and Thyrza Nichols Goodeve. *How Like a Leaf: An Interview with Donna Haraway*. London: Routledge, 2013.

Hardt, Michael. "The Common in Communism." *Rethinking Marxism. A Journal of Economics, Culture and Society* 22.3 (August 2010): 346-356.

Harman, Graham. *Tool-Being: Heidegger and the Metaphysics of Objects*. Open Court Publishing, 2002.

Harney, Stefano. "Hapticality in the Undercommons or From Operations Management to Black Ops.". *CuMMA Papers*, 2013. https://cummastudies.files.wordpress.com/2013/08/cumma-papers-9.pdf.

Harney, Stephano and Fred Moten. *The Undercommons: Fugitive Planning and Black Studies*. Wivenhoe, New York and Port Watson: Minor Compositions, 2013.

Harrist, Robert E., Jr. "Background Stories: Xu Bing's Art of Transformation." In Reiko Tomii et al., *Xu Bing*, London: Albion. 2011.

Hayek, Friedrich. "The Use of Knowledge in Society." *American Economic Review* 35.4 (1945): 519-30.

Hayles, N. Katherine. *How we became posthuman: Virtual bodies in cybernetics, literature, and informatics*. Chicago: University of Chicago Press, 2008.

Heaven, Douglas. "The Obsessioneers." *New Scientist* 2971 (2014): 38-41.

Heidegger, Martin. *Being and Time*. Trans. Joan Stambaugh. Albany: University of New York Press, 2010.

Herzongenrath, Bernd. "Introduction." *An [Un]Likely Alliance: Thinking Environment[s] with Deleuze|Guattari*. Ed. Bernd Herzogenrath. Newcastle Upon Tyne: Cambridge Scholars Press, 2008. 1-22.

Hoghe, Raimund. " 'Walzer.' Fragen, Themen, Stichpunkte aus den Proben." *Theatergeschichten von Raimund Hoghe*. Eds. Raimund Hoghe and Pina Bausch. Frankfurt am Main: Suhrkamp, 1986. 84–89.

Holland, Eugene. "Deleuze and Psychoanalysis". The *Cambridge Companion to Gilles Deleuze*. Eds. Daniel W. Smith and Henry Somers-Hall. Cambridge: Cambridge University Press, 2012. 307-336.

Hollnagel, Erik and David D. Woods. *Joint Cognitive Systems: Foundations of Cognitive Systems Engineering*. London: Taylor and Francis, 2005.

Hongisto, Ilona. "Documentary Imagination. The disappeared, the clue and the photograph." *Journal of Scandinavian Cinema* 3.1 (2013): 49–63.

Hongisto, Ilona. *Soul of the Documentary: Framing, Expression, Ethics*. Amsterdam: Amsterdam University Press, 2015.

Hornblow, Michael. *Sponging the Chair: Diagramming Affect through Architecture and Performance*. PhD Dissertation, Royal Melbourne Institute of Technology, 2013.

Hornblow, Michael. "O'megaVille: Excursions in Planetary Urbanism." International Symposium on Electronic Art, 2015a. Conference Presentation. http://isea2015.org/publications/proceedings-of-the-21st-international-symposium-on-electronic-art/

Hornblow, Michael. "A Sahara in the Head: The Problem of Landing." *Inflexions* 8 (2015b): 222-238. http://www.senselab.ca/inflexions/radicalpedagogy/main.html#Hornblow

Horsefield, Craigie. *Relations*. North Sydney: Museum of Contemporary Art, 2007.

Huhn, Rosi. "Moving Emissions and Hollow Spots in the Field of Vision." *Matrix-Borderlines*. Oxford: Museum of Modern Art, 1993: 5-10.

Hyppolite, Jean. *Logic and Existence*. Trans. Leonard Lawlor and Amit Sen. Albany: State University of New York Press, 1987.

Ivakhiv, Adrian J. *Ecologies of the Moving Image: Cinema, Affect, Nature*. Waterloo: Wilfred Laurier Press, 2013.

Iaconesi, Salvatore. "Conflict is Transgression." *Art is Open Source* (2015). http://www.artisopensource.net/network/artisopensource/2015/06/08/conflict-and-transgression/#.VYFEnaLnyuU.facebook

Jacobs, Jane. *The Death and Life of Great American Cities*, New York: Vintage Books, 1992.

Jacobs, Jane. *The Nature of Economies*. New York: The Modern Library, 2000

James, William. *The Will to Believe and Other Essays in Popular Philosophy*. New York: Longmans, Green, and co., 1912.

James, William. *Principles of Psychology*, vol. 1. New York : Dover, 1950a.

James, William. 1950b. *Principles of Psychology*, vol. 2. New York : Dover.

James, William. *The Meaning of Truth: A Sequel to Pragmatism*. New York: Greenwood, 1986.

James, William. *Essays in Radical Empiricism*. Lincoln: University of Nebraska Press, 1996a.

James, William. 1996b. *A Pluralistic Universe*. Lincoln : University of Nebraska Press.

Janesick, James. *Scientific charge-coupled devices*. Bellingham: SPIE Press, 2001.

Jones, Judith. *Intensity: An Essay in Whiteheadian Ontology*. Nashville: Vanderbilt University Press, 1998.

Jullien, François. *In Praise of Blandness. Proceeding from Chinese Thought and Aesthetics*. Trans. Paula M. Varsano. New York: Zone Books, 2004.

Jung, Heekyoung, Erik Stolterman, Will Ryan, Yonya Thompson, and Martin Siegel. "Toward a Framework for Ecologies of Artifacts: Digital Artifacts Interconnected within a Personal Life?" *NordiCHI 2008: Using Bridges*, 18-22. 2008.

Kandel, Eric. *In Search of Memory: The Emergence of a New Science of Mind*. New York: W. W. Norton, 2007.

Kaptelinin, Victor and Liam. J. Bannon. "Interaction Design Beyond the Product: Creating Technology-Enhanced Activity Spaces." *Human-Computer Interaction* 27.3 (2012): 277–309.

Kaufman, Eleanor. *Deleuze, The Dark Precursor: Dialectic, Structure, Being.* Baltimore: Johns Hopkins University Press, 2012.

Kember, Sarah and Joanna Zylinska. *Life after New Media: Mediation as a Vital Process*. Cambridge, MA: MIT Press, 2014.

Kjeldskov Jesper. *Designing Mobile Interactions: The Continual Convergence of Form and Context, Volume I and II*. PhD Dissertation. Aalborg University, Department of Computer Science. 2013.

Klarer, Mario. "Putting Television 'Aside': Novel Narration in House of Cards." *New Review of Film and Television Studies* 12.2 (2014): 203-220.

Kohn, Eduardo. "Natural engagements and ecological aesthetics among the Avila Runa of Amazonian Ecuador." *PhD Thesis*, University of Wisconsin, Madison. 2002.

Krippendorff, Klaus. *The Semantic Turn: A New Foundation for Design*. Boca Raton, London and New York: Taylor & Francis, CRC Press, 2006.

Langer, Susanne. *Feeling and Form: A Theory of Art Developed from Philosophy in a New Key*. New York: Charles Scribner's Sons, 1953.

Lapoujade, David. "From Transcendental Empiricism to Worker Nomadism: William James." *Pli* 9 (2000): 190-199.

Lapoujade, David. *Puissances du temps: versions de Bergson*. Paris: Minuit, 2010.

Lapoujade, David. *Powers of Time*. Helsinki/São Paolo: n-1 publications, 2013.

Latour, Bruno, Pablo Jensen, Tommaso Venturini, Sebastian Grauwin and Dominique Bouiller. "The Whole is Always Smaller Than Its Parts. A Digital Test of Gabriel Tarde's Monads." *The British Journal of Sociology* 63.4 (December 2012): 590-615.

Lazzarato Maurizio. *Videophilosophie. Zeitwahrnehmung im Postfordismus*. Berlin: b_books, 2002.

Lazzarato, Maurizio. "Video, Flows and Real Time." *Art and the Moving Image: A Critical Reader.* Ed. Tanya Leighton. London: Tate Publishing, 2007: 283–85.

Lazzarato, Maurizio. *The Making of Indebted Man: An Essay on the Neoliberal Condition*. Trans. Joshua David Jordan, 2012.

Levy, Malcolm. "Other-frames and the Moving Image." Unpublished essay.

Lewandowska, Marysia. "Museum commons. Research driven art practice and the public function of archives, collections and exhibitions." Keynote lecture at the *NECS* Conference, Lodz, Poland (20 June 2015). https://www.youtube.com/watch?v=aKCBdmmi9G4&feature=youtu.be

Libet, Benjamin, and Curtis Gleason, Elwood Wright, Dennis Pearl. "Time of Conscious Intention to Act in Relation to Onset of Cerebral Activity (Readiness-Potential). The Unconscious Initiation of a Freely Voluntary Act." *Neurophysiology of Consciousness*. Contemporary Neuroscientists Series. 1983. 249-268.

Lingis, Aphonso. *Violence and Splendor*. Illinois: Northwest University Press, 2011.

Liu Yuedi. "Calligraphic Expression in Contemporary Chinese Art: Xu Bing's Pioneer Experiment." *Subversive Strategies in Contemporary Chinese Art*. Ed. Mary Wiseman and Yuedi Liu. Brill, 2011.

Lorange, Astrid. *How Reading Is Written: A Brief Index to Gertrude Stein*. Middletown, CT: Wesleyan University Press, 2014.

Lorraine, Tamsin. "Oedipus and the Anoedipal Transsexual." *Between the Psyche and the Social: Psychoanalytic Social Theory*. Eds. Kelly Oliver and Steve Edwin. Boston: Rowman and Littlefield, 2002: 3-18.

Lotti, Laura. "'Making sense of power': Repurposing Gilbert Simondon's philosophy of individuation for a mechanist approach to capitalism (by way of François Laruelle)." *Platform: Journal of Media and Communication* 6 (2015): 22-33.

MacKenzie, Adrian. *Transductions: Bodies and Machines at Speed*. London: Continuum, 2002.

Malabou, Catherine. *From Sorrow to Indifference*. Provost's Lecture Series, Stony Brook University. October 22, 2013. https://www.youtube.com/watch?v=KoAd1lQ1bXM.

Manning, Erin. *Relationscapes. Movement, Art, Philosophy*. Cambridge and New York: The MIT Press, 2009a.

Manning, Erin. "Propositions for the Verge: William Forsythe's Choreographic Objects." *Inflexions* 2 (2009b). http://www.inflexions.org/n2_manninghtml.html.

Manning, Erin. "7 Propositions for the Impossibility of Isolation or, the Radical Empiricism of the Network." *eipcp: european institute for progressive cultural policies* (January 2011). http://eipcp.net/transversal/0811/manning/en. Eipcp 2011.

Manning, Erin. *Always More Than One: Individuation's Dance*. Durham and London: Duke University Press, 2013.

Manning, Erin. "Weather Patterns, or How Minor Gestures Entertain the Environment." *Complex Ubiquity Effects: Individuating, Situating, Eventualizing*. Eds. Jay David Bolter Ulrick Ekman, Lily Diaz, Morten Sondergaard, Maria Engberg. New York: Routledge. 2015.

Manning, Erin. *The Minor Gesture*. Durham: Duke University Press, 2016.

Manning, Erin. Forthcoming. "What Things Do When They Shape Each Other." *For a Pragmatics of the Useless,* Duke University Press.

Manning, Erin and Brian Massumi. "For a Pragmatics of the Useless: Propositions for Thought" (2013). https://www.youtube.com/watch?v=Mp5REJAi20o

Manning, Erin and Brian Massumi. *Thought in the Act, Passages in the Ecology of Experience*. Durham: Duke University Press, 2014.

Mason, Matt. *The Pirate's Dilemma. How Youth Culture is Reinventing Capitalism*. New York: Free Press, 2008.

Massumi, Brian. *A User´s Guide to Capitalism and Schizophrenia*. Cambridge and London: MIT Press, 1992.

Massumi, Brian. "The Autonomy of Affect." *Cultural Critique* 31 (Autumn 1995): 83-109.

Massumi, Brian. *Parables for the Virtual: Movement, Affect, Sensation*. Duke University Press, 2002.

Massumi, Brian. "Fear (The Spectrum Said)" *Positions* 13.1 (2005): 31-48.

Massumi, Brian. "National Enterprise Emergency. Steps Toward an Ecology of Powers." *Theory, Culture, and Society* 26.6 (2009): 153-186.

Massumi, Brian. "On Critique." *Inflexions* 4 (November 2010): 337-340. http://www.inflexions.org/n4_t_massumihtml.html

Massumi, Brian. *Semblance and Event. Activist Philosophy and the Occurent Arts*. Cambridge: MIT, 2011.

Massumi, Brian. *What Animals Teach Us about Politics*. Durham: Duke University Press, 2014.

Massumi, Brian. *Ontopower: Wars, Powers, and the State of Perception*. Durham: Duke University Press, 2015a.

Massumi, Brian. *Politics of Affect*. Cambridge: Polity Press, 2015b.

Massumi, Brian. *The Power at the End of the Economy*. Durham: Duke University Press, 2015c.

Massumi, Brian and Joel McKim. "Of Microperception and Micropolitics An Interview with Brian Massumi." *Inflexions* 3 (2008) http://www.inflexions.org/n3_massumihtml.html

Massumi, Brian, Jason Nguyen and Mark Davis: "Interview [with Brian Massumi]". *Manifold. Forms of Time* 2 (2008): 17-30.

Massumi, Brian and Mary Zournazi. "Navigating Moments: A Conversation with Brian Massumi." *Hope: New Philosophies for Change*. Ed. Mary Zournazi. Sydney: Pluto Press, 2002: 210-24.

Maturana, Humberto and Francisco Varela. *Autopoiesis and Cognition: The Realisation of the Living*. 1981.

Mauss, Marcel. *The Gift. Forms and Functions of Exchange in Archaic Societies*. Trans. Ian Cunnison. Mansfield Centre: Martino Publishing, 2011.

McKenzie, Scott. *Screening Québec: Québécois Moving Images, National Identity, and the Public Sphere*, Manchester: Manchester UP, 2004.

Meillassoux, Quentin. 2010. *After Finitude: An Essay on the Necessity of Contingency*. Trans. Ray Brassier. London: Bloomsbury.

Mittell, Jason. "Narrative Complexity in Contemporary American Television." *The Velvet Light Trap* 58 (2006): 29–40.

Mollison, Bill. *Permaculture, a Designer's Manual*. Canada: Tagari Publications, 1999.

Monbiot, George. *Feral: Rewilding the Land, Sea and Human Life*. Chicago: Chicago Press, 2014.

Moten, Fred and Adam Fitzgerald. "An Interview with Fred Moten: In Praise of Harold Bloom, Collaboration and Book Fetishes." *Literary Hub* (August, 2015). http://lithub.com/an-interview-with-fred-moten-pt-i/.

Munster, Anna. *An Aesthesia of Networks. Conjunctive Experience in Art and Technology*. Cambridge and London: MIT Press, 2013.

Munster, Anna. "Tuning in to the Signaletic: experiements with the imperceptible of real time." Keynote Address, *Tuning Speculaton III*. Toronto Canada, November 20-22, 2015.

Murphie, Andrew. "Putting the Virtual back into VR." *A Shock to Thought: Expression in the Philosophy of Gilles Deleuze and Félix Guattari*. Ed. Brian Massumi. London: Routledge, 2002: 188-214.

Murphie, Andrew. "Electronicas: Differential Media and Proliferating, Transient Worlds." *Melbourne DAC, the 5th International Digital Arts and Culture Conference*. Proceedings, 2003. 144-154.

Murphie, Andrew. "The World as Clock: The Network Society and Experimental Ecologies." *Topia: Canadian Journal of Cultural Studies*. Spring (2004): 117-139.

Murphie, Andrew. "Differential Life, Perception and the Nervous Elements: Whitehead, Bergson and Virno on the Technics of Living." *Culture Machine* 7 (2005). http://www.culturemachine.net/index.php/cm/article/view/32/39.

Murphie, Andrew. "Deleuze, Guattari and Neuroscience." *Deleuze, Science and the Force of the Virtual*. Ed. Peter Gaffney. Minneapolis: University of Minnesota Press, 2010: 330-367.

Murphie, Andrew. "Hacking the aesthetic: David Haines and Joyce Hinterding's new ecologies of signal." *Journal of Aesthetics and Culture*. 8.1 (2012).

Murphie, Andrew. "Convolving Signals: thinking the performance of computational processes", *Performance Paradigm*, 9 (2013): 1-21. http://www.performanceparadigm.net/wp-content/uploads/2013/12/murphie-andrew_convolving_signals_2.pdf.

Murphie, Andrew. "Making Sense: The Transformation of Documentary by Digital and Networked Media." *Studies in Documentary Film* 8.3 (2014): 188-204.

Nakatani, Hajime. "Imperious Griffonage: Xu Bing and the Graphic Regime." *Art Journal* 68. 3 (Fall 2009): 6-29.

Nancy, Jean-Luc. *Being Singular Plural*. Stanford, CA: Stanford University Press, 2000.

Nardi, Bonnie. A. and O'Day, Vicki. L. *Information Ecologies: Using technology with Heart*. MIT Press: Cambridge, MA, 1999.

Navon, David. "From Pink Elephants to Pyschosomatic disorders: Paradoxical Effects in Cognition." *Psycholoquy* 5.36 (1994). http://www.cogsci.ecs.soton.ac.uk/cgi/psyc/newpsy?5.36

Nelson, Elissa. "Windows into the Digital World: Distributor Strategies and Consumer Choice in an Era of Connected Viewing." *Connected Viewing: Selling, Streaming, & Sharing Media in the Digital Era*. Eds. Jennifer Holt and Kevin Sanson. New York and London: Routledge, 2013. 62-78.

"Neurons in human skin perform advanced calculations." *ScienceDaily*. September 1, 2014. http://www.sciencedaily.com/releases/2014/09/140901090301.htm.

Newfield, Christopher. "Corporate Open Source. Intellectual Property and The Struggle Over Value." *Radical Philosophy. Philosophy Journal of the Independent Left* 181 (September-October 2013): 6-11. http://www.radicalphilosophy.com/commentary/corporate-open-source

Newman, Michael Z. and Elana Levine. *Legitimating Television: Media Convergence and Cultural Status*. New York: Routledge, 2012.

Nguyen, Jason and Mark Davis. "In dialogue with Brian Massumi." *Manifold Magazine* 3 (Fall 2008): 9-18.

Nietzsche, Friedrich. *Thus Spoke Zarathustra: A Book for Everyone and Nobody*. Trans. Graham Parkes. Oxford: Oxford University Press, 2008.

Northwestern University. "Conventional wisdom of how neurons operate challenged: Axons can work in reverse." *ScienceDaily*. February 19, 2011. http://www.sciencedaily.com/releases/2011/02/110217171344.htm.

O'Neill, Lisa. "Placing the Participant in the Performing Role". *Intimate Transactions: Art, Exhibition and Interaction within Distributed Network Environments*. Ed. Jillian Hamilton. Brisbane: Australasian CRC for Interaction Design, 2006. 36-43.

Parikka, Jussi. *Insect Media: An Archeology of Animals and Technology*. Minneapolis: University of Minnesota Press, 2010.

Parikka,Jusi. "Media Ecologies and Imaginary Media: Transversal Expansions, Contractions, and Foldings." *The Fibreculture Journal*, 17 (2011). http://seventeen.fibreculturejournal.org/fcj-116-media-ecologies-and-imaginary-media-transversal-expansions-contractions-and-foldings/

Parikka, Jussi. "The Geology of Media." *The Atlantic*. October 11, 2013. http://www.theatlantic.com/technology/archive/2013/10/the-geology-of-media/280523/.

Parikka, Jussi. *The Anthrobscene*. Minneapolis: University of Minnesota Press, 2014.

Parisi, Luciana. "Symbiotic Architecture: Prehending Digitality." *Theory, Culture & Society* 26.2-3 (2009a): 346-374.

Parisi, Luciana. "Technoecologies of Sensation." *Deleuze|Guattari & Ecology*. Ed. Bernd Herzogenrath. London: Palgrave, 2009b: 182-199.

Parisi, Luciana. *Contagious Architecture: Computation, Aesthetics and Space*. Cambridge, MA: MIT Press, 2013.

Parisi, Luciana and Steve Goodman. "Extensive Continuum: Towards a Rhythmic Anarchitecture." *Inflexions* 2 (2009). http://www.inflexions.org/n2_parisigoodmanhtml.html.

Parisi, Luciana and Stamatia Portanova. "Soft Thought (in Architecture and Choreography)." *Computational Culture* 1 (2011). http://computationalculture.net/article/soft-thought>.

Parr, Adrian. "Deterritorialization /Reterritorialization" in *The Deleuze Dictionary*. ed. Parr, Adrian. Edinburgh University Press: Edinburgh, 2005.

Peirce, Charles Sanders. *Philosophical Writings of Peirce*. New York: Dover Publications, 1955.

Peirce, Charles. *The Essential Peirce, Volume 1: Selected Philosophical Writings (1867–1893)*. Eds. Nathan Houser, Christian J.W. Kloesel. Bloomington: Indiana University Press, 1992a

Peirce, C. S.. *Reasoning and the Logic of Things*. Cambridge: Harvard University Press, 1992b.

Peirce, C.S. *Pragmatism as a Principle and Method of Right Thinking: The 1903 Lectures on Pragmatism*. Albany: State University of New York Press, 1997.

Peirce, Charles Sanders. *Collected Papers of Charles Sanders Peirce, Volumes I and II: Principles of Philosophy and Elements of Logic (Volume II)*. Eds. Charles Hartshorne, Paul Weiss. Cambridge, MA: Belknap Press (Harvard University Press), 2009.

Pelbart, Peter Pál. *Cartography of Exhaustion: Nihilism Inside Out*. Trans. Hortencia Santos Lencastre. Helsinki and São Paulo: n-1 publications, 2013.

Peters, John Durham. *The Marvelous Clouds: Towards a Philosophy of Elemental Media*. Chicago: Chicago University Press, 2015.

Phillips, Justy. *Scoreography: Compose-with a hole in the heart!* PhD Dissertation. RMIT University, Melbourne. 2014.

Poniewozik, James. "It's Not TV. It's Arrested Development." *Time* 181.19 (May 20, 2013): http://content.time.com/time/magazine/article/0,9171,2143009,00.html

Poniewozik, James. "Veronica Mars Rising. A Fan Revival Proves You Can Go Home Again, Kind Of." *Time*. (March 24, 2014): 56.

Portanova, Stamatia. *Moving without a Body: Digital Philosophy and Choreographic Thoughts*. Cambridge, Massachusetts, London: MIT Press, 2013.

Pradeep, Kumar. 2011. "CCD vs CMOS." Classle, May 7. https://www.classle.net. Accessed 12/22/2015.

Prigogine, Ilya. *From Being to Becoming: Time and Complexity in the Physical Sciences*. San Francisco: Freeman and Co., 1980.

Prigogine, Ilya and Isabelle Stengers. *The End of Certainty: Time, Chaos and the New Laws of Nature*. New York, London, Toronto, Sydney and Singapore: The Free Press, 1996.

Putnam, Hilary. 1994. "Peirce's Continuum." In Kenneth L. Kettner, ed., *Peirce and Contemporary Thought: Philosophical Inquiries*. New York: Fordham University Press. 1-24.

Quaranta, Domenico. "The Postmedia Perspective". *Rhizome Blog*. January 12, 2011. https://www.rhizome.org/editorial/2011/jan/12/the-postmedia-perspective/

Rainer, Yvonne. "Some Retrospective Notes on a Dance for 10 People and 12 Mattresses Called 'Parts of Some Sextets,' Performed at the Wadsworth Atheneum, Hartford, Connecticut, and Judson Memorial Church, New York, in March, 1965." *The Tulane Drama Review* 10.2 (1965): 168.

Ricoeur, Paul. *Time and Narrative (Volume 1)*. Chicago: University of Chicago Press, 1990.

Rifkin, Jeremy. *The European Dream: How Europe's Vision of the Future Is Quietly Eclipsing the American Dream*. New York: Tarcher, 2005.

Riquier, Camille. "Bergson et le problème de la personnalité : la personne dans tous ses états." *Les études philosophiques* 81 (2007): 193-214.

Robbert, Adam. "Speculative Ecology: Matter, Media, and Mind." *CIIS Founders Symposium*. San Francisco CA. May 4, 2005. Conference Paper.

Robbert, Adam. "Earth Aesthetics: Knowledge and Media Ecologies." *Knowledge Ecology*. 2013a. http://knowledge-ecology.com/2013/07/14/earth-aesthetics-knowledge-and-media-ecologies-3/.

Robbert, Adam. "Geocentric Media Ecology." *Knowledge Ecology*. 2013b. http://knowledge-ecology.com/2013/10/14/geocentric-media-ecology/.

Roberston, Robin. "Some-thing from No-thing: G Spencer-Brown's Laws of Form". *Cybernetics and Human Knowing* 6.4 (April 1999): 43-55.

Rocha, Luis Mateus. "Adaptive Recommendation and Open-Ended Semiosis." *Kybernetes* 30.5/6 (2001): 821-854.Ume

Rowe, Colin. *The Mathematics of the Ideal Villa and Other Essays*. Cambridge, London: MIT Press 1988.

Schneider, Michael. "*Arrested Development* Creator Mitch Hurwitz Has Created a 22-Episode Season 4 Remix." *IndieWire*. July 27, 2016. http://www.indiewire.com/2016/07/arrested-development-creator-mitch-hurwitz-reedits-season-4-netflix-1201710496/ Accessed on October 3, 2017.

Schüll, Natasha Dow. *Addicted by Design: Machine Gambling in Las Vegas*. Princeton: Princeton University Press, 2012.

Sehgal, Melanie. "Wo anfangen? Wie überschreiten? William James und die Phänomenologie." *Journal Phänomenologie. Phänomenologie und Pragmatismus* 32 (2009): 9-20.

Serres, Michel. *The Birth of Physics*. Trans. Jack Hawkes. Manchester, UK: Clinamen Press, 2001.

Sha, Xin Wei. *Poiesis and enchantment in topological matter*. Cambridge, MA: MIT Press, 2013.

Shannon, Claude Elwood. "A mathematical theory of communication." *ACM SIGMOBILE Mobile Computing and Communications Review* 5.1 (2001): 3-55.

Shaviro, Steven. *Without Criteria: Kant, Whitehead, Deleuze, and Aesthetics*. Cambridge, MA: MIT Press, 2009.

Shaviro, Steven. *The Universe of Things*. Minneapolis: University of Minnesota Press, 2014.

Shaviro, Steven. *No Speed Limit: Three Essays on Accelerationism*. Minneapolis: Minnesota University Press, 2015.

Shouse, Eric. "Feeling, Emotion, Affect." *Media Culture Journal, Queensland University of Technology* 8.6 (2005). http://journal.media-culture.org.au/0512/03-shouse.php

Seising, Rudolf and Veronica Sanz. *Soft Computing in Humanities and Social Sciences*. New York: Springer, 2011.

Simondon, Gilbert. *On the Mode of Existence of Technical Objects*. Trans. Ninian Mellamphy. London, ON: The University of Western Ontario. 1980.

Simondon, Gilbert. "The Genesis of the Individual." In *Incorporations*. Eds. Jonathan Crary and Sanford Kwinter. Trans. Mark Cohen and Sanford Kwinter. 297-319. New York: Zone Books, 1992.

Simondon, Gilbert. "Form and Matter." Trans. Taylor Adkins. 2007. https://fractalontology.wordpress.com/2007/10/19/translation-simondon-completion-of-section-i-chapter-1-the-individual-and-its-physico-biological-genesis/

Simondon, Gilbert. "The Position of the Problem of Ontogenesis." *Parrhesia* 7 (2009): 4-16.

Smith, R., Iversen, O. S., Hjermitslev, T. and Borup, A. "Towards an Ecological Inquiry in Child-Computer Interaction." *IDC: Proceedings of the 12th Inter- action Design and Children conference*. New York: ACM, 2013. 183–92.

Smithson, Robert, and Jack D. Flam. *Robert Smithson, the collected writings*. Berkeley: University of California Press, 1996.

Solhdju, Katrin. "Self-Experience as an Epistemic Activity: William James and Gustav Theodor Fechner." *Introspective Self-Rapports. Shaping Ethical and Aesthetic Concepts 1850-2006*. Ed. Katrin Solhdju. Berlin: Max Planck Institute for the History of Science, 2006. 39-50.

Spencer-Brown, G. *Laws of Form*. New York: E.P. Dutton, 1979.

Spivak, Gayatri. *Other Asias*. Oxford: Blackwell, 2008.

Stavning Thomsen, Bodil Marie. "Alt stof udsender `billeder' – om det visuelle som begivenhed" In *Flugtlinier. Om Deleuzes filosofi*. Eds. Mischa Sloth Carlsen, Karsten Gam Nielsen, Kim Su Rasmussen. København: Museum Tusculanums Forlag, 2001. 217-245

Stavning Thomsen, Bodil Marie. "Signaletic, haptic and real time material." *Journal of Aesthetics and Culture* 4 (2012): 1–10. http://www.aestheticsandculture.net/index.php/jac/article/view/18148

Stein, Charles. "Introduction." In *Being = Space X Action: Searches for Freedom of Mind through Mathematics, Art and Mysticism*. Ed. Charles Stein. Berkeley, CA: North Atlantic Books, 1988. 1-54.

Stengers, Isabelle. "A 'Cosmo-Politics' - Risk, Hope, Change." *Hope: New Philosophies for Change*. Ed. Mary Zournazi. Sydney: Pluto Press, 2002: 244-272.

Stengers, Isabelle. *Cosmopolitics 1*. University of Minnesota Press: Minnesota, London. 2010.

Stengers, Isabelle. *Thinking with Whitehead*. Cambridge: Harvard University Press, 2011a.

Stengers, Isabelle. "William James – Naturalisme et pragmatisme au fil de la question de la possession." *Philosophie des possessions*. Ed. Didier Debaise. Paris: Éditions du réel, 2011b, 35-70.

Stevens, Tim. "Avegant's Virtual Retinal Display prototype takes Oculus Rift-style immersion to the next level." *CNET.com*. October 9, 2013. http://www.cnet.com/products/avegant-virtual-retinal-display/.

Stoppani, Antonio. "First Period of the Anthropozoic Era." Trans. Valeria Federeighi. *Making the Geologic Now: Responses to the Material Conditions of Contemporary Life*. Eds. Elizabeth Ellsworth and Jamie Kruse. New York: Punctum, 2013.

Tanizaki, Jun'ichirō. "Poetry and Characters." Trans. Thomas Lamarre. *In Shadows on the Screen: Tanizaki Jun'ichirō on Cinema and "Oriental" Aesthetics*. Ann Arbor: University of Michigan Press, 2005.

Taussig, Michael. *Walter Benjamin's Grave*. Chicago: University of Chicago Press, 2006.

Taylor, Charles. *A Secular Age*. Cambridge: Belknap/Harvard, 2007

Taylor, William M. *The Vital Landscape: Nature and the Built Environment in Nineteenth-Century Britain*. Farnham: Ashgate, 2004.

Terranova, Tiziana. "Red Stack Attack!" *Accelerate: The Accelerationist Reader*. Eds. Robin Mackay and Armen Avanessian. Falmouth: Urbanomic, 2014. 379-398.

Thacker, Eugene. *Biomedia*. Minneapolis: University of Minnesota Press, 2004.

Thain, Alanna. *Suspended (Re)Animations: Affect, Immediation and the Film Body*. PhD Dissertation. Duke University, 2005.

Thain, Alanna. "Anarchival Cinemas." *Inflexions* 4 (December 2010): 48-68. http://www.inflexions.org/n4_thainhtml.html

Tinnell, John. "Transversalising the Ecological Turn: Four Components of Felix Guattari's Ecosophical Perspective." *The Fibreculture Journal* 18 (2011). http://eighteen.fibreculturejournal.org/2011/10/09/fcj-121-transversalising-the-ecological-turn-four-components-of-felix-guattari's-ecosophical-perspective/.

Thompson, Evan. *Mind in Life: Biology, Phenomenology, and the Sciences of Mind*. Cambridge, MA: Harvard University Press, 2007.

Thompson, Kristen and David Bordwell. "Has 3D Already Failed?" *Observations on Film Art*. August 28, 2009. http://www.davidbordwell.net/blog/2009/08/28/has-3-d-already-failed/

Tinnel, John. "Transversalising the Ecological Turn: four components of Félix Guattari's ecosophical perspective." *The Fibreculture Journal* 18 (2011). http://eighteen.fibreculturejournal.org/2011/10/09/fcj-121-transversalising-the-ecological-turn-four-components-of-felix-guattari%E2%80%99s-ecosophical-perspective/.

Toscano, Alberto. "The Culture of Abstraction." *Theory Culture Society* 25.4 (2008): 57–75.

Trenkner, Sophie. *The Greek Novella in the Classical Period*. Cambridge: Cambridge University Press, 1957.

Tsao Hsingyuan. "Reading and Misreading: Double Entendre in Locally Oriented Logos." In *Xu Bing and Contemporary Art*. Ed. Hsingyuan Tsao and Roger T. Ames. Albany: State University of New York Press, 2011.

Uricchio, William. "Television's Next Generation: Technology / Interface Culture / Flow." *Television After TV: Essays on a Medium in Transition*. Eds. Lynn Spigel and Jan Olsson. Durham: Duke University Press, 2004. 163-182.

van Lawick-Goodall, Jane. *In the Shadow of Man*. New York: Delta, 1971.

Varela, Francisco. "The Extended Calculus of Indications Interpreted as a Three-value Logic." *Journal of Genetic Systems* 3 (1975a): 141-46.

Varela, Francisco. "A Calculus for Self-Reference." *International Journal of Genetic Systems* 2 (1975b): 15-24.

Varela, Francisco, Evan Thompson and Eleanor Rosch. *The Embodied Mind*. Cambridge, MA: MIT Press, 1992.

Varela, Francisco. *Ethical Know-How: Actions, Wisdom, and Cognition*. Stanford CA: Stanford University Press, 1999.

Varela, Francisco. "The Specious Present: A Neurophenomenology of Time Consciousness." *Naturalizing Phenomenology: Issues in Contemporary Phenomenology and Cognitive Science*. Eds. Jean Petitot, Francisco Varela, Bernard Pachoud, and Jean-Michel Roy. Stanford: Stanford University Press, 2000. 266-329.

Venturi, Paolo. "...sul Dono, la Condivisione e la costruzione dell'Identità." Tempi Ibridi (November 2014). http://www.tempi-ibridi.it/sul-dono-la-condivisione-e-la-costruzione-dellidentita/.

Verbrugge, Robert. "Language and Event Perception." *Persistence and Change: Proceedings of the First International Conference on Event Perception*. Eds. W.H. Warren and R.E. Shaw. Hillsdale: Lawrence Erlbaum Associates, 1985. 157-92.

Verhoeven, Daniel. "Introduction into Defining the Commons." Real Democracy Now! January 2015. https://niepleuen.wordpress.com/2015/01/15/introduction-to-the-commons-and-some-definitions/

Vermeulen, Timotheus and James Whitfield. "Arrested Developments: Towards an Aesthetic of the Contemporary US sitcom." *Television Aesthetics and Style*. Ed. Jason Jacobs and Steven Peacock. London: Bloomsbury, 2013. 103-111.

Vermeulen, Timotheus. "Borrowed Energy." *Frieze magazine* 165 (September 2014). http://www.frieze.com/issue/article/borrowed-energy/

Virno, Paolo. *A Grammar of the Multitude*. Trans. James Cascaito, Isabella Bertoletti and Andrea Casson. New York: Semiotext(e), 2004.

"Virtual Reality for Worms." *The Cellular Scale*. May 1, 2012. http://cellularscale.blogspot.com.au/2012/05/virtual-reality-for-worms.html.

Vitale, Christopher. "World as Medium: Or, How Self-Differing Substance makes strange bedfellows of Whitehead, Hegel, and Deleuze." *Networkologies*. November 15, 2009. http://networkologies.wordpress.com/2009/11/15/world-as-medium-or-how-self-differing-substance-makes-strange-bedfellows-of-whitehead-hegel-and-deleuze/.

von Uexküll, Jakob. *A Foray into the World of Animals and Humans: With a Theory of Meaning*. Trans. Joseph D. O'Neil. Minneapolis: University of Minnesota Press, 2010.

Wark, McKenzie. *Virtual Geography*. Indianapolis: Indiana University Press, 1994.

Wark, McKenzie. *A Hacker Manifesto*. Harvard: Harvard University Press, 2004.

Wark, McKenzie. "To the Vector the Spoils." *Cabinet* 23 (Fall 2006). http://www.cabinetmagazine.org/issues/23/wark.php.

Wark, McKenzie. *Molecular Red*. London: Verso, 2015.

Watson, Sean. "The Neurobiology of Sorcery: Deleuze and Guattari's Brain." *Body & Society* 4 (1998): 23-45.

Webb, Clement C.J. *God and Personality*. London: Henderson and Spalding, 1919.

Webster, Guy. "An Interview with Sound Artist Guy Webster by Jillian Hamilton and Jeremy Yuille." *Intimate Transactions: Art, Exhibition and Interaction within Distributed Network Environments*. Eds. Jacqueline Adair Jones in Jillian Hamilton. Brisbane: Australasian CRC for Interaction Design, 2006. 60-75.

Wegner, Daniel, David Schneider, Samuel Carter III and Terri L. White. "Paradoxical Effects of Thought Suppression." *Journal of Personality and Social Psychology*. 53.1 (1987): 5-13.

Wegner, Daniel and David Schneider. "Mental Control: The War on the Ghost in the Machine." *Unintended Thought*. Eds. J.S. Uleman and J.A. Bargh. New York: Guilford, 1989: 287-305.

White, Mimi. "The Attractions of Television: Reconsidering Liveness." *MediaSpace: Place, Scale and Culture in a Media Age*. Eds. Nick Couldry and Anna McCarthy. London and New York: Routledge, 2004. 75-92.

Whitehead, Alfred North. "Mathematics and the Good" and "Immortality." *The Philosophy of Alfred North Whitehead*. Ed. Paul Arthur Schilpp. New York: Tudor Publishing Company, 1951.

Whitehead, Alfred North. *The Function of Reason*. Boston: Beacon Press, 1958.

Whitehead, Alfred North. *Adventures of Ideas*. New York: Free Press, 1967a.

Whitehead, Alfred North. 1967b. *Science and the Modern World*. New York: Free Press.

Whitehead, Alfred North. 1968. *Modes of Thought*. New York: Free Press.

Whitehead, Alfred North. *Process and Reality: An Essay in Cosmology*. New Nork: Free Press, 1978.

Whitehead, Alfred North. 1996. *Religion in the Making: Lowell Lectures, 1926*, 2nd edition. New York: Fordham University Press.

Whitehead, Alfred North. 2007. *The Concept of Nature*. New York : Cosimo, Inc.

Williams, Raymond. 1977. *Marxism and Literature*. Oxford: Oxford University Press.

Williams, Raymond. *Television: Technology and Cultural Form*. London: Routledge, 2003.

Wright, John S. *Shadowing Ralph Ellison*. Jackson: University Press of Mississippi, 2006.

Wu Hung. "A 'Ghost Rebellion': Notes on 'Nonsense Writing' and Other Works." *Public Culture* (1994) 6: 411-418.

Xu Bing. *Three Installations by Xu Bing: November 30, 1991-January 19, 1992*. Madison: Elvehjem Museum of Art, University of Wisconsin, Madison, 1991.

Xu Bing. "The Living Word." *The Art of Xu Bing: Words without Meaning, Meaning without Words*. Seattle: University of Washingon Press, 2001.

Xu Bing. *Xu Bing in Berlin*. Berlin: American Academy in Berlin: Deutsche Gesellschaft für Ostasiatische Kunst: Museum für Ostasiatische Kunst Berlin, 2004

Xu Bing. "A Conversation with Xu Bing." *Asian Art: The Newspaper for Collectors, Dealers, Museums, and Galleries*. March 2, 2012. http://www.asianartnewspaper.com/article/conversation-xu-bing

Yong, Ed. "Intercontinental mind-meld unites two rats." *Nature News*. February 28, 2013. http://doi:10.1038/nature.2013.12522

Zalamea, Fernando. 2012. *Peirce's Logic of Continuity*. Boston: Docent Press.

Zhang Zhaohui. *Where Heaven and Earth Meet: Xu Bing & Cai Guo-Qiang*. Hong Kong: Timezone 8, 2005.

Zeeman, Christopher. "Catastrophe Theory." *Scientific American* (April 1976): 65-83.

Contents Immediation I

www.ingramcontent.com/pod-product-compliance
Lightning Source LLC
LaVergne TN
LVHW091126080826
845145LV00008B/2060

* 9 7 8 1 7 8 5 4 2 0 2 4 5 *